Modern World History
FOR AQA SPECIFICATION B

FOUNDATION

Tony Hewitt • Jane Shuter

Heinemann

Heinemann Educational Publishers
Halley Court, Jordan Hill, Oxford, OX2 8EJ
A part of Harcourt Education
Heinemann is a registered trademark of Harcourt Education

© Tony Hewitt and Jane Shuter 2001

First published 2001

10-digit ISBN: 0 435311 98 0
13-digit ISBN: 978 0 435311 98 8
06
10 9 8 7 6

Designed and illustrated by Ian Foulis and Associates

Picture research by Geri May

Printed and bound in Italy by Printer Trento S.r.l

Index compiled by Indexing Specialists

Photographic acknowledgements
The authors and publisher would like to thank the following for permission to
reproduce photographs:
AKG: 42E, 182A, 187E, 191K, 192A, 196G, 197H, 199C, 208D, 210F; AKG
London: 186D, 189H; Associated Press: 32G; Corbis: 22F, 58C, 64J, 72A, 235C,
236E, 248F; Corbis/Sygma: 79B, 83D; Daily Mirror: 277D; Daily Mirror/Centre for
the Study of Cartoon and Caricature: 11C, 276A; David King: 153J, 155L, 156M,
158B, 161E, 166D, 168I, 175I, 176J; David Low/Solo Syndication: 29E, 31F, 202G;
e.t. archive: 135D, 137H; Hulton Getty: 14A, 20A, 37C, 74E, 85F, 127F, 138J,
140N, 144A, 151E, 159D, 162A, 170A, 188G, 239C, 250A, 251B, 252C, 253E,
267A, 269B, 278F, 280H, 284G; Hulton Getty/Archive Photos: 86A; Imperial War
Museum: 97B, 103K, 110W, 111X, 123C, 125D, 133J, 135C, 143U; Imperial War
Museum/London Express: 105N, 105O; Jean-Loup Charmet: 53E; Krause: 90C; Les
Gibbard: 82B; Magnum: 73C; Mary Evans: 256; Nebelspalter: 45S; New Statesman:
63I; PA News: 261C; Peter Newark: 39H, 77I, 134A, 218A, 224C, 225E, 226F,
230L, 231A, 237A, 243F, 247E; Popperfoto: 59D, 71D, 80D, 126E, 148A, 154K,
167F, 201F, 204A, 233B, 263F, 279G; Public Record Office: 136F, 137G, 140O;
Punch: 25I, 51H; Royal Army Museum Collection, Brussels: 16E; Scholastic: 262D;
School of Slavonic Studies: 62G; Simplissimus: 190I; Solo Syndication: 129H; Solo
Syndication/Centre for the Study of Cartoon and Caricature: 54B, 69D;
Süddeutscher Verlag Bilderdienst: 214B; The Hoover Institution: 178B; The Press
Association: 257H; Topham: 130I, 228I, 273H

With thanks to John and Andrew Frost at John Frost Historical Newspapers for the
loan of the newspapers used in 264G and 265H

Cover photograph: © Hulton Getty

Written source acknowledgements
The authors and publisher gratefully acknowledge the following publications from
which written sources in the book are drawn. In some sentences the wording or
sentence has been simplified:
Daily Express, 30 September 1938: 44H; *Daily Herald*, 16 April 1921: 260B; *Daily
Mail*, February 1903: 12D; *Deutsche Zeitung*, 28 June 1919: 25J; *Peking People's Daily*,
1 January 1980: 82C; *The Guardian*, 11 November 1989: 88B; *The Times*, 23
February 1968: 73B, 22 August 1968: 74D, 23 March, 1972: 80C, 3 January
2000: 91D, 27 December 1979: 92C, 18 April 1922: 215C, October 1936: 272G;
Washington Daily News: 62H; *Yorkshire Post*, December 1938: 44K

Contents

Modern World History for AQA

Chapter 1

International History 1900-91

INTRODUCTION

Option V: 1900–49

At the beginning of the twentieth century, the Great Powers were divided into two alliances, the Triple Alliance and the Triple Entente. Each side built up its armies and navies because it thought the other side would attack it. At first they managed to avoid war but in 1914, when the heir to the Austro-Hungarian Empire was murdered at Sarajevo, a chain of events led to the outbreak of the First World War.

Triple Alliance

- Germany
- Austria–Hungary
- Italy.

Triple Entente

- Great Britain
- France
- Russia.

The First World War ended in 1918 and the Great Powers met in Paris in 1919 to reach a peace settlement with Germany. France wanted revenge. The USA wanted a lasting peace. They got neither. Germany was weakened by the loss of land. With the Wall Street Crash of 1929 the period when countries had tried to co-operate came to an end.

In 1933, Hitler came to power in Germany. Britain's policy of appeasement attempted to avoid war but Germany continued to push for more territory. Events in Czechoslovakia and Poland eventually led to the outbreak of the Second World War in 1939 and ended with the defeat of Germany in 1945.

There were two new superpowers in 1945 – the USA and the USSR. They had different ways of running their countries and did not trust each other. The USSR took control of Eastern Europe and the USA used the Truman Doctrine and Marshall Aid to support the rest of Europe, including Britain. This rivalry between the USA and the USSR led to the Cold War.

1904	Entente Cordiale
1905–6	First Moroccan Crisis
1907	Anglo-Russian Agreement
1908–9	Bosnian Crisis
1911	Agadir Crisis
1914	Assassination at Sarajevo
1919	Treaty of Versailles
1929	Wall Street Crash
1931	Manchurian crisis
1935	Abyssinian crisis
1938	*Anschluss* Munich Conference
1939	Invasion of Czechoslovakia Nazi–Soviet Pact Invasion of Poland
1945	End of Second World War – Yalta and Potsdam Conferences
1946	Churchill's Iron Curtain speech
1947	Truman Doctrine and Marshall Plan
1948	Berlin Blockade and Airlift
1949	Formation of West Germany and NATO

Option W: 1919–63

When the First World War ended in 1918 the Great Powers met in Paris in 1919 to try and reach a peace settlement with Germany. However, France wanted revenge. The USA wanted a lasting peace. They got neither. Germany was weakened by the loss of land. With the Wall Street Crash of 1929 the period when countries had tried to co-operate came to an end.

When Hitler came to power in Germany in 1933, Britain's policy of appeasement attempted to avoid war but Germany continued to push for more territory. The invasions of Czechoslovakia and Poland in 1939 eventually led to the outbreak of the Second World War in September 1939 and ended with the defeat of Germany in 1945.

Two new superpowers emerged in 1945 – the USA and the USSR. They had different ways of running their countries and did not trust each other. One was capitalist and the other communist. The USSR took control of Eastern Europe and the USA used the Truman Doctrine and Marshall Aid to support the rest of Europe including Britain. This rivalry and suspicion led to the Cold War.

In 1948, the USSR attempted to take over the whole of Berlin. The USA did not like this and set up NATO in 1949. The USSR reacted by setting up its own alliances known as Cominform and the Warsaw Pact. The tension spread across the world. In 1950, both sides got involved in the Korean War, although they did not directly fight each other.

The development of nuclear weapons increased the tension, but the only time the two sides came close to war was during the Cuban missile crisis of 1962. Afterwards, both sides realised how close they had come to war. This experience led the superpowers to begin a period of co-operation.

1919	Treaty of Versailles
1929	Wall Street Crash
1931	Manchurian crisis
1935	Abyssinian crisis
1938	*Anschluss* Munich Conference
1939	Invasion of Czechoslovakia Nazi–Soviet Pact Invasion of Poland
1945	End of Second World War – Yalta and Potsdam Conferences
1946	Churchill's Iron Curtain speech
1947	Truman Doctrine and Marshall Plan
1948	Berlin Blockade and Airlift
1949	Formation of West Germany and NATO
1950	Start of Korean War
1953	End of Korean War – death of Stalin
1955	Warsaw Pact
1956	Hungarian Rising
1957	Soviet Union launches Sputnik
1960	U2 spy plane incident
1961	Building of Berlin Wall
1962	Cuban missile crisis
1963	Nuclear Test Ban Treaty

Option X: 1945–91

When the Second World War ended in 1945 two new superpowers emerged – the USA and the USSR. Each had different ways of running their countries and did not trust each other. The USSR took control of Eastern Europe. The USA used the Marshall Aid scheme to support the rest of Europe including Britain, and to prevent countries becoming communist. This rivalry and tension led to the Cold War.

In 1948, the USSR attempted to take over the whole of Berlin. The USA did not like this and set up NATO in 1949. The USSR reacted by setting up its own alliances known as Cominform and the Warsaw Pact. The tension spread across the world. In 1950, both sides got involved in the Korean War, although they did not fight each other directly.

The development of nuclear weapons increased the tension, but the only time the two sides came close to war was during the Cuban missile crisis of 1962. Afterwards, both sides realised how close they had come to war. This experience led the superpowers to begin a period of co-operation, called Détente. A 'hot-line' phone link was set up between Washington and Moscow and both sides signed a test ban treaty to stop testing nuclear weapons. They even agreed to reduce the numbers of nuclear missiles they had through the Strategic Arms Limitation Talks (SALT).

The Cold War was not over though. In 1979, the Soviet invasion of Afghanistan angered the USA and it began to look at developing more nuclear missiles. By this time, the Soviet Union was short of money and its new leader, Mikhail Gorbachev, had to agree to further cuts in weapons spending. Gorbachev introduced a number of reforms in the USSR which led to protests in Eastern European countries. The peoples of eastern Europe decided they did not want to be under the control of the Soviet Union any longer and country after country broke away from the USSR. By 1989, the Soviet Empire had broken up and the Cold War was over.

1945 End of Second World War – Yalta and Potsdam Conferences

1946 Churchill's Iron Curtain speech

1947 Truman Doctrine and Marshall Plan

1948 Berlin Blockade and Airlift

1949 Formation of West Germany and NATO

1950 Start of Korean War

1953 End of Korean War – death of Stalin

1955 Warsaw Pact

1956 Hungarian Rising

1957 Soviet Union launches Sputnik

1960 U2 spy plane incident.

1961 Building of the Berlin Wall

1962 Cuban missile crisis

1963 Nuclear Test Ban Treaty

1968 Prague Spring and the invasion of Czechoslovakia

1972 SALT 1

1975 Helsinki Agreement

1979 Soviet invasion of Afghanistan

1980 USA boycott of Moscow Olympics

1981 USSR imposes martial law in Poland

1984 Soviet boycott of Los Angeles Olympics

1985 Mikhail Gorbachev becomes leader of Soviet Russia

1989 Disintegration of the Soviet Empire – Berlin Wall pulled down

1991 End of communist rule in Russia

1.1 Why did tension increase in Europe between 1900 and 1914?

The Great Powers in 1900

Germany

In 1871, two things happened that made Germany stronger:

- Prussia won a war with France. The Treaty of Frankfurt which ended the war gave Prussia the French province of Alsace-Lorraine as well as 200 million francs to pay for war damage.

- Prussia united all the German states into an empire ruled by a **Kaiser** (emperor). The first Kaiser was the ruler of Prussia.

By 1900, Germany was an important industrial nation. The Kaiser, Wilhelm II, wanted Germany to build a big German **empire**, to have what he called 'its place in the sun'.

To do this he needed a strong army and navy. Much of the steel from the new German steel works went straight to the new factories that made weapons for the army. Shipyards began building more and more warships.

France

France resented Germany. It wanted Alsace-Lorraine back and felt threatened by Germany's **colony**-grabbing overseas.

Source Ⓐ

Germany has gone beyond her rights in forcing an exhausted, defeated France to give up Alsace-Lorraine. One and a half million French people live here. Give us our freedom. Give us justice.

From a speech made to the German Parliament in 1874 by a deputy from Alsace-Lorraine.

THINGS TO DO

1 Read the text on pages 8 and 9.
  (a) Which country do you think a British politician would see as Britain's biggest rival in 1900? Why?
  (b) Which country do you think an Austro-Hungarian politician would see as his country's biggest rival in 1900? Why?

2 How does **Source A** suggest that France might see Germany as a rival after 1871?

Britain

Britain had a large overseas empire. Much of Britain's wealth came from trade. Britain already had a powerful navy to protect British ships that sailed all over the world. This navy also kept the British coast safe. Before 1900, as a rich and powerful island, Britain had not needed to make **alliances** with other Great Powers. After 1900, Germany was more and more of a threat to Britain's trade and empire.

Austria–Hungary

Austria–Hungary was a large empire, ruling many different peoples. These people, who included Germans, Slavs and Serbs, had different languages and customs. They often resented being part of Austria–Hungary. As Serbia became more powerful as an independent country, the rulers of Austria–Hungary feared their Serbs would want to break away and join Serbia.

Russia

Russia was the largest of the Great Powers. However, it was the least **industrialised**. Russia, like Austria–Hungary, was made up of many different nations, including Slavs. Both countries were arguing over land in the Balkans, where their two empires met.

Italy

Italy was united in 1861. By 1900, Italy had joined the Triple Alliance, with Germany and Austria–Hungary. However, like Russia, Italy shared a border with Austria–Hungary and was arguing over land on this border. Italy did not always side with its allies in disputes over land.

Source **B** A French cartoon of Kaiser Wilhelm II. He is standing in a ring of artists and photographers. He had a withered left arm (as shown in the cartoon) and is dressed in uniform.

THINGS TO DO

1 Look at **Source B**. What points do you think the artist is making in the following details:
   (a) he is the centre of attention
   (b) he is in uniform
   (c) his sword arm is withered?

2 What country do **Sources A** and **B** come from? Why might this be a problem to someone studying relations between Germany and France in 1900?

The Alliance System, 1900–14

Since the late 1800s the Great Powers had been making secret alliances to help each other if they were attacked. These alliances did not mean that the allies agreed or sided with each other in all disputes. The alliances were:

- **The Franco-Russian Treaty:** formed in 1894 between France and Russia. Russia made a separate agreement with Germany in 1905, but it soon fell apart.

- **The Triple Alliance:** formed in 1900 between Austria–Hungary, Germany and Italy.

- **The Entente Cordiale** (Friendly Agreement): formed between Britain and France in 1904. They also agreed not to fight each other over colonies.

- **The Triple Entente:** formed when Russia joined the Entente Cordiale in 1907.

The alliances between the Great Powers made a world war more likely because:

- They created two opposing camps.

- The details of the alliances were kept secret from the other side. So both sides came to fear that, while *their* alliance was only defensive, the other side was plotting an attack. Once they feared this, they prepared for war, which scared the other side and made a war more likely.

- Members of each alliance could be pulled into the disputes which their allies became involved in.

The countries in the Triple Alliance and Triple Entente.

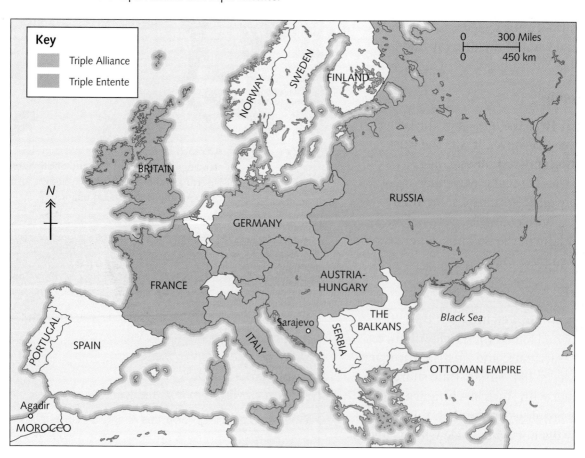

Rivalry increases

From 1900 to 1905, there was growing suspicion and tension between members of the Triple Alliance and those of the Entente Cordiale. They began to see each other as 'sides' who were more and more likely to start a war.

Events in Morocco, 1905–6

In 1905, Morocco was independent, but shared a long border with Algeria, a French colony. France wanted to take over Morocco. Its coastline would provide a safe border and trading ports. In 1905, **Kaiser Wilhelm II** visited Morocco and said he would help it stay independent. This upset the French, who protested. The British sided with the French.

A meeting was held at Algeciras in 1906 to sort out the disagreement. Russia, Spain and Italy sided with Britain and France. Only Austria–Hungary sided with Germany. So Germany had to leave Morocco alone. Britain and France asked Russia to join them to form the Triple Entente. Germany felt cut off and resentful.

The Bosnian crisis, 1908–9

Bosnia was a Slav state in the Balkans. Its capital was Sarajevo. Austria–Hungary took over Bosnia in 1908. **Serbia**, also a Slav state, wanted Bosnia for itself. Russia supported Serbia, because it did not want Austria–Hungary growing more powerful in the Balkans. Germany supported Austria–Hungary. It became clear that Germany and Austria–Hungary were prepared to fight.

The Russian **Tsar** did not think his army could take on Germany and Austria–Hungary. Britain and France waited to see what would happen. So, in 1909, Russia backed off and Austria–Hungary kept Bosnia.

Source C

A British cartoon, drawn in 1905. The cartoonist shows the Entente Cordiale making Britain and France strong enough to oppose Germany.

THINGS TO DO

1 List the members of the Triple Alliance and the Triple Entente under separate headings.

2 List the reactions to the Bosnian crisis of
(a) Austria–Hungary (b) Russia
(c) France.

Morocco again – the Agadir crisis, 1911

In 1911, the French helped the ruler of Morocco to stamp out a **rebellion**. In return, it looked as if he would let France take over Morocco.

The Germans sent a **gunboat** to Agadir, a Moroccan port, to try to stop a French takeover. Perhaps the Kaiser hoped the French would agree to share Morocco.

The British, worried that the Germans would turn Agadir into a base for their new navy, supported France.

After many talks, the French kept Morocco, but ruled it as a **protectorate**, a separate country, not part of their empire. They gave Germany some of the French Congo as part of the agreement. The land was mostly swamp and jungle, so it was not a good exchange. While Austria–Hungary and Germany had 'won' over Bosnia, it was clear that Britain and France had 'won' in Agadir.

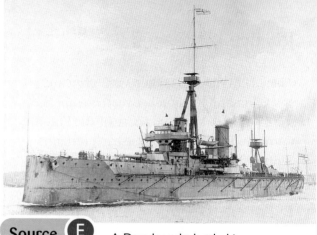

Source **E** A Dreadnought battleship.

The naval race, 1906–14

Britain is an island. It had a huge empire, spread all over the world. It had a fairly small army, so it needed a strong navy. In 1900, Britain had the strongest navy in the world.

When Germany began building up its navy, the British felt threatened. They began to build more ships themselves.

In 1906, Britain built the first of a new kind of ship, called **Dreadnoughts**. They were faster and better armed and protected than earlier battleships. Germany began to build Dreadnoughts, too. This gave Britain a problem: the British navy was bigger than the German one, but most of the ships in it were out of date.

Both sides began a 'naval race' to build the most Dreadnoughts. The British tried to get the Germans to agree to set a limit on the number of ships each side would build. The Germans refused. There was public pressure on both governments to spend more and more money on shipbuilding, to get ahead in the race. By 1914, Britain had 29 Dreadnoughts, while Germany had 17.

Source **D**

Great naval power in British hands is not a menace; in German hands it puts the whole world in danger. In recent years Germany has been aggressive. Lack of space at home is forcing Germany to try to take over other nations' colonies.

Written in the British newspaper, the Daily Mail, in February 1903.

The build-up of armies, 1900–14

As the Great Powers built up their armies (see table below) they created even more tension and mistrust. The build-up of armies, just like the naval race, became unstoppable. No one wanted to be the first to stop and let other countries overtake them. How did they build up their armies?

- After 1871, all the Great Powers except Britain set up **conscription** (men had to serve in the army for a number of years). In 1913, they increased the number of years that men had to stay in the army.

- All the Great Powers increased their spending on weapons and arms. Germany spent the most. Germany also encouraged people to be proud of their army – the Kaiser enjoyed being seen in public in uniform (see Source B on page 9).

- All the Great Powers made war plans, 'just in case'.

THINGS TO DO

1 Why is the writer of **Source D** so against Germany having a powerful navy?

2 Read pages 11–12.
   List the disputes, who sided with whom, and who 'won'?

3 Read pages 12–13.
   (a) Why was it so hard for the Great Powers to stop building up armies and/or navies?
   (b) Does the build-up mean they were sure they would have to go to war?

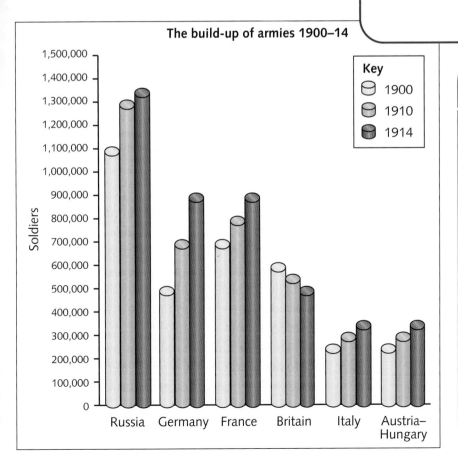

The build-up of armies 1900–14

Key
1900
1910
1914

SUMMARY

Relations between the Great Powers

1904 Entente Cordiale.

1905 First Moroccan crisis.

1906 Launch of the Dreadnought – the naval race begins.

1907 Triple Entente.

1908 Bosnian crisis.

1911 Agadir crisis.

1.2 Why did the assassination at Sarajevo lead to the outbreak of war in 1914?

Assassination at Sarajevo

On 28 June 1914, the heir to the throne of Austria–Hungary, the Archduke Franz Ferdinand, visited Sarajevo, capital of **Bosnia**.

A Serbian group which wanted Bosnian independence from Austria–Hungary set out to kill him. First, they threw a bomb into his car. Franz Ferdinand knocked the bomb away. It exploded behind the car, injuring several people.

The second attempt was successful. As the driver of the car stopped to turn the car (he had taken a wrong turn) two shots were fired. Franz Ferdinand and his wife were both killed. The **assassin** was called **Gavrilo Princip**.

Source (A) An artist's impression of the assassination of the Archduke Franz Ferdinand. This was drawn in 1914.

THINGS TO DO

1 Look at **Source A**. Do you think it is an accurate picture of the assassination? Explain your answer.

2 Look at **Source C**. Do you think the cartoonist supported Germany's invasion of Belgium? Use as many details from the cartoon as you can to explain your answer.

3 Read 'From assassination to war' on page 15. Draw a flow diagram showing the various steps to war that followed the assassination of Franz Ferdinand.

The last straw

The murder of Franz Ferdinand and his wife was the last of the incidents that had been pushing the Great Powers towards war since 1900. The Austro-Hungarian leaders had no proof that the leaders of Serbia had supported the actions of the group that assassinated Franz Ferdinand. Despite this, they gave Serbia a list of ten demands that had to be met to avoid war. The demands were harsh, so harsh that many thought that Austria–Hungary was forcing war on Serbia. They included the rooting out of all groups in Serbia that were against Austria–Hungary.

From assassination to war

Serbia had just finished fighting in the Balkans. Its leaders did not want to go to war again. Despite the fact that the Austro-Hungarian demands were harsh, Serbia accepted all but one of them: this was the demand that Austro-Hungarian investigators join the enquiry into the shootings. This would have been seen as Austria–Hungary interfering in Serbian courts. It was a clear threat to Serbian independence. The Serbian leaders stressed, however, that they would be happy for an international court, rather than just a Serbian one, to carry out the enquiry.

That was not enough for Austria–Hungary which declared war on Serbia on 28 July 1914. This declaration of war on Serbia was the first step to world war.

Steps to war

- **30 July:** the Russians **mobilised** their army, clearly getting ready for war against Austria–Hungary in support of Serbia. The British and French were not consulted before Russia did this.

- **1 August:** Germany declared war on Russia.

- **3 August:** Germany declared war on France, as one of Russia's allies. On the same day, the German army set out to invade France. To do this, it first had to invade Belgium.

BRAVO, BELGIUM!

Source C A British cartoon from August 1914. It shows Germany threatening Belgium. Germany is the man with a big stick. We know it is Germany because we can read part of the name on his hat and there are sausages hanging out of his pocket. Belgium is the small boy in clogs. He is defending his country, which is on the other side of the gate marked 'No Thoroughfare'. This sign is to remind people that Belgium was a neutral country.

- **4 August:** Britain declared war on Germany. Britain had been holding back from war, but the invasion of Belgium made it clear that France would be attacked, and Britain had said it would go to war if this happened. Also, Belgium was a **neutral** country, one that did not take sides. In 1839, with the Treaty of London, most European countries had promised to protect Belgium's neutrality and stop it being invaded. So Britain had two reasons for declaring war on Germany.

Source B

> I no longer have any doubts that Britain, Russia and France have agreed to go to war to destroy us. They have already surrounded us.
>
> *Said by Kaiser Wilhelm II in 1914, just before war broke out.*

Britain and the war

The Triple Entente between Britain, France and Russia did not mean they would always go to war to help each other. When Russia mobilised for war, it did not consult Britain and France first. It wanted war and did not expect their help. France was forced into war by Germany, but Britain hesitated. What was the British government's attitude to war?

A British postcard published in 1914.

Should Britain go to war?

- No one really wanted a war with Germany on Russia's behalf.

- Some politicians, such as Lord Grey, wanted to help France, especially if its northern coast (closest to Britain) was attacked.

- Other politicians only wanted to go to war if Belgium was invaded. A German invasion of Belgium broke the 1839 **Treaty of London** made to protect Belgium's neutrality. Belgium was a small country, but well placed to be a base for invading several others, including Britain.

- On 2 August, the British Cabinet said that Britain would go to war if Belgium was invaded. On 3 August, the Germans invaded Belgium. On 4 August, Britain declared war on Germany. The Kaiser was astonished that the British had joined the war over '**a scrap of paper**' (the Treaty of London).

THINGS TO DO

1 Why did the British government publish **Sources D** and **E**?

2 List the steps of the Schlieffen Plan.

3 Was Germany wise to use this plan?

THE "SCRAP OF PAPER"

These are the signatures and seals of the representatives of the Six Powers to the "Scrap of Paper"—the Treaty signed in 1839 guaranteeing the independence and neutrality of Belgium. "Palmerston" signed for Britain, "Bülow" for Prussia.

The Germans have broken their pledged word and devastated Belgium. Help to keep your Country's honour bright by restoring Belgium her liberty.

ENLIST TO-DAY

Source **E** A British poster showing the Treaty that should have protected Belgium from invasion.

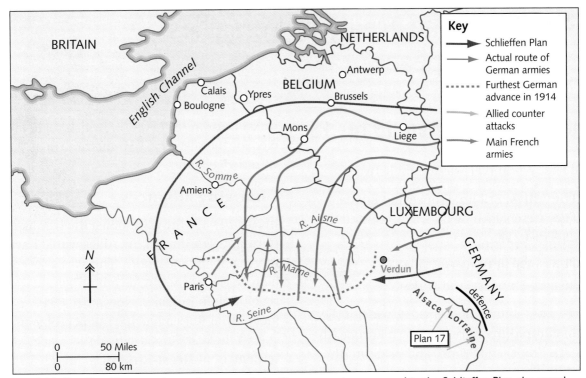

The Schlieffen Plan. This map shows the route of the German armies proposed in the Schlieffen Plan, the actual route, and counter attacks.

The Schlieffen Plan

France and Russia had been allies since 1894. If Germany had to fight both countries it meant fighting on two fronts, which would stretch the army very thinly. So, well before war broke out, **Count Alfred von Schlieffen**, the German War Minister, made a plan (see map above). It involved moving large armies quickly over huge distances. If it worked Germany would only have to fight on one front at a time. This was the theory behind the plan:

- Russia was a big country with poor roads. Schlieffen estimated it would take the Russian army six weeks to reach the German border.

- So Germany had to beat France on the Western Front before Russia could mobilise. Schlieffen felt the German army could beat France quickly if it made its main attack through Belgium and the Netherlands.

The general in charge in 1914, General von Moltke, changed Schlieffen's plan: he attacked through Belgium only and sent more troops to Alsace-Lorraine. The Germans soon found that they had underestimated the strength of Belgian resistance, the British army and the speed of Russian mobilisation.

SUMMARY

Events leading to war

28 June	Assassination of Franz Ferdinand.
23 July	Austrian ultimatum to Serbia.
28 July	Austria–Hungary declares war on Serbia.
1 August	Germany declares war on Russia.
3 August	Germany declares war on France.
	German troops enter Belgium.
4 August	Britain declares war on Germany.
5 August	Austria–Hungary declares war on Russia.

1.3 How did the Treaty of Versailles establish peace?

The First World War, 1914–18

The First World War was fought between:

- **The Allies:** Britain, France and Russia. They were joined by Italy in 1915 and the USA in 1917.

- **The Central Powers:** Germany, Austria–Hungary and Turkey.

There was fighting all over the world but the main **campaigns** were in eastern Europe (the Eastern Front) and France and Belgium (the Western Front).

During the war both sides sent millions of men to fight on the Western Front. But they were bogged down in **trenches**. In 1917, the British attacked the Germans at **Passchendaele**. 250,000 British soldiers died for the sake of a 750-metre strip of waterlogged land.

Changing alliances

In April 1917, the USA joined the war against Germany. This meant the Allies would have more supplies and troops. This was a severe blow to Germany. But, a communist revolution in Russia in November 1917 meant that Russia had too many problems to stay in the war. Russia signed the peace settlement of **Brest-Litovsk** in March 1918 and gave Germany a lot of Russian land. Now Germany could concentrate all its troops on the Western Front.

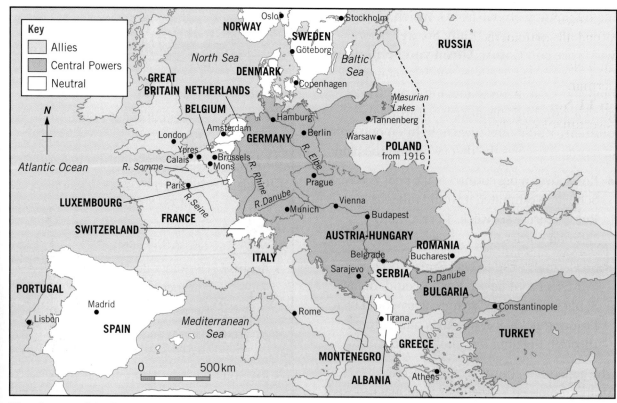

The alliances of the First World War.

Germany's gamble fails

The German generals knew Germany had to defeat the Allies before large numbers of US soldiers arrived in France. So the generals attacked heavily on the Western Front, where the Allies were weakest. They began to push the Allies back. Could they win? They had big problems:

- They could not push the Allies back far enough or fast enough. The Allies halted the retreat then, in July, pushed the Germans back.

- US troops began pouring into France.

- Germany was starving. A **blockade** of German ports meant that there was no food getting into Germany.

- A violent flu outbreak killed thousands of already weakened Germans and lowered morale still further.

- In October 1918, both the army and the navy had serious **mutinies** (uprisings).

- By early November, Germany's allies (Bulgaria, Turkey and Austria–Hungary) had all surrendered.

On 9 November, the Kaiser resigned. The German government **surrendered at 11 am on 11 November 1918**. A new German government was set up.

The impact of the war

France

- 2 million people homeless
- 750,000 homes destroyed
- many roads, railways and factories destroyed
- much farmland ruined.

Belgium

- people made homeless
- many roads, railways and factories destroyed
- much farmland ruined.

Britain

- over 1000 people killed in air attacks
- war debts, about £1 billion, to USA.

Germany

- starvation
- defeat; made worse by the fact its leaders had hidden the worsening situation from the population.

Russia

- suffered very heavy casualties
- loss of much farmland and industrial land to Germany with the peace of Brest-Litovsk in March 1918. Would Russia get the land back?

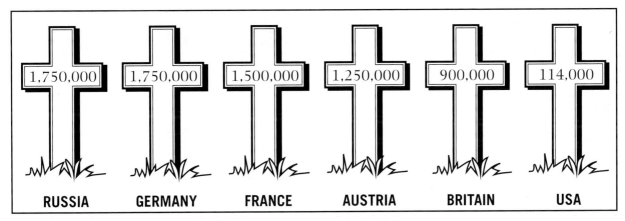

RUSSIA	GERMANY	FRANCE	AUSTRIA	BRITAIN	USA
1,750,000	1,750,000	1,500,000	1,250,000	900,000	114,000

Numbers of casualties in the First World War.

The city of Ypres, Belgium, after an intensive bombardment. Many cities and towns in France also suffered badly.

Source **A**

Source **B**

We must not let revenge or greed prevent a just peace. We will fight the next election on the grounds of such a peace.

From a speech by Lloyd George to Parliament on 12 November 1918.

Source **C**

If you elect me, I will make sure Germany pays war damages. We will squeeze everything we can out of her.

Part of a speech made by Eric Geddes during the 1918 general election campaign.

Source **D**

We will demand the whole cost of the war from Germany.

Part of a speech made by Lloyd George during the 1918 general election campaign.

THINGS TO DO

1 (a) What are Lloyd George's views in **Sources B** and **D**?
  (b) Can **Source C** help to explain the difference?

The main personalities and their attitudes to the defeated countries

When the war ended, it was time to negotiate a **peace settlement**. Many of the Allies were torn between a desire for revenge and a need to make sure the peace settlement was fair.

In January 1919, representatives of the Allies met in Paris to agree a peace treaty. Neither the defeated countries nor Russia, who had agreed a separate peace with Germany and was now a communist country, were allowed to take part.

The leaders of the USA, France and Britain dominated the discussions.

Woodrow Wilson, President of the USA

Woodrow Wilson wanted a perfect solution. The USA was less concerned with punishing Germany than the other Allies. There had been no fighting in the USA, so there was no war damage. The USA had joined the war late, in 1917. Far fewer US soldiers had been killed than soldiers of other allied countries.

Wilson's biggest concern was to prevent another world war. So:

- He wanted everyone to be happy with the peace settlement, even Germany. Germany should not be made to pay the crippling cost of the war.

- He wanted a **League of Nations** to settle international disputes before they could lead to war.

- He wanted everyone to accept a set of rules, the **Fourteen Points**, that would run international relations. The most important of these was 'self-determination'. This meant that each nation had a right to rule itself, and not be part of another nation's empire.

Some of the Fourteen Points

1. No secret treaties

2. Free access to the seas in peacetime and wartime

3. Free trade between countries

4. Disarmament

5. Colonies to be able to have a say in their own futures

6. German troops to leave Russia

7. Independence for Belgium

8. France to regain Alsace-Lorraine

13. Poland to become an independent state with access to the sea

14. A League of Nations to be set up to keep the peace

Source E

It is a privilege to open the discussion in this conference on the League of Nations. We have two reasons for being here – to make the peace settlements and to secure the future peace of the world. We need the League for both actions.

From a speech by Woodrow Wilson to the Paris Peace Conference, January 1919.

David Lloyd George, Georges Clemenceau and Woodrow Wilson.

David Lloyd George, Prime Minister of Britain

Lloyd George was an experienced politician. Like Wilson, he wanted lasting peace. But Britain had had a hard war, too. So:

- He wanted a fair settlement. However, many British people had only re-elected him in 1918 because he promised to 'squeeze Germany until the pips squeak'.

- He wanted Germany punished, but not so harshly that its leaders became resentful and likely to go to war again.

- He wanted the German economy to recover so Britain could begin trading with Germany again.

- He wanted to set a limit on Germany's navy.

Georges Clemenceau, Prime Minister of France

France had been devastated by the war. Clemenceau was a tough politician who had come to power promising to beat Germany and get Alsace-Lorraine back. So:

- He wanted Germany to pay for the way the French had suffered from being occupied and having the war fought in France. He wanted Germany to provide the money that would be needed to rebuild French industries, homes and farmland.

- He wanted to take Alsace-Lorraine back and also take land from Germany on the French–German border to make a buffer between France and Germany.

THINGS TO DO

Write short speeches for Wilson, Clemenceau and Lloyd George for the peace conference. For each person make sure you:
- list what he wants
- explain why.

The Treaty of Versailles, June 1919

On 28 June 1919, the Treaty of Versailles was signed by the Allies at the Palace of Versailles, 16 km from Paris. It was very complicated, over 200 pages long with over 400 clauses (sections). Two representatives of the new German government were sent for. They were not allowed to discuss any of the clauses. They had no choice but to sign.

Territorial changes

The map below shows the loss of land that Germany had to accept:

- France was given Alsace-Lorraine back.

- France was to run the Saar coalfields for the League of Nations.

- Belgium was given Eupen and Malmédy.

- Denmark was given Northern Schleswig.

- Poland was given West Prussia, part of Upper Silesia and Posen.

- Lithuania was given Memel.

- Danzig became a free city, controlled by the League of Nations. Poland could trade from Danzig.

- Germany lost all the land taken from Russia at Brest-Litovsk in 1918.

- Germany was forbidden to unite with Austria.

- All Germany's colonies were taken away and given to other nations to rule until they were able to rule themselves.

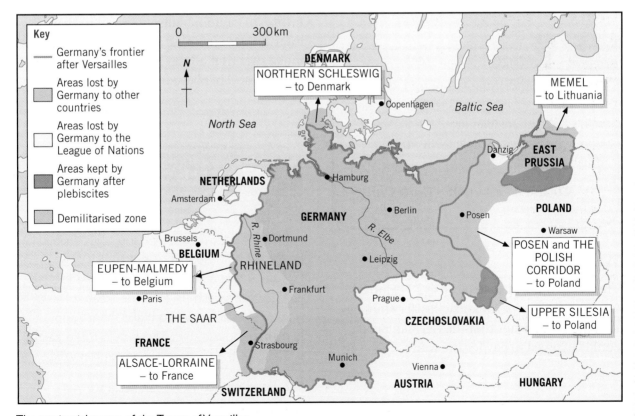

The territorial terms of the Treaty of Versailles.

Military restrictions

Germany had restrictions placed on its army and navy:

- army limited to 100,000 men

- no conscription; all soldiers to be volunteers

- no tanks, submarines or military planes

- only allowed six battleships

- no German troops could go into the Rhineland, near the French border. The Allies kept an army there to make sure this happened for fifteen years.

Reparations

Once Germany accepted Clause 231 and accepted responsibility for war damage, it could be made to pay for it. The payments were called '**reparations**'. The amount was not set in the Treaty of Versailles. It was set, in 1921, at £6600 million. Germany was to pay a certain amount each year. In fact, the amounts were reduced in later years and in 1930 Germany stopped paying.

Source G

The Allied governments say, and Germany accepts, that Germany and her allies are responsible for all the loss and damage suffered by Allied countries during the war.

Clause 231, the War Guilt Clause.

War guilt

The **War Guilt Clause** (Clause 231) forced Germany to accept responsibility for starting the war. This meant that the German people could be forced to pay for the war.

Source H

It is a people's treaty, because it sets peoples free. The Allies do not demand land for themselves. The people of Europe do not want to be ruled by masters, they want to choose their governments. This is the most important idea behind the treaty.

From a speech made by Woodrow Wilson in the USA in 1919. He was touring to get American support for the Treaty of Versailles.

The League of Nations

The League of Nations was set up to settle future international disputes and to keep international peace. It was also supposed to make sure that all the clauses of the Treaty of Versailles were obeyed.

THINGS TO DO

1 Think back to what Wilson, Clemenceau and Lloyd George wanted.
   (a) Make a list for each of the leaders. Say which parts of the Treaty of Versailles would make them happy.
   (b) Pick one thing that would make each of them unhappy, and explain why.

2 Read **Source H**. Is it an accurate description of the Treaty?

Reasons for resentment and bitterness in Germany

Most Germans did not believe Germany started the war, so they saw reparations as unfair. The government that had replaced the Kaiser (who led Germany to war) had surrendered and agreed to an **armistice**.

The Germans had expected to be allowed to negotiate with the Allies.

November Criminals

Most Germans had not wanted the new government to sign the peace treaty, or end the war. They believed that these 'November Criminals' (because they stopped the war in November 1918) had betrayed Germany.

Land and population

The Treaty of Versailles took from Germany:

- 10 per cent of its land
- all its colonies
- 12.5 per cent of its people
- 50 per cent of its iron and steel industries
- 16 per cent of its coalfields.

The Germans resented these losses. The Fourteen Points and the idea of self-determination that Wilson was so keen on were not to apply to German people in land that no longer belonged to Germany. Germans ignored the fact that their allies (Turkey and Austria–Hungary) were treated in the same way. They also ignored the fact that Germany's terms in the Treaty of Brest-Litovsk (imposed on Russia in March 1918) had been very harsh.

THE FINISHING TOUCH.

Source A cartoon from *Punch*, 1919.

War guilt

The War Guilt Clause was seen as a humiliation. The newspaper *Deutsche Zeitung* published the treaty on a front page surrounded by a black mourning band.

Source J

Vengeance! German Nation!

Today at Versailles a disgraceful treaty is being signed. Never forget it! On the spot where, in 1871, the German Empire began, German honour is today buried. Never forget it! There will be vengeance for the shame of 1919.

From the front page of the Deutsche Zeitung, 28 June 1919.

1.4 Why did the League of Nations frequently fail in its aims to keep peace?

The League of Nations was set up in 1919–20 as part of the peace treaties. It was built into Woodrow Wilson's Fourteen Points. No one wanted another world war. Most people hoped the USA would head the League and keep the rest of the world in line.

The powers, membership and peace-keeping role of the League

Each of the separate peace treaties signed at the end of the war began with the **Covenant**. This was a set of 26 rules that all members agreed to keep. The rules encouraged nations to cut down their armies, trade with each other and work to improve standards of living worldwide. The most important rule was Article 10. This said everyone had to protect any member who was threatened with war. This was called '**collective security**'.

At first, 42 countries joined. By the 1930s, there were 59 members. However:

- The defeated countries (Germany, Austria and Turkey) were not allowed to join.

- Russia was not allowed to join, because it was communist.

The USA fails to join

Woodrow Wilson expected the USA to join the League. So did other countries. But the US Senate voted not to join because:

- Many Americans had not wanted to get involved in a war in Europe in the first place.

- After the war, even more people thought it was a good idea to practise '**isolationism**' – stay out of quarrels in other countries.

Source **A**

We have US interests to guard in Asia and the Pacific. The less we act as umpire in Europe, the better.

I must think of America first. The United States is the world's best hope. If you pull her into the quarrels of other nations, you will destroy her power for good.

From a speech made in August 1919 by Senator Henry Cabot Lodge, an opponent of Wilson.

- The USA had many citizens from all over Europe. They included people from Allied countries and defeated countries. They wanted these people to live peacefully as Americans.

Wilson tried to persuade the Senate to change its mind. When Wilson died in 1921 the next President, Warren Harding, was firmly in favour of isolationism. The failure of the USA to join the League made it less of a world power.

Source **B**

If America does not join the League I predict that there will be another world war within a generation.

From a speech made by Woodrow Wilson in 1919.

The structure of the League of Nations

THE ASSEMBLY

Every country in the League sent a representative to the Assembly. It recommended action to the Council and could vote on the budget, admitting new members, and so on.

The Assembly met once a year at the League's headquarters, Geneva in Switzerland. Its decisions had to be agreed by all members of the Assembly.

THE COUNCIL

The Council was a smaller group that met several times a year and in emergencies. It was set up to have five permanent members: Britain, France, Italy, Japan and the USA (the USA never joined). It also had non-permanent members, elected by the Assembly for three-year periods.

Each permanent member had the power to stop any action being agreed by voting against it.

THE SECRETARIAT

The Secretariat kept records of meetings and prepared reports. Many of its staff spoke several languages. English and French were the main languages used.

THE PERMANENT COURT OF INTERNATIONAL JUSTICE

The Court was based at the Hague in the Netherlands. It was made up of judges from the member countries. It was set up to settle disputes between members, but had no way of enforcing its decisions.

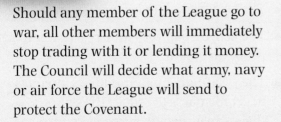

Source C

Should any member of the League go to war, all other members will immediately stop trading with it or lending it money. The Council will decide what army, navy or air force the League will send to protect the Covenant.

Article 16 of the Covenant of the League of Nations.

THINGS TO DO

Read **Source A**. How might the following people react to Cabot Lodge's arguments:

(a) an American woman whose two sons were killed in the First World War

(b) a Frenchwoman living in the USA?

Source Ⓓ A British cartoon from 1920. The keystone is the most important part of a bridge.

Powers of the League

The Covenant gave the League three ways to settle disputes:

- a **hearing** by a country not involved in the dispute

- a **decision** by the International Court of Justice

- an **inquiry** by the Council of the League.

If a country ignored the League's decision, the League could:

- exert **moral pressure** (try to get world opinion against the country's actions)

- use **economic sanctions** (stop League members trading with the country)

- use **military force** (use troops from several League countries to force obedience).

Strengths of the League

Most countries began by supporting the League. Most Great Powers joined it. Better communications helped the League to work efficiently.

The League solved some political disputes in the 1920s:

- In 1921, it settled a dispute between Sweden and Finland over the Aaland Islands.

- In 1925, a Greek army invaded Bulgaria. The League persuaded the Greeks to leave and let the League settle their argument.

Weaknesses of the League

- The USA did not join the League.

- The USSR was not allowed to join the League.

- The League had no army of its own.

- The League had very little real power to get people to obey it.

- The Disarmament Committee's attempts to get members to reduce the size of their armies had no success. Countries were still too distrustful of each other.

In the 1930s, the League could not stop the rise of dictators in Japan, Germany and Italy. It was not strong enough.

Japanese expansion into Manchuria and China

Effects of the Wall Street Crash

In the 1920s, the world economy recovered from the war and was doing well. There was a boom in world trade, centred on the USA.

But, in 1929, the US stock market collapsed in what became known as the Wall Street Crash. Many banks and businesses went bankrupt. Millions of people lost their jobs.

World trade was badly affected and the countries that the USA had lent money to (almost all of Europe) were asked for the money back. Countries stopped trading freely, to protect their own industries. The USA stopped importing goods from Japan; Japan faced unemployment and starvation.

THINGS TO DO

Sources **E** and **F** were drawn by the same artist. Think about how he shows the League of Nations.
(a) What did he think about it in 1920?
(b) What did he think about it in 1933?

A cartoon from the *London Star*, November 1920. It suggests that the League of Nations faced a lot of opposition to its desire for world peace.

" KEEP THE HATE-FIRES BURNING "

The Japanese army

The Japanese army leaders had not been happy with the way other nations treated Japan. They were also unhappy that Japan's government had agreed to limit its navy to three ships to every five built by Britain and the USA.

While Japan's economy was booming, the army leaders got very little support from the Japanese people. When the Japanese government failed to cope with the problems caused by the Wall Street Crash, the army leaders said the answer was to take more land to grow more food and expand trade.

People began to listen to them. Support for the army grew and it became harder for the government to ignore its demands.

Manchuria

Manchuria was a **province** of China. It was perfect for a takeover because:

- It had **raw materials**, like coal and iron, that Japan needed.

- It had farmland that Japan also needed.

- China was weak. A revolution in 1911 had meant that it was broken up into lots of different provinces led by **warlords** who fought each other.

- Japan had special trading rights in Manchuria.

- A Japanese army was in southern Manchuria.

- Japan owned the South Manchurian Railway.

The Japanese takeover of Manchuria

In September 1931, there was an explosion on the South Manchurian Railway. The Japanese blamed Chinese **sabotage**. The Chinese claimed that, while they had soldiers in the area, they were innocent. The Japanese did not accept this and, in February 1932, put a Chinese ruler, controlled by Japan, in charge of Manchuria. They renamed the province **Manchukuo**.

The Japanese invasion of Manchuria. You can see how important the South Manchurian railway was to the invasion.

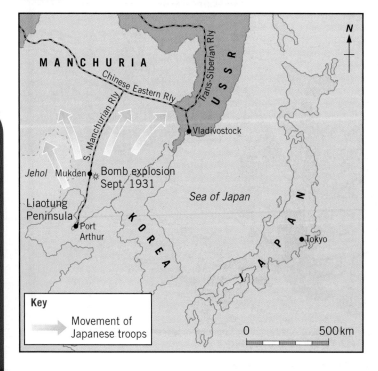

The reaction of the League of Nations

The Chinese complained to the League of Nations. The Japanese told the League that Japan was simply 'protecting its interests' as it had a trade agreement and the railway to protect. Japan was a leading member of the League and there was some truth in its arguments. On the other hand, it was clear that the arguments were a cover for an army takeover.

- The League told Japan to withdraw its troops from Manchuria.

- Instead, the Japanese army took over more land there.

- The League sent a commission to run an enquiry into the incident. It took a long time to get there and to collect information. The report was not published until September 1932. It said Japan should give Manchuria back to China.

- The League presented Japan with the report and asked it to give Manchuria back.

- Japan ignored the report, left the League in 1933 and kept Manchuria.

The Japanese invade China

Japan moved westward through China to gain more territory. In 1933, it moved into the **Jehol province**. The League did nothing.

Japan got bolder. In 1937, it began a major invasion of China. Japan's main trading partner, the USA, was not in the League. Britain traded with Japan, but did not want to use economic sanctions (controls) in case trade was harmed. The League did not want to raise an army and so was powerless against an aggressive dictator who wanted to invade another country.

THINGS TO DO

1 List as many reasons as you can why the League could not stop Japan. Which do you think was most important, and why?

2 Why was Japan's takeover of Manchuria so important in the history of the League?

THE DOORMAT.

Source A cartoon from the London *Evening Standard*, 19 January 1933.

International History 1900–91

31

The Italian conquest of Abyssinia

The background

Abyssinia was an African country that had not yet been made a European colony. It had good farmland and many **minerals**. It was surrounded by European colonies, including Eritrea and Somaliland, both Italian.

- In 1896, Italian troops invaded Abyssinia, but were beaten at the Battle of Adowa.

- In 1928, Italy signed a treaty of friendship with Abyssinia.

- In the 1930s, it became clear that the Italian dictator, **Mussolini**, was preparing to go to war to take Abyssinia.

Mussolini and the League of Nations, January–October 1935

The League did not want a clash with Mussolini. Britain and France wanted him to be their ally against Hitler in Germany. Mussolini decided that neither the League nor Britain and France would act if he took Abyssinia.

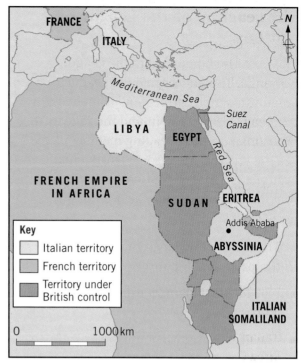

Foreign possessions around Abyssinia, 1935.

Italy attacks Abyssinia, October 1935

In October 1935, Italy invaded Abyssinia. The Italians used modern weapons, including tanks, planes and poison gas. The Abyssinians did not have weapons like these. The only hope for their Emperor, **Haile Selassie**, lay in the size of the country, the poor state of the roads and an appeal to the League of Nations.

Source Destruction after an Italian bombing raid on Abyssinia in December 1935.

The League's response

This was clearly a case of the strong invading the weak. The League should have defended Abyssinia. The first step, according to the League's Covenant, was economic sanctions. The League set up a committee to decide on sanctions:

- The sale of weapons and some goods to Italy was banned.

- No League member was to buy Italian goods or lend Italy money.

But:

- Vital oil and coal were still sold to Italy, to protect US and British trade.

- Italian ships were still allowed to use the **Suez Canal** – Mussolini's main supply route to Abyssinia.

The Hoare–Laval Pact

Meanwhile, the British and French foreign ministers, Hoare and Laval, drew up a plan to end the war. They suggested that Abyssinia should be split into two.

Italy would get the best area for farming and minerals. Haile Selassie would get the poor, mountainous land. The plan was leaked to the press and there was a huge outcry. Britain and France were clearly putting their interests ahead of the interests of the League. Hoare and Laval were forced to resign. This damaged the League's reputation.

Mussolini triumphs

The Italians continue fighting in Abyssinia. In May 1936, they captured the capital city, Addis Ababa. Haile Selaisse managed to escape to Geneva and appealed to the League for more help.

The next step for the League would be to gather an army to turn Mussolini out of Abyssinia. The League did nothing.

Source H

I am here to claim the justice due to my people and help promised to it eight months ago, when 50 nations agreed that Italy's aggression broke international treaties.

From a speech made by Haile Selassie to the League of Nations, 30 June 1936.

The end of the League of Nations

In March 1936, the German dictator, Hitler, had sent troops into the Rhineland, breaking the Treaty of Versailles. The League had done nothing.

Its failure to act in Abyssinia marked the end of the League's influence, even though it was not formally broken up until 1946. In October 1936, Hitler and Mussolini made the **Rome–Berlin Axis** agreement. Another world war was looming.

Source I

The real death of the League was in 1935. One day it was a powerful body and seemed more effective than ever before. The next day it was seen as all show and had the support of no one. Hitler watched.

Written by the historian A. J. P. Taylor in 1966.

The reasons for and implications of the League's failure

Why did the League fail?

- The League did not meet often. It needed all decisions to be agreed by every member. These things made it difficult for the League to make quick decisions.

- The USA was not a member. The USSR did not join until 1934. Germany and Japan left in 1933. Italy left in 1937.

- Sanctions, especially without US support, did not work.

- The League had no army, did not want to fight and had trouble raising an army from its members.

- The League was supposed to uphold the peace treaties of 1919–20. These were now seen as unfair.

What were the implications of the League's failure?

- Japan, Italy and Germany all broke League rules and kept the lands they invaded. The only action they faced was the disapproval of other countries.

- The only way the League could save itself from failure was by rapid action. It was not set up to act quickly. It was not able to agree to raise an army to defend its weaker members.

- This showed that the League could not make collective security work.

- Weak nations realised they could not rely on the League to protect them.

- Britain and France saw the League did not work against dictators. They began to build up their armies.

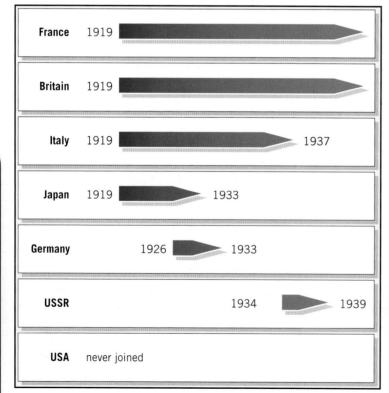

France	1919	
Britain	1919	
Italy	1919	1937
Japan	1919	1933
Germany	1926	1933
USSR	1934	1939
USA	never joined	

The most powerful members of the League of Nations, 1919–46.

THINGS TO DO

Do you think the League of Nations could have been a success? Explain your answer.

1.5 How did Hitler challenge and exploit the Treaty of Versailles in the period 1933 to March 1938?

The Treaty of Versailles

Section 1.3 of this chapter gave the terms of the Treaty of Versailles. Very few people were happy with the treaty.

- The USA thought it was too hard on Germany.

- France thought it was not hard enough, especially when only a fraction of the reparations set in 1921 were actually repaid.

- Germany was humiliated by the way the treaty had been imposed, by the amount of land taken from it, by the War Guilt Clause and by the size of reparations it had to pay (£6600 million).

The German economy recovered rapidly after the war, especially with US help. Germany joined the League of Nations and began trading with other countries.

However, German anger over the Treaty of Versailles remained and gained Hitler support for his aggressive foreign policy in the 1930s.

Hitler's aims

In 1924, Hitler led a rising in Munich to take over the government. It failed. He was sent to prison where he wrote *Mein Kampf*, setting out his aims for the future. They were to:

- rearm Germany and recapture land taken by the Treaty of Versailles

- unite all German-speaking people under German rule

- expand eastwards, taking *lebensraum* (living space) from other countries.

To do this, Germany had to destroy France's power, win Italy's friendship and make Britain an ally.

Hitler's foreign policy

The economic problems caused by the Wall Street Crash pushed Germany into a **depression** and led Germans to elect Hitler and the Nazis to power. Now Hitler could act on his ideas.

German rearmament

Hitler rearmed Germany in stages. He moved slowly, because he did not want to have to fight when the German army was too weak.

1. Germany left the World Disarmament Conference in 1933, although Hitler said Germany would disarm if everyone else did.

2. Germany left the League of Nations.

3. Conscription was introduced in 1935. This broke the Treaty of Versailles but no one stopped Hitler. The British government supported Germany's right to rearm.

4. In 1935, Germany and Britain signed a naval agreement allowing Germany more than the six warships in the Treaty of Versailles. The German fleet still had to be 35 per cent smaller than the British one.

The Saar Plebiscite, 1935

The Treaty of Versailles gave the League of Nations control of the Saar area of Germany. After fifteen years a **plebiscite** (vote) was held in the Saar region. Everyone living there voted on whether the Saar should be given back to Germany.

The plebiscite was held in January 1935 and 90 per cent said 'yes'. The Nazis called this a great victory and the first step to righting the wrongs of the Treaty of Versailles.

The re-militarisation of the Rhineland, 1936

The Treaty of Versailles had said that the German army could not enter the Rhineland, on the French–German border, despite the fact that the Rhineland was German land. On 7 March 1936, Hitler's army marched into the Rhineland and set up bases there. Hitler feared that Britain or France might try to stop him. They did nothing. The occupation of the Rhineland made Hitler popular and more confident about his next move.

Was the Rhineland a missed opportunity?

Why did Britain and France not act against Hitler when he occupied the Rhineland? The German army was still small and could have been defeated without a full-scale war. There were several reasons:

- France wanted to act, but wanted British support.

- The British government did not want to fight Germany. It thought the reoccupation of the Rhineland was just Hitler 'marching into his own backyard'. Many people thought the Treaty of Versailles had been unfair and that Hitler would stop once Germany had a 'fair' settlement.

- The French and British were caught up in a dispute with Mussolini over his invasion of Abyssinia. Mussolini was seen, at this time, as more of a threat than Hitler.

- Hitler was careful to try to keep the peace at this stage. He stressed the unfairness of Versailles. He offered to sign a 25-year peace treaty, to show he was not aiming for war. His tactics worked. While the League of Nations condemned what Hitler had done, it did not act to force his armies out of the Rhineland.

Source B

Germany and Italy are rearming faster than England. In three years, Germany will be ready.

Said by Hitler in a private talk with Mussolini's son-in-law, October 1936.

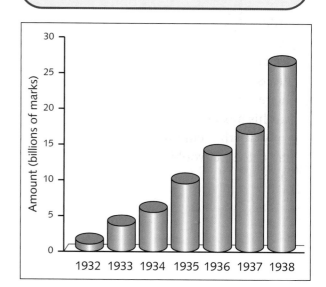

German spending on armaments in the period 1932–8. It shows that rearmament began as soon as Hitler came to power and increased rapidly. There is an especially big increase in 1938, as Hitler was certain he was going to war.

German troops marching into the Rhineland, 7 March 1936.

Anschluss, 1934–8

Hitler wanted to unite Germany and Austria as his next step. This joining together (*Anschluss*) was forbidden in the Treaty of Versailles. In 1934, Austrian Nazis killed the Austrian Chancellor and tried to take over the government.

The man who then became Chancellor, Schuschnigg, opposed them. The Nazis backed down, but Hitler was still looking for a chance to take over.

Source

Even later, when Hitler was fighting almost the entire world, he always said the re-militarisation of the Rhineland was his most daring act. 'We had no army worth mentioning. If the French had acted we would have been beaten easily.'

Albert Speer, one of Hitler's advisers, wrote this after the war.

THINGS TO DO

1 Which two demands of the Treaty of Versailles do you think Germans resented most? Explain your answer.

2 Why did Britain not try to stop German rearmament in the 1930s?

3 Look at **Source C** and read **Source D**. How do you explain their different views of the German army that occupied the Rhineland?

The Spanish Civil War

In 1936, a civil war broke out in Spain. Hitler and Mussolini supported the Spanish **fascist**, **General Franco**. The war had two benefits for Hitler. He used the war to give his new troops practice in dive-bombing and tank formations. The war also brought Hitler and Mussolini together. In 1936, they signed the **Rome–Berlin Axis** agreement. Shortly after, they were joined by Japan in a new treaty, the Anti-Comintern Pact. In this pact they agreed to help each other to stop the spread of communism.

The annexation of Austria (*Anschluss*), 1938

- In 1938, Hitler ordered the Austrian Nazi Party to begin campaigning for Austria to be united with Germany.

- Demonstrations and riots followed. The Chancellor, **Schuschnigg**, began to set up a plebiscite (vote) on union.

- Hitler was too quick for him. He moved his army to the German–Austrian border.

- Schuschnigg resigned and Hitler was invited into Austria 'to restore order'.

- The army marched in, imprisoning over 80,000 of Hitler's opponents.

- Austria and Germany were united on 14 March 1938.

- Only after this was a plebiscite held: 99.75 per cent of people said they agreed with the *Anschluss*.

Hitler had organised the *Anschluss* well. He had reached an agreement with Mussolini before starting the process, so Mussolini would not interfere. He had tested whether Britain and France would go to war by first taking the Rhineland. He then presented the *Anschluss* to them as part of righting the wrongs of Versailles. They had accepted this. Hitler was now ready to move on to his next target, Czechoslovakia.

Source E

The union of Austria and Germany is our life's work, to be done by any means.

An extract from Hitler's Mein Kampf.

Source F

Hitler threatened to march into Austria if his demands were not met. Schuschnigg left the room to get advice. Hitler called for **General Keitel** (who was in charge of the German army). When Keitel arrived and asked what his orders were, Hitler said: 'No orders, I just wanted you here.'

An eyewitness description of part of the negotiations between Hitler and Schuschnigg over the plebiscite in 1938.

Source G

I promise Czechoslovakia has nothing to fear from the Reich.

Said by Hitler to Chamberlain after the Anschluss.

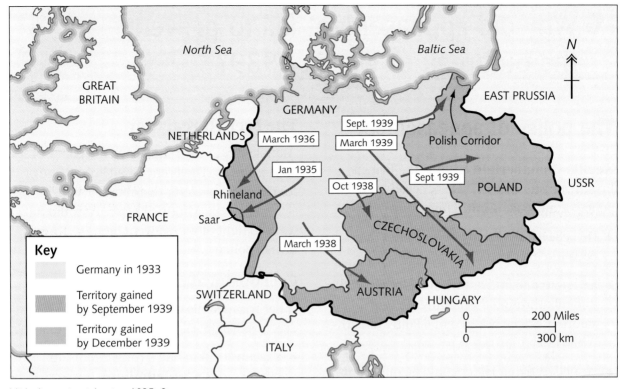

Hitler's territorial gains, 1935–9.

The people of Vienna welcome the arrival of German troops in March 1938.

THINGS TO DO

1 How did the Spanish Civil War help Hitler's plans?

2 (a) When did Hitler hold the plebiscite (vote) in Austria over *Anschluss*?

(b) Why did he do it then?

3 Read **Source F**.

(a) Who was Keitel?

(b) Why did Hitler send for him?

4 What did Hitler learn from European reaction to the *Anschluss*?

The policy of appeasement

Neville Chamberlain became the British Prime Minister in 1937. He believed in the policy of **appeasement**. This meant:

- He believed the Treaty of Versailles had been too hard on Germany.

- He wanted to find out what Hitler wanted and talk through these things to find a solution. So, he believed in dealing directly with Hitler, meeting in person.

- He believed that Hitler could be talked into limiting his demands and that he had to be trusted to do so.

Many British people supported appeasement. They did this for various reasons:

- Many remembered the horrors of the First World War; they did not want another war.

- Britain had not rearmed and so did not have the troops to fight.

- Others were more frightened of the Communist USSR than Germany. Having Germany as an ally could block any USSR expansion.

Source A

Do not misunderstand when the government says it is preparing our defences. I promise there will be no great rearmament.

Said by Stanley Baldwin, the British Prime Minister, during the 1935 election.

The French reaction

After 1937, France supported the policy of appeasement. The French had built a line of **fortifications** along their border with Germany – the **Maginot Line**. They did not want to fight alone, so went along with British policy.

Czechoslovakia, 1938

Hitler planned his next advance into Czechoslovakia. He did this for several reasons:

- Czechoslovakia had strong mountain borders in the **Sudetenland**. It was rich in coal and other minerals.

- Czechoslovakia had been formed by the Treaty of Versailles. So it was a good next step as part of Hitler's policy of undoing the wrongs of the Treaty.

- Czechoslovakia had about 3 million German-speakers from the old Austro-Hungarian empire. Most of these lived in the Sudetenland.

Hitler began by taking the political route, as he had in Austria. He told the leader of the Czech Nazi Party to push the Czech government to give Sudeten Germans special rights. He was to keep on asking for more and more rights. Then, as in Austria, Hitler collected an army on the Czech border.

The Czech President, Benes, mobilised all his troops to fight off the Germans. Britain and France persuaded Benes to give the Sudeten Germans more freedom, to prevent war. They kept on pushing until it was clear that Hitler was determined to invade.

Appeasement in action

- On 12 September 1938, Hitler told the Sudeten Germans that he would support them. This was a definite encouragement to them to rebel. Riots broke out. They were crushed by the Czech army.

- On 15 September, Chamberlain met Hitler and discussed his demands. He then went to see Benes and persuaded the Czech government to transfer the German-speaking parts of the Sudetenland to Germany.

- On 22 September, Chamberlain met Hitler again, telling him what the Czech government had agreed to do.

- Hitler refused to accept the agreement. He said he wanted all of the Sudetenland.

- Chamberlain knew he could not get the Czechs to agree to this. He went back to Britain and began to prepare for war.

- Mussolini persuaded Hitler to take part in talks at Munich, instead of going to war. There was one last chance.

The Munich Conference, September 1938

There were four people at the conference in Munich:

- Chamberlain, the British Prime Minister

- Mussolini, the Italian leader

- Hitler, the German leader

- Daladier, the French Prime Minister.

The Czechs were not invited to send a representative.

The conference agreed that Hitler could have all of the Sudetenland. The Czechs were told to allow Hitler to take over. His army marched in on 1 October 1938. Chamberlain returned home with a separate agreement between Britain and Germany which said that they would never go to war with each other. While some people were worried by events, most people greeted Chamberlain as a hero. He had avoided war.

 Source B

Hitler said that the aim of German foreign policy was to defend and enlarge Germany. We had to begin by taking over Czechoslovakia and Austria. Hitler believed that Britain and France had already written off the Czechs.

From notes taken secretly at a meeting between Hitler and the commanders of his armed forces in November 1937.

 Source C

How horrible, how incredible it is that we are digging trenches and trying on gas masks because of a quarrel far away between people we do not know.

From a radio broadcast by Neville Chamberlain, 22 September 1938.

 Source D A cartoon of the time, entitled 'Still hope', shows Chamberlain on his way to Munich to negotiate a settlement.

The occupation of Czechoslovakia, March 1939

Czechoslovakia now had serious political problems.

- It had lost the Sudetenland.

- Other groups in Czechoslovakia were now demanding their independence.

- In October 1938, Poland gained Polish-speaking Czechoslovakia.

- In November 1938, Hungary gained Hungarian-speaking Czechoslovakia.

- In early 1939, the Slovaks in Czechoslovakia began to demand independence.

- The new Czech President, Hacha, decided to ask a strong neighbour for help. He asked Hitler. On 15 March 1939, Hitler's army marched into the Czech capital, Prague. The army did not help Hacha regain control. It took over.

The Czech government had invited the German army into Czechoslovakia. So, although it then took over, it had not invaded. However, this was the point at which Chamberlain and the other supporters of appeasement realised that Hitler was not going to stop at righting the wrongs of Versailles. He was going to keep taking more and more land. Appeasement was based on trust, and Hitler had shown he could not be trusted.

After the occupation of Czechoslovakia, Britain and France rearmed more quickly. Britain introduced conscription in peacetime for the first time. As Hitler moved into the province of Memel, set up by the Treaty of Versailles, France and Britain worked out that his next target would be Poland.

The threat to Poland

In April 1939, they promised to help Poland if it was attacked by Germany. However, Poland was on the other side of Europe. The country that was best placed to help Poland was the Soviet Union (USSR).

THINGS TO DO

1 Explain what 'appeasement' means.

2 Read **Source F**. Look at the map on page 39. Some historians have criticised the Soviet Union for the Nazi–Soviet Pact.
  (a) How does the Soviet historian in **Source F** excuse the signing?
  (b) How does the map support this?
  (c) Do any events before the Munich Conference not support it?

Source **E** German troops entering Prague in March 1939.

Talks with the USSR

Britain began talks with the USSR, hoping for an alliance to protect Poland. Hitler hated communism and would want to take over German-speaking Soviet land. So this made the USSR a natural ally for Britain.

However, the Poles did not trust the USSR. While the British were still trying to persuade the Poles to accept Soviet help they were shocked to hear that the USSR had signed a pact with Germany.

The Nazi–Soviet Pact, 1939

The Nazi–Soviet Pact, signed on 23 August 1939, was an agreement not to fight each other; it also had secret clauses dividing up Poland. Germany would attack Poland from the west, the USSR from the east. Hitler was sure Britain and France would not help Poland. They had backed down over Czechoslovakia and would do so again.

Why did **Stalin**, leader of the USSR, sign the Pact?

- He was impatient at the time Britain was taking to sign their agreement.

- He was suspicious that Britain and France were pushing Hitler's attention eastwards, to make the USSR face fighting first.

- He was still angry about not being invited to the Munich Conference.

The attack on Poland, 1 September 1939

On 1 September 1939, the German army invaded Poland. Chamberlain asked Germany to withdraw and negotiate. Hitler refused. So, on 3 September, Britain declared war on Germany, followed shortly after by France.

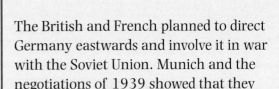

Source F

The British and French planned to direct Germany eastwards and involve it in war with the Soviet Union. Munich and the negotiations of 1939 showed that they did not want to fight Hitler themselves.

The USSR was forced to make a treaty with Germany in the summer of 1939. The Soviet government knew what Hitler's aims were; the treaty gave them a breathing space to prepare their defences.

A Soviet historian writing in 1969 about the Nazi–Soviet Pact.

SUMMARY

1919	Treaty of Versailles.
1933	Hitler takes power.
1934	Germany begins to rearm.
1935	The Saar Plebiscite.
	Mussolini invades Abyssinia.
1936	Re-militarisation of the Rhineland.
	Spanish Civil War.
	Rome–Berlin Axis.
1938	*Anschluss.*
	Munich Agreement.
1939	Invasion of Czechoslovakia.
	Nazi–Soviet Pact.
	Invasion of Poland.

What are the verdicts on the Munich Agreement?

Source G

The Sudetenland is the last problem to be solved. It is my last territorial claim in Europe. Ten million Germans were exiled beyond the borders of the Reich and wished to return.

Hitler speaking in Berlin in 1938.

Source H

Thank God! People of Britain, your children are safe. Your husband and sons will not have to fight. Chamberlain is our victor, his conquests are great and lasting – millions of happy homes and relieved people.

From the Daily Express newspaper, 30 September 1938.

Source I

It is peace for our time ... peace with honour.

From a radio broadcast about the Munich Agreement by Neville Chamberlain, 1 October 1938.

Source J

We have suffered a total defeat. Soon the Nazis will take over Czechoslovakia. This is only the beginning.

From a speech by Winston Churchill in Parliament, October 1938.

Source K

By repeatedly giving in to force, Chamberlain is encouraging it. He fatally misunderstands the way dictators think.

From the Yorkshire Post newspaper, December 1938.

Source L

The settlement forced Czechoslovakia to give Germany 11,000 square miles of land, including all its fortifications. Its rail, road, telephone and telegraph systems were disrupted. It lost 66 per cent of its coal, 86 per cent of its chemicals, 70 per cent of its electric power and 40 per cent of its timber. A wealthy industrial nation was split up and made bankrupt overnight.

Written in 1959 by the US historian William Shirer.

Source M

'Hitler says he has no more territorial ambitions in Europe. Do you believe him?'
Yes: 7 per cent   No: 93 per cent
Results of a British public opinion poll after Munich.

Source N

Those who welcomed the Munich Conference and its settlement saw it as a victory for appeasement. The opponents of Munich saw it as Britain and France failing to live up to their responsibilities. Others saw it as giving in to fear or pushing the Nazis into fighting Soviet Russia. It was all of these things.

Written in 1969 by the British historian A. J. P. Taylor.

Source O

'That fellow Chamberlain has ruined my entry into Prague.'

'Do you know why I finally yielded at Munich? I thought the Home Fleet might open fire.'

Hitler speaking in 1938 after Munich.

Source P

From the military point of view time is in our favour. If war with Germany has to come, it would be better to fight her in six to twelve months time.

Chamberlain's military advisers 1938.

Source Q

They are little worms. I saw them at Munich.

Hitler's opinion of Britain and France expressed in April 1939.

Source R

The Pact of Munich is signed. Czechoslovakia as a power is out. The genius of the Führer and his determination not to avoid even a world war have again won victory without the use of force. The hope remains that the doubters have been converted and will remain that way.

A German general speaking after Munich.

Source S

A Swiss cartoon about Munich, drawn at the time. 'Pax' means 'peace'. Under the sheet marked 'Pax' you can see the shapes of soldiers and a big gun.

THINGS TO DO

1 Some people saw Munich as a success, others as a failure. Divide the sources on pages 44 and 45 under these two headings.

2 What does **Source M** tell us about how popular the Munich agreement was in Britain?

3 What view does the artist of **Source S** have of Munich? What might affect the reliability of this view?

1.7 Why did the USA and USSR become rivals in the period 1945 to 1949?

Communism and capitalism

The USA and the USSR had been allies during the war, but they had very different political systems.

The USSR was communist:

- no free elections because there was only one political party to choose from

- state-owned industry.

The USA was capitalist:

- free elections with a choice of political party (this was a democratic system)

- industry owned by individuals and companies.

After the Second World War, the USSR feared that the USA wanted to destroy communism. At the same time the USA thought that the USSR wanted to destroy capitalism and undermine democratic countries. These two superpowers and their allies argued but avoided fighting. This was called the Cold War.

The Yalta Conference

In February 1945, before the war had ended, the three leaders of the Allies, Roosevelt (USA), Churchill (Britain) and Stalin (USSR) met at the town of Yalta. They agreed to:

- divide Germany into four zones (Britain, France, the USSR and the USA to get one each)

- allow the USSR to have some sort of control over eastern Europe. The countries in eastern Europe were to have elections to decide who would govern them.

The Potsdam Conference, July 1945

By the time the Allied leaders met again, Roosevelt had died and Churchill was no longer Prime Minister of Britain. Stalin was the only leader who had been at Yalta. He did not get on with the new US President, Truman, and they had a number of disagreements. The USA and USSR distrusted each other more and more. The Cold War had begun.

Reparations and the atom bomb

The two main disagreements at Potsdam were about reparations and the **atom bomb**.

At the end of the First World War, Germany had been made to pay for the damage it had caused during the war. Many people believed that this was unfair and had in some way helped to cause the Second World War. They did not want reparations to cause a third world war. However, the USSR had suffered very badly during the Second World War and so wanted the money or goods reparations would provide.

Modern World History for AQA

Source

> The Soviet government is alarmed by the attitude of the US government. The American attitude cooled once it became clear that Germany was defeated. It was as though the Americans were saying that the USSR was no longer needed.
>
> *Stalin talking about the American President, Harry S. Truman, in May 1945.*

The Iron Curtain.

Growing divisions between East and West

In March 1946, **Winston Churchill** made a speech where he described the differences between East and West as being so great as to be like an **iron curtain** coming down between them.

Churchill might have made this speech to make sure that the Americans kept an army in Europe. This would help to make sure that no more countries became communist.

USSR and eastern Europe: the Iron Curtain

At Yalta, both sides had agreed to allow free elections to decide the governments of countries in eastern Europe. The USSR made sure, sometimes by force, that communist governments, loyal to the USSR, were set up in many countries.

While it was agreed that Germany should pay reparations, the western Allies soon realised that a weak Germany might be taken over by the USSR. They began to strengthen the German economy. Stalin was suspicious of this.

At the same time, the USA announced it was going to use the atom bomb to force Japan to surrender. The US government told the USSR only eleven days before the bomb was used. The USSR was worried that the USA might use the bomb against communist countries too.

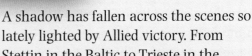

A shadow has fallen across the scenes so lately lighted by Allied victory. From Stettin in the Baltic to Trieste in the Adriatic, an iron curtain has descended across the continent.

Extract from Churchill's speech at Fulton, USA, in March 1946.

PEEP UNDER THE IRON CURTAIN

Source C A British cartoon, published in March 1946, commenting on the Iron Curtain between East and West.

Communist satellite governments (controlled by the USSR) were set up in Poland, Hungary, Romania, Bulgaria and Albania.

The Western Allies saw this as part of Stalin's plan to spread communism throughout Europe.

The Truman Doctrine

In 1947, it looked as if communists would take control in Greece and Turkey. In March 1947, President Truman promised to help any country threatened by communism. The Americans believed that the countries in eastern Europe had been forced to become communist; they were determined to prevent this happening again. This was known as the 'Truman Doctrine'.

The USA gave :

- $400 million aid to help Greece and Turkey.

- US ballistic missile (nuclear weapons) sites were set up in Turkey (facing the USSR).

The Greek government defeated the communists and the Turkish government was strengthened. The USSR did not have nuclear weapons at this time and came to mistrust the USA even more.

The Marshall Plan

The Marshall Plan was another part of the Truman Doctrine. The USA offered European countries economic aid after the war to help them resist any threat from the USSR.

- $15 billion was made available to Europe.

Stalin would not let eastern European countries take any of the money. He did not want communist countries to become dependent on the USA nor start trading with it.

Source D

Our policy is directed not against any country or doctrine but against hunger, poverty, desperation and chaos. Any country that is willing to assist in the task of recovery will find full co-operation on the part of the US government.

George C. Marshall, the US Secretary of State, speaking about his plan for aiding Europe, June 1947.

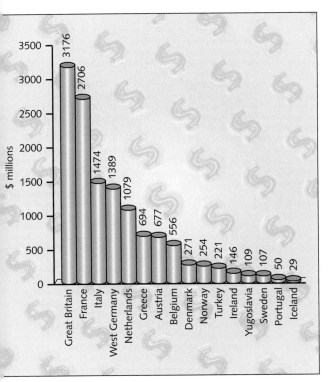

Aid received under the Marshall Plan.

European recovery

Altogether sixteen nations in western Europe asked the USA for help. These countries included Allies, such as Britain, and former enemies, such as West Germany. Between 1948 and 1950 industrial production in western Europe had increased by 25 per cent. By 1952, most western European economies were on their way to recovery.

Stalin was not pleased. He asked Soviet **satellites** to withdraw their applications for Marshall Aid. This meant that he was forced to offer these countries help instead. In order to provide this help the Council for Mutual Economic Assistance, or **Comecon**, was set up. However, as the Soviet Union did not have enough money to help other countries Comecon was never effective.

Stalin was very suspicious of the Marshall Plan as he saw it as an attempt by the USA to gain more control in Europe. Stalin's fears increased the divisions within Europe.

The Cominform

In 1947 **Cominform** (Communist Information Bureau) was set up. This was designed to help spread communism and protect communist states from US aggression. Stalin did not want any opposition at all, and in 1948 Stalin asked for Tito, the communist leader of Yugoslavia, to be expelled as Tito refused to do as Stalin wished. The West saw Cominform as a serious challenge and relations between the superpowers got even worse.

The post-war division of Germany

After the Second World War, Germany had been divided into four zones controlled by the USA, Britain, France and the USSR. Berlin, the capital city of Germany was divided up in the same way (see map on the next page).

The problem was that Berlin was right in the middle of the Soviet zone. To get there from the West you had to travel through '**corridors**'. The West depended on the good will of the Soviets to keep their contact with Berlin. The Allies lost this good will when the West made some decisions that the Soviets did not like.

What did the West do to anger the Soviets?

- The West gave its zones help in the form of Marshall Aid.

- The West gave extra help to West Berlin.

- The West joined the British, French and US zones together.

- The West planned to bring in a new German currency, the **Deutschmark**, to help the German economy.

How did Stalin, the leader of the USSR react to all this?

The Berlin Blockade

Stalin felt that a richer Germany was not a good idea. He thought that it might eventually threaten the Soviet countries near Germany. On 24 June 1948 he decided to act. He closed all roads, canals and railways between the West and West Berlin. He wanted to force the West to give up West Berlin by starving the two million people living there. The people of West Berlin only had fuel and food to last six weeks.

Truman, the US President, had two choices. He could let the USSR have West Berlin or he could go to war. He did not want to do either. In the end, the governments of the West came up with a less dangerous plan. They decided to fly in supplies. This became known as the **Berlin Airlift**.

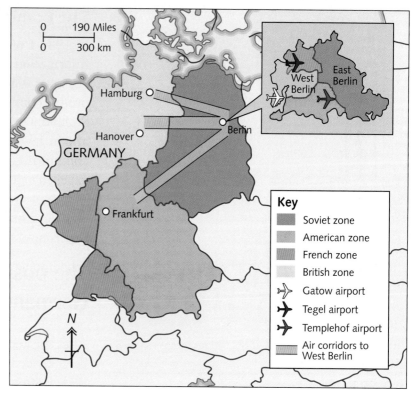

The occupied zones of Germany in 1945.

Key
- Soviet zone
- American zone
- French zone
- British zone
- Gatow airport
- Tegel airport
- Templehof airport
- Air corridors to West Berlin

The Berlin Airlift

People living in West Berlin needed 4000 tons of fuel and food supplies each day if they were to survive the **Blockade**. The Allies (Britain, United States and France) used the three air corridors (see the map above) to deliver what they needed.

Source **E**

When Berlin falls, Western Germany will be next. If we withdraw our position in Berlin, Europe is threatened. Communism will run rampant.

> *General Clay, the American commander in Berlin, on the dangers of the Blockade.*

THINGS TO DO

1 How did the West try to help Germany?

2 Why did the USSR not like this?

3 Which three countries got the most help from the United States? Use the graph on page 49 to help you.

4 Read **Source E.** Why did the West fear the loss of Berlin to the USSR?

Supplies to Berlin

- **26 June 1948:** airlift began, but deliveries were only 600 tons a day

- **September 1948:** aircraft landing every three minutes with fresh supplies

- **Spring 1949:** 8000 tons a day being delivered.

Stalin tried to put the Berliners under more pressure. He ordered electricity supplies to be cut off and offered Berliners extra rations if they moved to the Soviet sector.

The Allied aircraft were tracked to make sure that they did not fly outside the agreed air corridor. This was little more than a gesture. Stalin dared not order the shooting down of these aircraft or a third world war might follow. It also became clear that the Berliners were prepared to suffer rather than become part of the communist USSR. Stalin called off the Berlin Blockade in May 1949.

The cost of the Berlin Airlift

- 79 British and US airmen lost their lives.

- Any hopes of uniting Germany were over.

- The West had shown how determined it was to fight communism.

- The USA became determined to show East Berlin what it was like to live in the West. It made West Berlin a showcase for everything that was good in the capitalist West.

Two new countries

In 1949, the three Allied zones were joined to form **West Germany**.

The USSR made its zone East Germany.

Source **F**

When we refused to be forced out of Berlin, we demonstrated to Europe that we would act when freedom was threatened. This action was a Russian plan to probe the soft spots in the Western Allies' positions.

President Truman speaking in 1949 about the Berlin crisis.

Source **G**

The crisis was planned in Washington, behind a smoke-screen of anti-Soviet propaganda. In 1948 there was the danger of war.

The self-blockade of the Western powers hit the West Berlin population with harshness. The people were freezing and starving. In the spring of 1949 the USA was forced to yield; their war plans came to nothing

A Soviet version of the Berlin crisis.

THE BIRD WATCHER

Source **H** A *Punch* cartoon from July 1948. It shows Stalin watching the Allied 'storks' flying supplies to Berlin during the Blockade.

Exam-style assessment – OPTION V

In the exam, the questions will follow the same pattern in each option. In the examples in the book, this does not always apply in order to show the variety of questions that can be set. In the examination, if you choose Option V, you must answer two of the three questions in the section.

Question 1: The alliances and the outbreak of war in 1914

Study **Sources A** and **B** and then answer the following questions.

Source A: The formation of the Triple Entente 1904–7

In 1904 Britain signed the Entente Cordiale with France. To Britain this was a colonial agreement which solved areas of dispute between Britain and France. The diplomatic support promised to France made Morocco the centre of European disputes in the next few years. The completion of the Triple Entente three years later marked the division of Europe into two rival camps. It was no military alliance but, since France was Russia's ally, most European statesmen believed that Britain had cast her vote on the side of Russia and France against the Triple Alliance.

From *Europe since Napoleon* by David Thomson, a British historian, published in 1957

Source B: An Austrian comment on the assassination at Sarajevo 1914

The assassination at Sarajevo is not the crime of a single fanatic; assassination represents Serbia's declaration of war on Austria–Hungary.

From a speech by Conrad von Hotzendorf, the Chief of Austrian General Staff, made immediately after the assassination

(a) According to **Source A**, what was the importance of the alliances Great Britain made in 1904 and 1907? **(3 marks)**

(b) Describe what happened at Sarajevo on 28 June 1914. **(6 marks)**

(c) How reliable is **Source B** to an historian writing about the importance of the assassination at Sarajevo? Use **Source B** and your own knowledge to answer the question. **(6 marks)**

(d) Was the system of alliances that existed in 1914 the main cause of World War One? Explain your answer. **(10 marks)**

Question 2: Attempts to keep peace after World War One

Study **Source C** and then answer the following questions.

Source C: The Manchurian Crisis 1931–2

For some years past unpleasant incidents have taken place in the region of Manchuria where Japan has special trade interests and treaty rights. The area has been subject to the raids of Chinese bandits and in September a detachment of Chinese troops destroyed the tracks of the South Manchurian Railway near Mukden and murdered Japanese guards. The Japanese army had to act swiftly to restore order.

From an official report of the Japanese Government published in September 1931

(a) According to **Source C**, why did the Japanese invade Manchuria in 1931? **(3 marks)**

(b) Do you think that **Source C** is a reliable account of the causes of the invasion? Use **Source C** and your own knowledge to answer the question. **(6 marks)**

(c) Describe how the League of Nations tried to solve the Manchurian Crisis. **(6 marks)**

(d) Was the Manchurian Crisis the most important reason for the failure of the League of Nations? Explain your answer. **(10 marks)**

Question 3: From World War Two to Cold War

Study **Sources D** and **E** and then answer the following questions.

Source D: The Yalta Agreement February 1945

> At Yalta, the USA, the USSR and Great Britain agreed that Germany would be divided up into four zones of Allied occupation, as would Berlin. The three powers agreed that they would assist any European state which had been freed from German control, to form a government which was representative of all democratic elements in the population. They pledged themselves to the establishment through free elections of governments responsible to the will of the people.

From a British historian writing in 2000

Source E: The spread of Communism

This French cartoon was published after World War Two. It shows the Russian leader, Stalin, spreading communism to other countries.

(a) According to **Source D**, what was agreed at Yalta ? **(3 marks)**

(b) Describe the main problems facing the Allied leaders when they met at Potsdam in May 1945 and how they solved them. **(6 marks)**

(c) How reliable is **Source E** to an historian writing about the Soviet expansion in Eastern Europe after World War Two? Use **Source E** and your own knowledge to answer the question. **(6 marks)**

(d) In the period 1945 to 1949, Germany was often at the centre of the Cold War. Explain why this was so. **(10 marks)**

1.8 How did the Cold War develop in the period 1949 to 1963?

Nato and the Warsaw Pact

The success of the Truman Doctrine, the Marshall Plan and the Berlin Airlift showed that the Americans were not going to return to the policy of **isolationism** they had had in 1919.

In 1949, the western Allies formed the **North Atlantic Treaty Organisation** (NATO). This was a **military alliance**. Its twelve member countries (USA, Canada, Britain, France, Belgium, the Netherlands, Iceland, Luxembourg, Italy, Norway and Portugal) agreed to act together to protect **democracy** and freedom.

NATO would stop the spread of communism by surrounding the Soviet states; all members agreed to go to war if any one of them was attacked. Greece and Turkey joined in 1952 and West Germany in 1955.

When West Germany joined NATO, the Soviet Union once again began to fear a stronger Germany. So, in 1955, the Communist countries joined together to form the **Warsaw Pact**. These eight countries (Albania, Bulgaria, Czechoslovakia, East Germany, Hungary, Poland, Romania and the USSR) agreed to defend themselves against NATO.

The setting up of NATO and the Warsaw Pact made the tensions of the Cold War even worse.

Source A

A Soviet cartoon expressing the fear that Germany would emerge again to threaten the USSR.

Source B

A British cartoon, dated 2 March 1948, commenting on the spread of communism in Europe.

"WHO'S NEXT TO BE LIBERATED FROM FREEDOM, COMRADE?"

North Atlantic Treaty Organisation			
1949	1952	1955	1982
Belgium	Greece	West Germany	Spain
Britain	Turkey		
Canada			
Denmark			
France			
Iceland			
Italy			
Luxembourg			
Netherlands			
Norway			
Portugal			
USA			

Warsaw Pact
Albania (Expelled 1968)
Bulgaria
Czechoslavakia
East Germany
Hungary
Poland
Romania
USSR

Membership of NATO and the Warsaw Pact.

Soviet and US involvement in Korea

Between 1910 and 1945, the Japanese had controlled Korea. In 1945, Japan was defeated in the Second World War and had to leave Korea. Soviet forces occupied the north and American forces occupied the south.

Both sides promised to leave Korea after free elections had taken place. This did not happen. In the north, the USSR decided to keep control through Kim Il Sung. Elections in the south saw an anti-communist government led by Syngman Rhee, who was elected to run the country from Seoul.

Korea is divided

Once new governments had been elected in the north and the south of the country the USSR and the USA withdrew their troops. The country was divided along the 38°N parallel while both sides claimed that all of Korea was theirs.

In 1949, when all of China became communist, South Korea was on its own surrounded by communist countries. The United States was very worried that South Korea would be the next to become communist, as part of the **domino theory** (the theory that, like a row of standing dominoes, as soon as one country became communist others would follow).

Stalin and the Chinese leaders encouraged Kim Il Sung to attack South Korea. They even provided money and weapons but avoided sending in any of their own troops. In June 1950, North Korea attacked the South and the Korean War began.

The Korean War

- Between June and September 1950, North Korea was very successful. South Korean troops were forced back to the Pusan Pocket in the south-east (see map on page 56).

- South Korea was desperate. It asked the United Nations for help. The permanent members of its Security Council declared that North Korea was the **aggressor** (in the wrong) and promised to send help to the South.

- Sixteen nations under the leadership of the US **General Douglas MacArthur** went to Korea. A surprise landing on 15 September 1950 at Inchon forced the communists back. North Korean resistance collapsed and the Americans and their allies forced the North Koreans back towards China and the Yalu River.

- Communist China was worried by this and warned the UN not to go near the Yalu River. MacArthur, against the orders of his President, did so and was sacked.

  In November 1950, the Chinese sent 200,000 troops to help North Korea. They pushed the United Nations forces back past the 38°N parallel and into the South.

- Between July 1951 and July 1953 there was **stalemate**. Neither side gained the advantage and yet many soldiers lost their lives.

  After the death of Stalin in 1953, the USSR decided that problems at home were more important and agreed to a cease-fire which divided Korea, yet again, by the 38°N parallel.

The maps on this page show how the Korean War progressed. This is described on page 55.

1 June – September 1950

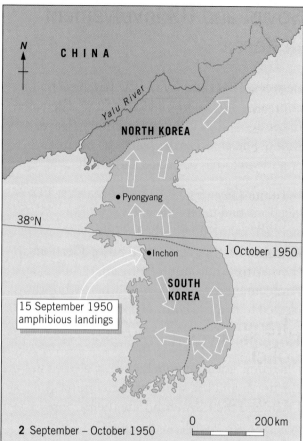

2 September – October 1950

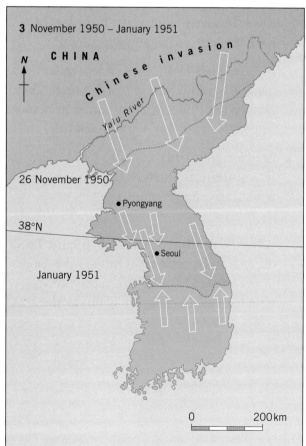

3 November 1950 – January 1951

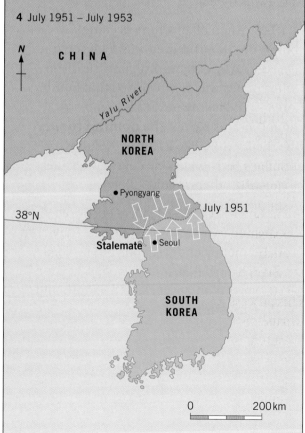

4 July 1951 – July 1953

The Korean War, 1950–3.

The impact of the Korean War

- The Cold War grew worse. It spread across the world.

- The **South East Asian Treaty Organisation** (SEATO) was formed in 1954. It was like NATO – it was designed to stop communism in the Far East.

- The USA thought that it had kept communism back.

- China was now a world power.

- It showed that the United Nations could work together much better than the League of Nations.

Changing attitudes and policies in the 1950s

Krushchev and co-existence

When Stalin died in 1953, the Soviet people were relieved that the **regime** which saw thousands killed or imprisoned by the secret police was over (see Chapter 4).

In 1955, **Nikita Khrushchev** took over and began to change the way the USSR was run.

- In 1956 Khruschev made a speech at the 20th Party Congress of the Communist Party criticising Stalin.

- Stalin's body was removed from the **Kremlin** (government headquarters) and statues of him were taken down.

- Krushchev allowed more consumer goods such as washing machines to be produced which helped many people.

This process was called **destalinisation**. Khrushchev became more popular in the West too. He wanted the two systems to live side by side. This was called **peaceful co-existence**. In terms of the Cold War, this time became known as a '**thaw**'.

How was Eastern Europe affected?

Seeing the changes in the Soviet Union, some of the satellite states (countries under Russian control) began to hope for change. They wanted more freedom and political and social reforms.

Khrushchev was not willing to see too many changes. He did not trust the West enough to lose control of the satellite states. Three of these states revolted against the USSR:

- East Germany in 1953

- Poland and Hungary in 1956.

Each time Khrushchev crushed the revolts with tanks and troops. This led to the end of the 'thaw' and a worsening in relations between East and West.

THINGS TO DO

1 Why did the United Nations become involved in Korea?

2 What were the results of the Korean War?

Challenging the West

Khrushchev was determined to show the rest of the world that communism did really work and that the Soviet Union could compete with the West.

- The Soviet Union wanted to shows its sporting ability. The Olympic Games were important for this.

- Khrushchev travelled abroad offering aid to third world countries. These visits raised people's opinion of the Soviet Union.

- The Soviet Union continued to test and develop **nuclear weapons**. It exploded its first atom bomb in 1949. The **nuclear race** worsened the Cold War situation.

- The Soviet Union took part in a **space race** with the USA. In 1957, it launched the first satellite, **Sputnik**, and even put a dog into space (see Source C). In 1961, the first man to orbit the earth was a Russian.

The Hungarian Rising, 1956

The Hungarians thought that life in Hungary should change. There were three main reasons for this:

- the death of Stalin

- the new leadership of Khrushchev and the policy of **co-existence**

- a **revolt** in Poland in June 1956 which had led to some changes there.

The Hungarians wanted to end Soviet control of their country. They wanted more freedom and more contact with the West. Some even hoped that Soviet troops would leave Hungary.

Reform in Hungary

In October 1956, **Imre Nagy** was elected Prime Minister of Hungary after a series of demonstrations in the capital, Budapest. The demonstrations had caught the government of the Soviet Union out. It was not ready to deal with this, so it made the decision to withdraw.

The Soviet Union could beat the Hungarians easily but hoped that withdrawal would allow things to calm down.

Laika, the first dog in space.

D   A photograph taken in Budapest in November 1956.

Nagy began to introduce reforms:

- Control of newspapers, magazines and radio stations was lifted;

- Non-communists were allowed to be part of the government;

- Hungary was to leave the Warsaw Pact;

- Free elections were promised.

The Rising is crushed

Khrushchev would not accept these changes. Nagy had gone too far.

On 4 November 1956 the Soviet armies returned in strength and crushed the revolt. The Hungarians fought hard but were no match for them. Over 30,000 Hungarians were killed. Over 200,000 fled to western Europe. The Soviet authorities promised Nagy safety, but he was later arrested and executed. All the reforms were cancelled.

What did the West do?

The West did nothing. Britain and France were too involved in their own problems in Egypt over the Suez Canal to help Hungary. The USA did not want to get involved in a war which might end up using nuclear weapons (*both* sides had nuclear weapons now).

The thaw was over. Khrushchev was not prepared to see changes to the countries that protected the USSR from the West. The hopes of 1953–4 were disappearing fast because Khrushchev was going to take on the West. The Cold War began hotting up once more.

Source   **E**

There is no stopping the wild onslaught of communism. Your turn will come, once we perish. Save our souls! Save our souls! We implore you to help us in the name of justice and freedom.

A broadcast to the West from Hungarian fighters on 4 November 1956.

International History 1900–91

The nuclear arms race, 1945–63

For four years after the war the USA was the only country in the world with nuclear weapons. During this time the USSR could do nothing to reply to a nuclear attack. However, in 1949 the Soviets exploded their first atom bomb. This now meant that the Americans and the Soviets were on more equal terms if it came to war. This was made worse when the Americans exploded a much more powerful **H-bomb** in 1952 and the Soviets did the same a year later. These H-bombs could destroy a whole city.

Key developments in the nuclear arms race:

1945   Atom bomb dropped on Hiroshima

        Atom bomb dropped on Nagasaki

1949   First Soviet atom bomb exploded

1952   First American H-bomb tested

1953   First Soviet H-bomb tested

1957   First satellite in space (the Soviet satellite, Sputnik)

1958   USA responds by developing own rockets and satellites

1960   First **Polaris-type submarine** launches missile. These missiles had a range of over 1600 kilometres and were fired from under the sea.

Nuclear deterrent

By the early 1960s both sides realised that if one side launched an attack on the other, the other side now had the weapons and the technology to strike back.

This meant that neither side would dare risk using nuclear weapons against the other. But both sides thought they must go on developing nuclear weapons so as to keep one step ahead.

This was called the **nuclear deterrent**.

> ## THINGS TO DO
>
> In your own words, explain the term 'nuclear deterrent'.

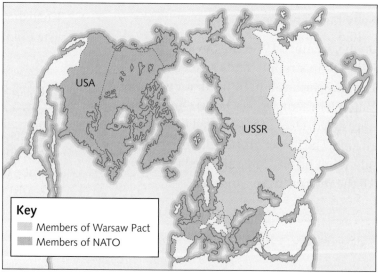

This map shows how the world was divided between communist and capitalist, East and West, NATO and the Warsaw Pact (see page 54).

Key
- Members of Warsaw Pact
- Members of NATO

The beginnings of the space race

Date	Country	Event
4 October 1957	Soviet Union	Sputnik 1 first artificial Earth-orbiting satellite
3 November 1957	Soviet Union	Sputnik 2 first animal in space, a dog called Laika
31 January 1958	USA	First US satellite in space
12 September 1959	Soviet Union	Luna 2 hits the surface of the Moon
4 October 1959	Soviet Union	Luna 3 takes pictures of the far side of the Moon
12 April 1961	Soviet Union	First man, Yuri Gagarin, put into orbit in Vostock 1
5 May 1961	USA	Alan Shepherd becomes first American in space
20 February 1962	USA	Colonel John Glenn becomes the first American to orbit the Earth
16 June 1963	Soviet Union	Valentina Tereshkova becomes the first woman in space

Key events in the space race, 1957–63.

Although American pride was hurt when the Russians put Sputnik into space in 1957, they were probably more worried about the powerful rocket which took it there. A powerful rocket could also launch a nuclear weapon at the enemy. The USA had worked this out too. This led to the development of **inter-continental ballistic missiles** (ICBMs) by both sides. By 1960, both sides had enough weapons to destroy the earth.

Peaceful co-existence?

Both sides felt another war would be disastrous. They began to talk about 'peaceful co-existence', about controlling separate parts of the world and leaving each other alone. Both sides would benefit.

- Communism seemed to be a match for capitalism.

- Both sides decided peaceful co-existence had to work.

- Fear on both sides prevented another world war breaking out.

- The huge cost of scientific developments led to scientific co-operation between the USSR and the USA.

- The cost of the arms/space race almost **bankrupted** the Soviet economy in the 1980s and led to the end of the Soviet Union (see pages 86–91).

(see pages 86–91).

Source F

The Sputniks prove that communism has won the competition between the communist and the capitalist countries. The economy, science, culture and the creative genius of people in all spheres of life develop better and faster under communism.

Khrushchev comments on the successes of communism.

THINGS TO DO

1 Why did the Soviet Union take part in the space race against the USA?

2 How useful is **Source E** to an historian studying the Hungarian Rising?

Crises in the early 1960s and their causes and results

The U2 Incident, 1962

There was little progress in ending the Cold War between the Hungarian Rising of 1956 and the beginning of the 1960s. Both the arms race and the space race continued. However, at the beginning of 1960, there was a chance that the thaw might begin again. A meeting of the big four was arranged to take place in Paris. The big four were:

- President Eisenhower (USA)
- First Secretary Krushchev (Soviet Union)
- President De Gaulle (France)
- Prime Minister Macmillan (Great Britain).

The hopes were that at last the leaders of capitalism and communism could patch up their differences and begin a new period of friendly relations and peace. These hopes were ruined before leaders even arrived in Paris.

The 'Spy in the Sky'

In the 1950s, the Americans had developed a plane that could fly at 75,000 feet. Even if Soviet **radar** saw it, it was too high for Soviet planes to do anything about. It also had a very powerful camera, so it could take good pictures of Soviet military bases without the Soviets knowing.

The pilot of the U2 spy plane, Gary Powers, set off from Peshawar in Pakistan on 1 May 1960, just two days before the summit was due to start. The flight went well and he took hundreds of photographs of Soviet military bases. As he was passing over the town of Sverdlovsk, his plane was shot down by a Soviet SAM-2 missile. He managed to eject from his plane and landed safely only to be captured by the Soviet forces on the ground. His plane crashed but was also found by the Soviets. It was recovered so that Soviet scientists could study it.

Source G

A Soviet cartoon, called 'The Art of Camouflage', comments on the USA's attitude to peace. The dove of peace is being painted onto the U2 spy plane.

Source H

Instructions to Mr Powers and other pilots are to feel free to tell the full truth about their mission. We think this is a firmly American way of behaviour – we can leave the bald-faced lying to the Soviets. We have to do this work, but we can be manly about it.

An extract from the Washington Daily News after Gary Powers' release from the Soviet Union.

The intended route of Powers' U2 spy plane.

The end of hopes for peace

Khrushchev claimed the Americans did not know how to stop planning for a war. He demanded an apology from the Americans. Eisenhower refused to apologise claiming he had to do whatever would stop his country suffering from a surprise attack.

Khrushchev stormed out of the meeting. He cancelled an invitation to President Eisenhower to visit the Soviet Union. The Cold War has just got colder at a time when people thought there would be a thaw.

Postscript: Gary Powers

Gary Powers was tried in Moscow on charges of spying. He was sentenced to ten years imprisonment. Seventeen months later he was released in exchange for a top Soviet spy from a US prison.

The American response

As soon as the Americans knew that the U2 plane had been hit they saw that the Paris talks could be ruined. So they tried to cover up what had happened. They said:

- the U2 was a research plane and not a 'spy in the sky' plane
- that it was studying weather conditions and not military bases
- it had disappeared over Turkey and not over the Soviet Union.

But the Americans did not know that:

- the plane had been recovered
- Gary Powers had been captured and had admitted being a spy
- the Soviet Union had also captured thousands of photographs.

On 7 May the Soviet Union demanded an apology.

Source   A cartoon from a British newspaper in 1960.

The Berlin Wall

Berlin was a big embarrassment to the USSR. People in West Berlin were able to buy luxury goods thanks to the economic aid sent by the USA after 1945. People in East Berlin, on the other hand, worked long hours and had to put up with food shortages. The people in East Berlin rebelled in 1954 but the rebellion was crushed by the army.

The 'Iron Curtain' was intended to stop western ideas entering eastern Europe. The only problem was that there was a 'hole' in it. That hole was in Berlin itself.

There was nothing stopping people from moving between East Berlin and West Berlin. Many East Germans thought that life in the West was better. Between 1945 and 1960, people were moving to the West at a rate of 500 a day. Up to 1961 over two million people left East Berlin for West Berlin. Many of them were well-qualified young people.

This was an embarrassment for communism as well as a drain on the resources of East Germany. It spread a message that communism did not work. Something had to be done.

Source J   The Berlin Wall.

Building the Wall

On 13 August 1961, the East Germans began to build a 160-kilometre barrier between East and West Berlin. At first it was a border of machine guns and barbed wire fence, but a concrete wall was soon built. It sealed off West Berlin from East Germany.

Many people still tried to leave East Berlin. Between 1961 and 1989, 86 people are known to have died trying to get across the wall and through the barbed wire.

Propaganda

Relations between the superpowers were already poor after the Gary Powers U2 incident. The Americans now asked why, if communism was so good, they had to build a barrier to cage people in.

In 1963, President Kennedy visited West Berlin. The people turned out in their thousands to see and hear him say 'Ich bin ein Berliner' (I am a Berliner). He had taken the opportunity to show how much the USA was committed to the people of West Berlin. The Soviet Union was furious and saw the visit as a deliberate attempt to cause trouble.

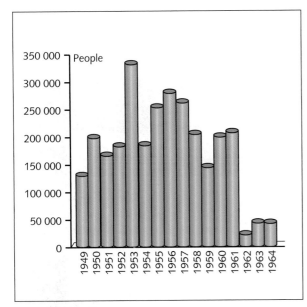

This graph shows the number of people who escaped from East Germany to West Germany, 1949–64.

Source **K**

In no part of the world are so many spies of foreign states to be found as in West Berlin. Nowhere else can they act with such freedom. These spies are smuggling agents into East Germany, causing sabotage and riot.

The view of the East German government, 1961.

Source **L**

Democracy may not be perfect but we never had to put up walls to keep our people in.

The view of J. F. Kennedy, 1962.

THINGS TO DO

1 Why did so many young people leave East Berlin for the West?

2 Why did the East German authorities want to stop people leaving East Berlin?

3 Do you think East Germans had a right to build the wall? Explain your answer.

4 How did the West use the wall as a reason to criticise communism?

5 Why did saying, 'I am a Berliner' please the crowd of West Berliners?

6 Why were the Soviet authorities angry with this visit?

1.9 How close to war did the world come over Cuba in 1962?

Communist rule in Cuba

Cuba is a large island only 150 kilometres away from the USA. The USA gave Cuba financial aid and bought Cuban goods such as sugar cane and tobacco. During the 1950s Cuba was so badly run by **Fulgencio Batista** that the country went bankrupt.

The Cuban people, led by **Fidel Castro**, rebelled. In January 1959, Castro overthrew Batista and set up his own government, which seemed to be pro-communist. The USA became increasingly worried that communist ideas might spread from Cuba to Central and southern America.

The US government stopped the trade in Cuban sugar and tobacco. Castro made a trade agreement with several communist countries, including the USSR. He took control of all industries and businesses in Cuba, most of which were owned by Americans. The USA now had a neighbour which was allied to its greatest rival, the USSR.

The Bay of Pigs, 1961

In April 1961, President Kennedy allowed 1400 supporters of Batista to attack Cuba. They landed at the **Bay of Pigs** in April 1961 but failed to gain any local support and were easily destroyed by Castro's men.

President Kennedy and the USA felt humiliated by this easy defeat. Worse, the fact that they had tried to help Batista and overthrow Castro meant that Castro felt threatened by the USA and looked to the USSR for help and protection.

The Cuban missile crisis, 1962

- In June 1962, shipments of arms were sent by the Soviet Union to Cuba.

- In September, Khrushchev decided to send inter-continental ballistic missiles (ICBMs) to Cuba. The Americans knew about these shipments but the Soviets insisted that the weapons were only for defence.

- On 14 October a U2 spy plane from the USA spotted and photographed the missile sites on Cuba.

- The spy plane also spotted 20 ships carrying missiles to Cuba.

The missiles had a range of 4000 kilometres (2500 miles) and the USA realised that nearly all its major cities were now at risk of nuclear missile attack from Cuba (see the map on page 67).

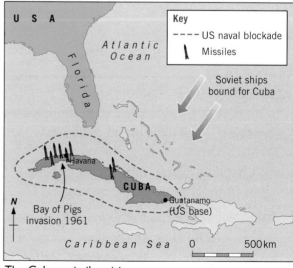

The Cuban missile crisis.

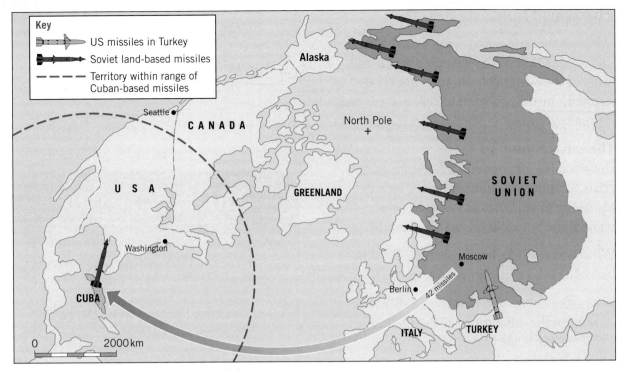

Key
- US missiles in Turkey
- Soviet land-based missiles
- Territory within range of Cuban-based missiles

Alaska

Seattle

CANADA

North Pole

USA

GREENLAND

SOVIET
UNION

Washington

Moscow

CUBA

Berlin

42 missiles

0   2000 km

ITALY   TURKEY

The threat from nuclear missiles based on Cuba.

President Kennedy had to do something. He did not want to use nuclear weapons against Cuba but he had to show that he was not weak and that the USA would not be threatened by the Soviet Union.

Kennedy's options:

- Do nothing.

- Make a **diplomatic protest** to the Soviets.

- Stop any ships getting in or out of Cuba.

- Launch air strikes against the missile sites.

- Invade Cuba and seize the bases.

- Attack Cuba with non-nuclear weapons.

- Attack Cuba with nuclear weapons.

What did Kennedy do?

- He could not sit by and do nothing.

- He did not want to use nuclear weapons.

- He did not want, therefore, to invade or attack Cuba with non-nuclear weapons either, in case of nuclear retaliation from the Soviets.

So, on 22 October 1962, Kennedy opted to place a naval blockade around Cuba. He even went on television to tell the waiting world that he had decided to do this to prevent Soviet missiles reaching Cuba. On 24 October the first Soviet ships carrying missiles met the American naval blockade. Many people all over the world began to think a third world war was about to start.

Source A

Even when people were enjoying themselves having a drink in the student bar, the conversation turned to Cuba. What would happen? Would it mean the end of the world? Everyone felt so helpless. There was nothing you could do to prevent destruction except pray. The end of the crisis was greeted with a tremendous feeling of relief.

Memories of a 19-year-old British university student in 1962.

The world holds its breath

On 24 October, three days after the blockade had started, Khrushchev backed down and ordered the Soviet ships to turn back. Like Kennedy, he did not want to risk nuclear war. He realised he had pushed things too far.

The crisis continues

However, this did not end the Cuban missile crisis. President Kennedy was still worried about the missile sites in Cuba. Kennedy wanted the Soviets to dismantle the sites.

What was Khrushchev's reaction? He sent two letters to Kennedy on 26 and 27 October.

- The first letter said that the USSR would remove the missile sites if the USA called off the blockade and promised not to invade Cuba.

- The second said that Khrushchev would only remove the missile sites if the USA removed its missiles from Turkey, on the Russian border.

Kennedy did not want to back down. He answered Khrushchev's first letter saying that he accepted the terms of the letter of 26 October. He gave Khrushchev until 29 October to reply, otherwise US forces would invade Cuba.

The crisis ends

On 28 October, the Soviet government agreed to remove its missiles from Cuba. Missiles were withdrawn on 3 November and the US blockade was called off on 20 November.

THINGS TO DO

1 Why did the USA oppose Soviet missiles on Cuba?

2 Do you think Kennedy chose the correct option of the six alternatives? Explain your answer.

3 What does **Source A** tell us about feelings in Britain about the Cuban crisis?

4 **Source C** suggests that the USSR was victorious in the Cuban crisis. Do you agree?

5 Is **Source D** an accurate interpretation of the Cuban crisis? Explain your answer.

Source B

You are worried about Cuba because it is 90 miles from America, but Turkey is next to us. We agree to remove from Cuba those means which you find offensive. The United States will for its part remove its missiles from Turkey.

Extract from Khrushchev's letter of 27 October 1962.

Results of the crisis

The Cuban missile crisis was the closest the world had come to a nuclear war. The leaders of the two superpowers realised something had to be done to improve relations.

- Both sides realised that each of them had to help save the face of the other.

- The USA promised not to invade Cuba.

- The USSR removed the missiles from Cuba.

- Both sides worked towards reducing Cold War tension.

- A test ban treaty was signed in August 1963 to stop the testing of nuclear bombs in the air or underwater.

- A direct 'hot-line' telephone was set up between the Kremlin in Moscow and the White House in Washington.

Not everything went well. Many communists thought Khrushchev had given in too easily. By the end of 1964 he was no longer the leader of the USSR.

Source **C**

We agreed to remove our missiles and bombers on condition that there would be no invasion of Cuba by US forces or anybody else. Finally Kennedy gave in and agreed to this. It was a great victory for us, a spectacular success without having to fire a single shot.

From Khrushchev Remembers published in 1971.

SUMMARY

1945	USA uses the atom bomb.
1949	USSR tests the atom bomb.
1950	Korean War begins.
1952	USA tests the H-bomb.
1953	USSR tests the H-bomb. Death of Stalin.
1956	Hungarian Rising.
1957	USSR launches Sputnik I.
1960	U2 Incident – failure of Paris Summit.
1961	Berlin Wall. Bay of Pigs.
1962	Cuban missile crisis.
1963	Test Ban Treaty.

Source **D** British cartoon showing Kennedy and Khrushchev struggling over the Cuban crisis with nuclear war only the press of a button away.

Exam-style assessment – OPTION W

In the examination, if you choose Option W, you must answer two of the three questions in the section.

Question 1: The Treaty of Versailles

Study **Sources A** and **B** and then answer the following questions.

Source A: Comment on the Treaty of Versailles

Severe as the Treaty seemed to many Germans, it should be remembered that Germany might easily have fared much worse. If Clemenceau had had his way, the Rhineland would have become an independent state, the Saar would have been annexed to France and Danzig would have become a part of Poland.

From *A History of Germany* by W Carr, a British historian, published in 1972

Source B: Peace and Future Cannon Fodder

The Tiger: "Curious! I seem to hear a child weeping!"

A cartoon published in Britain in 1920.

(a) According to **Source A**, why should Germany have been satisfied with the Treaty of Versailles? **(3 marks)**

(b) The cartoon in **Source B** shows Clemenceau, Lloyd George and Woodrow Wilson, who all attended the Paris Peace Conference in 1919. What were their aims at that conference? **(6 marks)**

(c) How accurate is the view of events shown in the cartoon in **Source B**? Use **Source B** and your own knowledge to answer the question. **(6 marks)**

(d) Why did many people in Germany hate the Treaty of Versailles? **(10 marks)**

Question 2: The policy of appeasement

Study **Sources C** and **D** and then answer the following questions.

Source C: Chamberlain and appeasement

Neville Chamberlain followed a policy of appeasement because he believed that Hitler would be satisfied if all German-speaking people were governed by Germany. He considered that the best way to avoid war was to settle Hitler's legitimate demands. The memory of the death of seven million young men in World War One greatly influenced Chamberlain who commented that in war 'there are no winners, but all are losers'. Britain was afraid of the growth of the communist USSR and saw a strong Germany as a useful buffer against this danger. In any case, Chamberlain's military advisers urged him to play for time as rearmament had only just begun.

From a British historian writing in 1996

Source D: Sudeten Germans greet German troops

A private photograph taken in the Sudetenland in October 1938.

(a) According to **Source C**, why did Britain try to appease Hitler? **(3 marks)**

(b) Describe how Hitler took over the Sudetenland in Czechoslovakia in 1938. **(6 marks)**

(c) How useful is **Source D** to an historian writing about the German entry into the Sudetenland in October 1938? Use **Source D** and your own knowledge to answer the question. **(6 marks)**

(d) Was the policy of appeasement the most important reason for the outbreak of the Second World War? Explain your answer. **(10 marks)**

Question 3: The Cold War 1950–62

Study **Sources E** and **F** and then answer the following questions.

Source E: The effect of Khrushchev's speech in 1956

In 1956 the new Soviet Premier, Khrushchev, attacked Stalin's leadership of the USSR. This speech gave people in the satellite states of the USSR new hope. They wanted a higher standard of living, less direction from Soviet Russia in economic life and more political freedom from the Soviets. Each satellite state wanted to develop a new communist state of its own.

From *The Great Power Conflict after 1945* by P Fisher, a British textbook published in 1985

Source F: Khrushchev's views on Soviet communism and the West in 1958

The launching of the Soviet sputniks first of all shows that a serious change has occurred in the balance of forces between communist and capitalist countries, in favour of the communist nations.

Extract from a speech by Khrushchev made in 1958

(a) According to **Source E**, what were the aims of Soviet Russia's satellite states after 1956? **(3 marks)**

(b) Describe how Hungary tried to achieve these aims in 1956. **(6 marks)**

(c) How accurate is Khrushchev's view of the balance of power between the USSR and USA stated in **Source F**? Use **Source F** and your own knowledge to answer the question. **(6 marks)**

(d) Why did the USA oppose the USSR in Korea in 1950 and in Cuba in 1962? **(10 marks)**

Czechoslovakia, 1968

After the Cuban missile crisis there seemed to be a thaw in the Cold War. Events in Czechoslavakia in 1968, however, suggested that the Cold War was still as intense as in 1962.

Czechoslovakia had been under Soviet control since 1948 but many Czechs were unhappy with Soviet rule. They could remember better times before the war. They had very little say in their own government. Czech industry produced goods for the Soviet Union but very few for the Czech people.

Source Alexander Dubcek.

The reforms of the 'Prague Spring'.

Reforms shown in diagram:
- Increased standard of living
- Powers of the secret police curbed
- Provision of basic human rights
- End of press censorship
- Czechoslovak reforms of early spring 1968
- Less state control
- Free elections
- Encourage competition
- Opposition parties allowed
- Plans to increase trade with the west
- Freedom to travel abroad

Dubcek and the Prague Spring

In January 1968, Alexander Dubcek became the new Czech leader. He saw the need to change things in Czechoslovakia. These changes were known as the **Prague Spring**.

Dubcek promised 'communism with a human face'. He hoped people would have a better life. To do this he wanted to sell goods to the West and borrow money from the USA to help his country.

The Soviet Union was worried, but Dubcek promised to stay part of the Warsaw Pact and remain a military friend of the Soviet Union.

The Soviet response

Brezhnev, the Soviet leader, was not convinced that Czechoslovakia would remain a member of the Warsaw Pact. He thought:

- reform in Czechoslovakia might encourage other communist countries to follow its example

- if that happened the Soviet Union's power would be weakened

- the 'Iron Curtain' might even come down

- the Warsaw Pact might break up.

If the Soviet Bloc (the Eastern European communist countries) collapsed, Russia itself might be at risk. This was too much for Brezhnev.

Dubcek's reform programme was popular in Czechoslovakia because it offered the possibility of free, democratic government, human rights and an improved standard of living. However, the other Warsaw Pact members supported Brezhnev and demanded Dubcek stop the reforms. Dubcek decided to do even more and promised to allow opposition parties and hold free elections.

The Soviet Union and the rest of the Soviet Bloc were angered by this and decided to use force. 500,000 troops invaded Czechoslovakia on 20 August 1968.

Source **B**

The effects of the change in leadership in January were felt almost within days. Books that had been held up for months or years were suddenly freed for publication. Banned films that had been gathering dust were distributed.

From the newspaper **The Times,** *23 February 1968.*

Source **C**   A drawing on a wall in a Prague street in 1968.

The invasion of Czechoslovakia, 1968

In Hungary in 1956, the Soviet Union had sent in troops to end a similar uprising (see Section 1.8 on pages 58–9). The people fought hard but had no chance against the Soviet army. Hundreds of people had been killed.

The Czechs knew of the events in Hungary and did not try to defeat the Soviet army. They protested through sit-ins, demonstrations and peaceful protest. This was called **passive resistance**.

However, some Czechs did turn to violence. Home-made bombs called **molotov cocktails** were thrown at tanks. Jan Palach, a 21-year-old student, set himself alight in protest, in Prague, in January 1969. He was badly burnt and died two days later. Students crowded into Wenceslas Square to protest at his death. They even renamed the square Jan Palach Square in

Source **D**

Youths with flaming rags and newspapers set fire to Russian tanks encircling the Prague radio building. Others threw wooden crates, rubbish bins and mattresses at the occupying forces who had moved swiftly into the city.

Snipers kept up fire much of the day. Scores of people were injured and several killed. I saw four young Czechs killed, minutes after a machine gun from a Russian tank had opened fire upon their vehicle.

The Times, *22 August 1968.*

Source **E** Czech youths attacking a Soviet tank on the streets of Prague in August 1968.

memory of his death and in protest at the invasion. Secret radio and TV stations broadcast events to the world until they were discovered and shut down.

The Soviet forces quickly stopped any more protests. Supporters of Dubcek were imprisoned and Dubcek was taken to Moscow and made to abandon his reform programme. He was sent abroad as **ambassador** to Turkey, but was later forced to resign. He was expelled from the Communist Party and given a job in the forestry department where he no longer had any political influence.

The Brezhnev Doctrine

Following the invasion of Czechoslovakia, the Soviet leader, Brezhnev, told the leaders of all the communist countries that any attempts to change things would be seen as a threat to all of them. He warned that troops would be used if any country stepped out of line. He was determined that events of the Prague Spring would never happen again.

East–West relations

Countries such as Britain and the USA welcomed the changes that began in Czechoslovakia, but were not willing to do anything to protect the Czech people when the Soviet forces invaded in 1968. This was because:

- they did not want a war to start over Czechoslovakia
- they realised that the Soviet Union would not let communist countries become westernised
- the Cold War continued.

Source F

Go to your places of work. Carry out passive resistance. Do not resist. We are incapable of defending these frontiers.

Radio Prague, 21 August 1968.

Source G

When hostile forces try to turn a socialist (communist) country towards capitalism, the suppression of these forces ... is the concern of all socialist countries.

The Brezhnev Doctrine, August 1968

THINGS TO DO

1 Explain the meaning of the following terms:
   - Prague Spring
   - molotov cocktail
   - passive resistance.

2 **Source C** shows a child giving flowers to a Soviet soldier in 1945. Why is the child dead in 1968?

3 Study **Source E**. Few Soviet tanks were damaged in the invasion. Why, then, has this photo been taken?

4 Why did the Soviets treat Dubcek the way that they did?

Détente

In the late 1960s and through most of the 1970s, the word 'détente' was used to describe the relaxing of tensions between the USSR and the USA, the East and the West. Some people called it a thaw in the Cold War.

Modern World History for AQA

Source H

In the Cold war everything moved on the level of a cheap western. You have an enemy that is the source of all evil. The policy of détente is more difficult to grasp. You have to realise that despite having major differences you might still have some things you could agree on.

Georgi Arbatov, a member of the Soviet Central Committee, looking back in 1983 at the period of détente.

Reasons for Détente

The Cuban missile crisis (pages 66-9) was an example of how dangerous the Cold War could be. Following this crisis the superpowers had started to try to improve relations, but they were still suspicious of each other.

During the 1960s, the USA became more and more involved in fighting the communists in **Vietnam**. Events in Czechoslovakia too seemed to have ended any chance of improved relations between East and West.

Problems at home

During the 1960s and 1970s, the USA and USSR each had problems of their own at home and did not really want to get involved in conflict with each other. They shared some of the same problems:

- Inflation.

- High expenditure on defence. Both sides had stockpiles of weapons – enough to destroy the earth many times over.

- The possibility of oil supplies being held up in the Suez Canal in Egypt because of war in the Middle East.

- The power of China. The Soviet Union and China were co-operating over Vietnam but quarrelled over other issues. The USA was concerned that the Soviet Union and China – both communist countries – would reach agreements which could harm the USA.

- The Vietnam War was causing a crisis of confidence in the USA and the economy of the USA was suffering because of the costs of the war.

- The economy of the USSR was in a poor state. Industry was inefficiently run and the people had a low standard of living. Khruschev wanted to increase trade with the West to improve this low standard of living.

Because of all these problems both sides wanted to improve working relations and to reduce Cold War tension.

Consequences of the Vietnam War

Vietnam had been split into two countries, North Vietnam and South Vietnam. North Vietnam was communist and South Vietnam was capitalist. The USA supported the government in the South because it was anti-communist, even though it was harsh and **corrupt**. The USA helped the South by sending in advisers. These advisers helped to train the South Vietnamese armed forces.

Soon the USA found itself fighting a full scale war. Between 1962 and 1968 more and more US troops were stationed in Vietnam (see below).

Year	Numbers of troops
1962	9,000
1963	15,000
1964	16,000
1965	60,000
1966	268,000
1967	449,000
1968	535,000
1969	415,000

Communist countries, such as China and the USSR, were very suspicious of US involvement in Vietnam. At the same time the war became more and more difficult for the USA to fight. Many South Vietnamese hated the Americans and supported communism.

As the war took more American lives and cost more and more money, demonstrations against the war became common, with some ending in violence. The war did not help the USA's reputation in the world either. The USA looked weak, as a small country was standing up to one of the world superpowers.

 Source I

A US anti-war poster from the Vietnam War.

 Source J

This cartoon was published in a British newspaper in 1976. It shows Kissinger of the USA on the left and Brezhnev of the Soviet Union on the right.

détente is... ...the exchange of sweet nothings

détente is... ...covering up his treaty violations

détente is... ...knowing when to give something for nothing

Attempts at arms control and improving human rights

The 1963 Test Ban Treaty banned tests by the Soviet Union, the USA and Britain of nuclear weapons in the atmosphere, outer space or under water. The 1968 **Nuclear Non-proliferation Treaty** aimed to stop other countries building their own nuclear weapons.

When **Richard Nixon** became US President in 1969, both he and President Brezhnev of the Soviet Union began talking about ways in which to slow down the arms race. The **Strategic Arms Limitation Talks** (SALT) started in 1969 and led to the SALT I agreement in 1972.

SALT I (1972)

- This was a five-year agreement.

- It limited the number of ICBMs (inter-continental ballistic missiles) and ABMs (anti-ballistic missiles).

- It allowed spy satellites to check on what the other side was doing.

Helsinki Agreement (1975)

This agreement marked the high point of Détente.

- 35 countries signed to accept the **frontiers** (borders) of eastern Europe and the USSR.

- West Germany officially accepted that East Germany existed.

- USSR agreed to buy US grain.

- USA agreed to buy USSR oil.

- Agreements on **human rights** (freedom of speech, of religion, of movement).

Source **A** A cartoon about the reasons for the SALT talks. It was published in the USA in 1970.

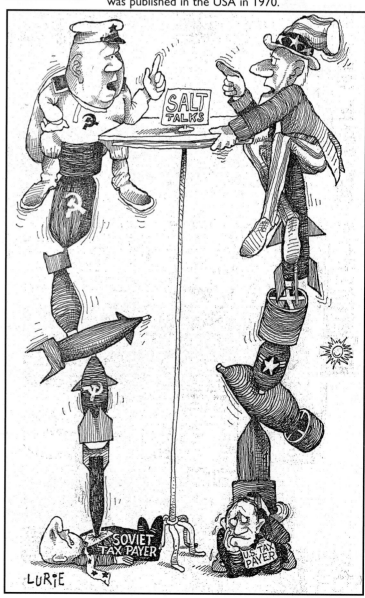

Presidents Nixon and Brezhnev meeting in 1974, when Brezhnev visited the USA.

How successful was the Helsinki agreement?

The Soviet Union was pleased that its borders had been recognised by the West, but human rights abuses continued within the Soviet Union. People who spoke out against communism were:

- put in prison

- had very poor conditions while in prison

- were sometimes put under arrest in their own homes (house arrest)

- were not allowed to travel where they wanted

- were not allowed to write to or speak to people outside the Soviet Union.

Other contacts between the superpowers in the 1970s

It is important to remember that the 1970s saw a great improvement in relations between the East and the West. Various social, sporting and cultural visits took place.

For instance in 1972 President Nixon visited Moscow, the first US President to do so since Roosevelt in 1945. In return Brezhnev, the Soviet President, visited the USA in 1974.

Events in Germany also helped to ease relations. In 1972 East and West Germany recognised each other's borders and agreed to develop trade between the two countries.

There was also co-operation in space. In 1975 the Apollo and Soyuz spacecraft docked (met) in space. The crews were able to see each other's space technology. This was a very obvious sign of détente.

At the same time in the early 1970s, the USA made greater efforts to build a better relationship with China.

- The USA agreed that China should be allowed to join the United Nations (1971).

- The US table tennis team visited Peking (Beijing), the Chinese capital (1971).

- At the same time politicians from both sides met. This was called 'ping pong diplomacy'. President Nixon visited Peking and met Mao Zedong, the Chinese leader in 1972.

Meanwhile relations between the Soviet Union and China remained poor, mostly because of border conflicts, and this helped the USA during the period of détente.

Stars and Stripes Flies Over the Kremlin

Mr Nixon began his visit to the Soviet Union today, becoming the first American President to visit Moscow since 1945.

The Times, *23 March 1972.*

The failings of Détente in the later 1970s

The mid-1970s was the high point of détente. However, the West became more and more annoyed over the low priority the USSR was giving to human rights. The USA also suspected that the USSR was not keeping to the terms of the SALT I agreement.

SALT II (1977-9)

The SALT I agreement was only for five years, so it ended in 1977. The new US President, Jimmy Carter, tried to get further reductions in arms through the SALT II talks. However, he wanted to link the talks to human rights.

The talks went on and on until an agreement was reached towards the end of 1979. Although an agreement was made it was not expected to come into effect until 1980.

Before the agreement could come into effect the Soviet Union invaded Afghanistan during Christmas 1979 and the agreement was abandoned. The Cold War seemed to have started again.

THINGS TO DO

1 What was détente?

2 Why did it come about?

3 What were its most important consequences:
   (a) for the USA
   (b) for the Soviet Union?

Source D

The badge worn by the American crew who took part in the Apollo–Soyuz space link-up.

1.12 How and why did Détente collapse in the late 1970s and early 1980s?

Soviet involvement in Afghanistan

Background

Although Afghanistan was a poor country its position was very important. It was near the oil fields of the Persian Gulf which made it important to the Soviet Union and to the USA. Both powers wanted to have some kind of influence over Afghanistan.

In 1921, Afghanistan became an independent country and became a friend of the Soviet Union. This friendship was strengthened in 1955 when Khrushchev visited and promised aid and arms.

Revolution in Iran

Meanwhile, in 1979 there was a Muslim revolution in neighbouring Iran to overthrow the US-backed leader (the Shah). Iran became anti-American. In November that year, 53 American hostages were held in Tehran and kept there for over a year. The USA and its leader, President Carter, felt humiliated.

Revolution in Aghanistan

In 1979 Hafizullah Amin seized power in Afghanistan. Although he was a communist, he was not friendly with the Soviet Union. Large Muslim groups in Afghanistan opposed him. The Soviets also feared these Muslim groups would try to take control, as they had done in Iran. They were also worried that Muslims in the Soviet Union might want to set up their own governments.

Soviet invasion

On 25 December 1979, Soviet troops invaded Afghanistan.

- They captured the airport.

- Within a week 50,000 Soviet troops had arrived in Afghanistan.

- The President's palace was captured.

- President Amin was killed.

On 1 January 1980, a new government was set up. The new leader, **Babrak Karmal**, had been living in exile in the Soviet Union. He was brought in by the Soviets to make sure the new government had better relations with the Soviet Union.

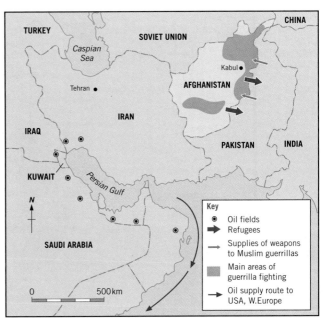

A map showing why Afghanistan was so important.

International History 1900–91

Reactions from other world powers

President Brezhnev claimed the invasion was justified to help restore order. He told the US President that his troops had been invited into Afghanistan to protect its government. Brezhnev said he would withdraw his troops when the situation was more stable.

President Carter was very angry and claimed that world peace was threatened (look at Source A). The Chinese government also reacted angrily and promised to support the **Mujaheddin** (Islamic Afghan fighters carrying out **guerrilla warfare** against the Soviet troops).

President Brezhnev said that the USA and China were interfering in things that did not concern them.

Source A

The leaders of the world must make it clear to the Soviets that they cannot upset world peace without paying for severe consequences.

President Carter's response to the Soviet invasion of Afghanistan.

Source C

Russia's actions are a stepping-stone for a southward thrust towards Pakistan and the Indian sub-continent. There will be no peace in southern Asia with Soviet soldiers in Afghanistan.

Peking People's Daily, 1 January 1980.

President Carter acted to show the USA's disapproval of the invasion:

- He pulled the USA out of the 1980 Moscow Olympics.

- He advised the US Senate not to agree to the SALT II treaty on weapons with the Soviet Union.

- He sent a US Navy Task Force of 1800 marines to protect oil routes in the Arabian Sea.

- He stopped exports of grain, the sale of computers and the sale of oil drilling equipment to the Soviet Union.

Source B

In this cartoon from *The Guardian* in 1980, President Carter views the Soviet invasion of Afghanistan.

The war continues

After a few months the Soviet troops controlled the towns and the Mujaheddin controlled the countryside. The Mujaheddin were fighting to get rid of Soviet troops and to make Afghanistan a Muslim country. They were well equipped thanks to the support and weapons they received from China and the USA.

The Mujaheddin attacked Soviet supply routes and shot at Soviet planes. The Soviets lost more and more men as this guerrilla war went on. By the early 1980s there were 125,000 Soviet troops in Afghanistan. They launched a massive attack on the Mujaheddin in 1982 but even that failed.

The Soviet Union was even becoming unpopular in other Muslim countries like Pakistan. The Soviet leadership began to worry about the 30 million Muslims within the Soviet Union. What might they do? Might they revolt and support the Mujaheddin?

The end of the war

In 1985, a new Soviet leader, **Mikhail Gorbachev**, realised the war could not be won. He started talks with the USA in 1987. The following year, an agreement was reached with US President **Ronald Reagan**. The last Soviet troops left Afghanistan in 1989.

THINGS TO DO

1 Why did the Soviet Union invade Afghanistan in December 1979?

2 Why could the Soviet Union, a superpower, not defeat the rebel forces of Afghanistan?

3 What were the consequences of the Soviet invasion of Afghanistan?

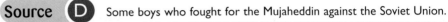

Source **D** Some boys who fought for the Mujaheddin against the Soviet Union.

Consequences of the war

- The Soviet Union lost 20,000 troops.

- One million Afghan people lost their lives.

- Over three million refugees left Afghanistan.

- Farmland had been destroyed and food shortages followed the end of the war.

- The high cost of fighting the war damaged the Soviet economy.

- Fighting continued in Afghanistan between rival groups that had fought together against the Soviets.

The renewed Cold War under Reagan and Brezhnev

By the early 1980s relations between the USA and the Soviet Union were very bad. In January 1980, Brezhnev had said that 'the USA is an absolutely unreliable partner whose leadership is capable at any moment of cancelling treaties and agreements.'

In late January 1980 President Carter withdrew the USA from the Moscow Olympics. He said that 'the Soviet Union is an unsuitable site for a festival meant to celebrate peace and good will.'

In January 1981, **Ronald Reagan** became the new US President. His tough, anti-communist views had helped him get elected. He called the Soviet Union an 'evil empire'. Détente was dead.

Development of new weapons

The new US President, Ronald Reagan, began developing new weapons:

- Between 1981 and 1986 he increased defence spending from $178 billion to $367 billion.

- He developed new weapons like the **Cruise missile**.

- 464 Cruise missiles were based in western Europe so that the Soviet Union was within their range.

- The United States began developing a **neutron bomb**, which would kill people but not damage much property.

- The United States began developing the MX missile to launch these weapons.

The nuclear weapons in the USA and USSR could destroy the whole world. It was this fear of **Mutually Assured Destruction** (MAD) that many people thought meant that neither side would risk using them.

The Strategic Defense Initiative (SDI)

US scientists began working on the so-called 'Star Wars' project in 1983. It was a satellite anti-missile system which would mean that Soviet missiles could be shot down before they reached the USA.

Despite the development of new weapons and the SDI, talks continued between the two sides to try to limit the number of nuclear weapons in Europe. These were called START (**Strategic Arms Reduction Talks**). President Reagan knew the USA could do this because it already had a lot more weapons than the USSR. It could also help save him some money. The USA had large debts and could not afford to keep spending money on defence.

Source **E** A cartoon from the *Sunday Times*, 29 November 1981.

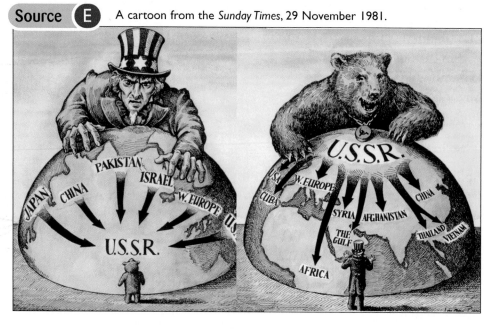

Solidarity in Poland

Meanwhile the Soviet Union had its own problems.

- In 1980 there were protests in Poland due to high prices and food and fuel shortages.

- The shipyard workers went on strike.

- They were led by **Lech Walesa** who had created the first trade union in Poland.

- This trade union was called **Solidarity**.

- The Pope, John Paul II, who was from Poland, encouraged people to speak out about the situation.

The strikes spread to other parts of Poland and soon nine million Poles were members of Solidarity. Many people thought the Soviet Union would invade Poland but they were too busy fighting a war in Afghanistan.

At first the government seemed to support Solidarity. However, the Soviet army was ordered to carry out 'training manoeuvres' near the Polish border and the Polish secret police watched what was going on. They bugged Solidarity meetings and tapped people's phones.

The government clamps down

In 1981 a new government under General Jaruzelski took action.

- The army was brought in to run the country (martial law).

- 10,000 strikers and members of Solidarity, including Lech Walesa, were arrested.

- Solidarity was declared illegal.

Solidarity survives!

Rather than destroying Solidarity, Lech Walesa's imprisonment turned him into a national hero. Solidarity continued to work in secret. In 1982 Lech Walesa was released from prison and in 1983 he was awarded the Nobel Peace Prize.

A new leader for the Soviet Union

In 1985, **Mikhail Gorbachev** became the new leader of the Soviet Union. He wanted to improve relations with the US President, Ronald Reagan, to make positive achievements.

Gorbachev wanted things to change even in Poland and this encouraged Solidarity to take action. There were more strikes and demonstrations. By the end of the 1980s Jaruselski's government had little support and he was forced to allow free elections to take place. Solidarity won the elections and in 1989 Lech Walesa became the new President of Poland.

Lech Walesa photographed in the early days of Solidarity.

Source **F**

Changing Soviet and US attitudes

Mikhail Gorbachev

Mikhail Gorbachev became a member of the **Politburo**, the most powerful group in the Soviet Communist Party in 1980. In 1985, he was chosen as leader. He was only 54 and became the youngest leader of the Soviet Union since the 1920s. He listened to new ideas and wanted to see things change in the Soviet Union. He also wanted to see progress in the Soviet Union's relationships with the rest of the world, including the USA.

He knew that too much money had been spent on weapons and on the war in Afghanistan. The standard of living in the Soviet Union was low. Factories were producing less and what they made was of a poor quality. The people had far fewer consumer goods than the people of western Europe and the USA.

New Soviet policies

Many people thought nothing could be done. Gorbachev knew that something had to happen. He introduced two new policies: *perestroika* and *glasnost*.

- *Perestroika* means **restructuring**. Gorbachev wanted to allow more competition between businesses to enourage the production of better quality goods.

- *Glasnost* means **openness**. Gorbachev wanted people to believe in the government. He wanted people to be free to criticise the government and to talk about what needed to happen in the Soviet Union to make it better.

Gorbachev also decided that the Soviet Union would have to stop trying to control other countries including Afghanistan and Poland.

Source A

Ronald Reagan and Mikhail Gorbachev in 1987.

US attitudes

President Reagan was pleased with this change in the Soviet Union. It gave him the chance to save money too. Because the Soviet Union planned to cut its defence expenditure, Reagan felt it was safe for the USA to do the same.

Arms reduction

Reagan and Gorbachev met several times in the 1980s:

- In 1985, in Geneva, they agreed to cut offensive (attack) weapons by 50 per cent.

- In 1986, in Iceland, the Soviet Union announced its withdrawal from Afghanistan and confirmed it would not test nuclear weapons unless the USA did first.

- In December 1987, both sides agreed to get rid of medium- and short-range missiles just a few years after they had been busy building them.

Reforms in the Soviet Union

At the same time, Gorbachev introduced reforms in the Soviet Union. Political prisoners who had disagreed with communist policies were released from prison; others, such as writers, were allowed to return from **exile** (other countries). In 1987 people were allowed to buy and sell goods at a profit for the first time in over 60 years.

However, many communists thought he had gone too far. Many other people wanted to see change happen quickly. Their expectations (hopes) for a better life were very high. Once people were allowed to say what they wanted without the risk of being sent to prison, some suggested that communism should be got rid of too. This was especially true in Eastern Europe.

The end of Soviet control of Eastern Europe

By the end of the 1980s, Soviet control of Eastern Europe had almost disappeared. The speed of the loss of Soviet control shocked the world.

- In 1982, the Polish opposition leader, Lech Walesa, was freed from prison.

- In 1983, Lech Walesa was awarded the Nobel Peace Prize.

- In 1985, Mikhail Gorbachev became President of the Soviet Union.

- In 1986, Hungarians made public protests using the banned Hungarian flag.

- In March 1989, Gorbachev told the communist leaders of the Eastern European countries that the Soviet Red Army would not help them if the people chose to oppose them.

- In early 1989, public demonstrations continued in Hungary and Gorbachev began the withdrawal of Soviet troops.

Poland

In June 1989, free elections were held. Lech Walesa, the leader of Solidarity, became the first non-communist leader of an Eastern European country since 1945. After this, the **Soviet Bloc** began to disintegrate (fall apart).

East Germany

By the autumn of 1989, thousands of people were fleeing East Germany through **Austria**.

There were massive demonstrations when Gorbachev visited East Germany and told the unpopular leader, Erich Honecker, to allow reforms. Honecker ordered troops to fire on the crowds but they refused. Honecker resigned and, on 10 November 1989, thousands of East Germans marched to the Berlin Wall and pulled it down. The symbolic barrier between East and West was removed.

Czechoslovakia

Two weeks after the Berlin Wall came down huge demonstrations took place in Czechoslovakia. Alexander Dubcek and the popular playwright, Vaclav Havel, appeared in public to encourage the demonstrations. The communist leader resigned and was replaced by Havel. Free elections were held in 1990.

Hungary

The Hungarian communists accepted the need for change. They changed their name to the Socialist Party. Other political parties were allowed and free elections were promised for 1990.

Romania

In December 1989 there was a short but bloody revolution. The hated communist dictator (absolute leader), Nicolae Ceausescu, and his wife were executed and their bodies were shown on television.

Source **B**

Citizens of united city overcome their disbelief

Yesterday Berlin ceased to be a divided city. Tens of thousands of East Berliners streamed to the West, unhindered for the first time since the Wall was put up 28 years ago. Most crossed just for the experience of freedom they had been denied so long.

Huge crowds built up on the Western side of the Wall as West Berliners witnessed the historic developments, some even crossing over into the East for a walk. In front of the Brandenburg Gate and elsewhere, they perched precariously on top of the Wall, clapping and calling for it to go.

East Berliners have been offered free tickets for a football match today in West Berlin as well as to a number of concerts and the opera. It was unclear last night how many East Berliners planned to stay in the West. Although the West German cities of Bremen and Hanover said they could take no more refugees, Berlin was still offering a warm welcome.

'After all we are not just one people, we are also one city,' said one West Berliner, who described the last 24 hours as 'simply unbelievable'.

Article from **The Guardian** *newspaper, 11 November 1989.*

Bulgaria

In November 1989, the communist leader resigned and free elections were held the next year.

The Baltic states

Latvia, **Lithuania** and **Estonia** declared themselves independent of the Soviet Union in 1990.

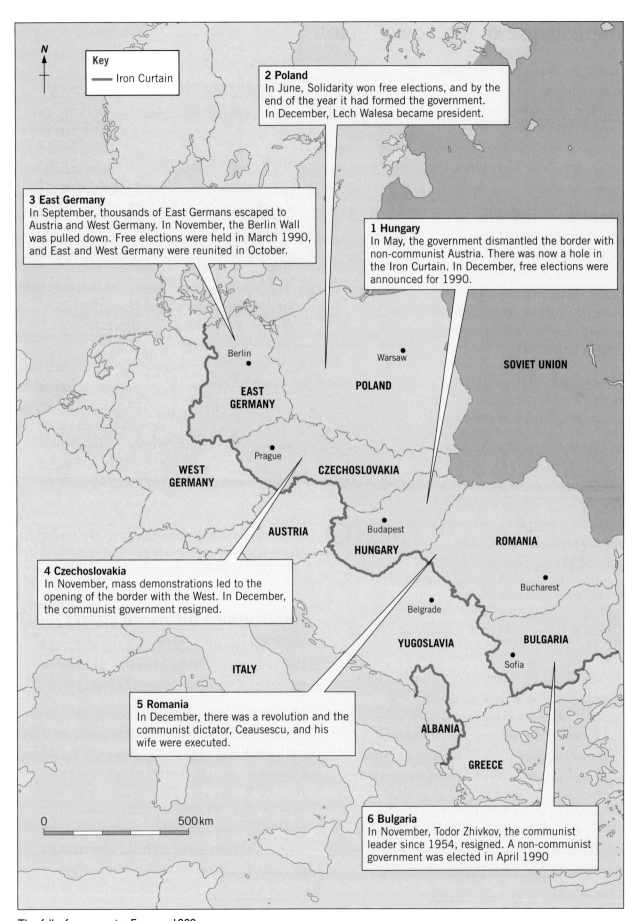

Key
— Iron Curtain

2 Poland
In June, Solidarity won free elections, and by the end of the year it had formed the government. In December, Lech Walesa became president.

3 East Germany
In September, thousands of East Germans escaped to Austria and West Germany. In November, the Berlin Wall was pulled down. Free elections were held in March 1990, and East and West Germany were reunited in October.

1 Hungary
In May, the government dismantled the border with non-communist Austria. There was now a hole in the Iron Curtain. In December, free elections were announced for 1990.

4 Czechoslovakia
In November, mass demonstrations led to the opening of the border with the West. In December, the communist government resigned.

5 Romania
In December, there was a revolution and the communist dictator, Ceausescu, and his wife were executed.

6 Bulgaria
In November, Todor Zhivkov, the communist leader since 1954, resigned. A non-communist government was elected in April 1990

Berlin

Warsaw

SOVIET UNION

EAST GERMANY

POLAND

WEST GERMANY

Prague

CZECHOSLOVAKIA

AUSTRIA

Budapest

HUNGARY

ROMANIA

Bucharest

Belgrade

YUGOSLAVIA

BULGARIA

Sofia

ITALY

ALBANIA

GREECE

0   500km

The fall of communist Europe, 1989.

The collapse of the Soviet Union

Gorbachev had done very little to prevent the fall of communism in eastern Europe. Many people in the USSR saw this as a weakness. There were other problems too.

Economic reforms in the Soviet Union did not seem to be working. There were still food shortages and rising prices. Many wanted to see the collapse of the communist system, not just reforms within it.

In February 1990, 250,000 people demonstrated in Moscow against communism.

In May 1990, Gorbachev was booed at the May Day parade in Moscow's Red Square. Gorbachev was much admired in the West but the people of the Soviet Union criticised him, either for taking reform too far or for not reforming enough.

Source **C**

A cartoon from *The Guardian* in January 1990, showing a hammer and sickle (the symbol of the Communist Party in the USSR) in tears.

The new President of the Russian republic, **Boris Yeltsin**, wanted to see the break up of the USSR.

In August 1991, extreme communists took over and arrested Gorbachev who was imprisoned in his own home. Boris Yeltsin led a demonstration against the communist takeover, demanding that reforms continue and Gorbachev be freed. Yeltsin was seen as a hero and he disbanded (broke up) the Communist Party in Russia. He formally ended the Soviet Union in December 1991. Gorbachev resigned as Soviet President because there was no longer a Soviet state to rule.

Implications for world affairs

The Cold War had ended and the arms race was now over. The communists were no longer in control of eastern Europe.

However, new problems arose as ethnic groups sought independence for their own nationalities. For example, in January 1993, Czechoslovakia split into two separate states – the Czech Republic and Slovakia. Yugoslavia was divided. Serbs and Croats wanted their own countries and civil war followed, and with it the horrors of '**ethnic cleansing**'.

In 1991, East and West Berlin were reunited and East and West Germany became a single country. The new Germany faced many new, economic problems in reducing the gap in living standards between the two parts of the country.

Although the Cold War lasted for so long and caused great distrust and suspicion between the USA and the USSR some people think that it had a positive effect. Compared to the first half of the twentieth century there had been no world war. Can this peace continue?

THINGS TO DO

1 Write down three reasons why Gorbachev needed to bring in new reforms.

2 How important were public demonstrations in bringing an end to communism?

3 Study **Source C**.
   - Why are the hammer and the sickle in tears?
   - How would you draw them in January 1992?

Source **D**

America's unique blend of confidence and self-doubt should guarantee another era of dominance

When the phrase 'the American century' was first used in 1941, it was at a time when America was being told off for not carrying out its duty as 'the elder brother of nations'. America then dominated the Second World War and the post-war world.

In the year 2000 America is more dominant in the world than ever before – its economy booming, its military power unmatched, its technology thriving, and its culture over all the globe.

Yet only ten years ago in 1990 the USA appeared to have overstretched itself. Japan's economy was roaring, China was a rising power and a united Europe was coming to life. Meanwhile increasing US debt, economic problems and government indecision seemed to be attacking America from inside.

However, at the end of the 1990s it is clear that the last decade of the twentieth century has been more America's than any decade before it. Japan is still struggling out of economic problems, the euro cannot compete with the dollar, and the Cold War is over. The astonishing success of the 1990s has been typical of American success in the twentieth century.

The Times, *3 January 2000.*

Exam-style assessment – OPTION X

The three questions provided here are on the period 1970–91. In the real examination for Option X, the questions will cover the whole period of 1945–91. A question covering the earlier part of this option can be found on the overlapping Option W's questions on pages 70-1.

Question 1: Détente in the 1970s

Study **Source A** and then answer the following questions.

SOURCE A

America cannot live in isolation if it expects to live in peace. We have no intention of withdrawing from the world. The only issue before us is how we can be most effective in meeting our responsibilities, protecting our interests, and thereby building peace.

From a speech by President Nixon to Congress and the American people, February 1970

(a) What was Nixon saying in **Source A** about US involvement in world affairs? **(3 marks)**

(b) How reliable is **Source A** to an historian studying US foreign policy in 1970? **(6 marks)**

(c) Describe attempts at arms control and improving human rights under détente in the 1970s. **(6 marks)**

(d) Détente broke down because of the Soviet Union's invasion of Afghanistan in 1979. Is this true? Explain your answer. **(10 marks)**

Question 2: The renewed Cold War in the early 1980s

Study **Sources B** and **C**, and then answer the following questions.

SOURCE B: Why the USSR invaded Afghanistan

The USSR has been invited in by the Afghan Government to come and protect it from threats by other nations. The USSR will remove its forces from Afghanistan as soon as the situation has stabilised.

Brezhnev using the hot-line to President Carter of the USA, 28 December 1979

SOURCE C: The invasion of Afghanistan

The Soviet Union made a massive airlift into Kabul over Christmas on December 25/26 and now have concentrated five divisions along the border.

From a British newspaper, The Times, 27 December 1979

(a) According to **Source B**, will Soviet troops stay in Afghanistan for long? **(3 marks)**

(b) Which **Source, B** or **C**, is more reliable for studying the invasion of Afghanistan in December 1979? Explain your answer. **(6 marks)**

(c) Describe how the Solidarity movement in Poland in the 1980s gradually succeeded. **(6 marks)**

(d) Why did the Cold War become worse in the early 1980s? **(10 marks)**

Question 3: The end of the Cold War

Study **Sources D** and **E** and then answer the questions which follow.

SOURCE D: Gorbachev's wish for world peace

Force or the threat of force neither can nor should be how foreign policy is carried out. The principle of the freedom of choice is essential. Refusal to recognise this principle will have serious consequences for world peace.

From a speech to the United Nations by Gorbachev, 7 December 1988

SOURCE E: Gorbachev explains the problems within the USSR

I knew that an immense task awaited me. The USSR was at the end of its strength. Production figures were slumping. The people's standard of living was clearly declining. Corruption was gaining ground. We wanted to reform by launching a democratic process. It was similar to earlier reform attempts.

Gorbachev writing in 1992, after he had lost power

(a) What was Gorbachev saying in **Source D** about the USSR's relations with other countries? **(3 marks)**

(b) How reliable is **Source E** for studying why Communism collapsed in the USSR? **(6 marks)**

(c) Describe how Communist rule ended in ONE East European country in 1989. **(6 marks)**

(d) Explain the immediate consequences for the world of the collapse of Communism in Eastern Europe and the end of the USSR, 1989–91. **(10 marks)**

2 Britain in the First World War

INTRODUCTION

Britain went to war with Germany in 1914. The German Schlieffen Plan was made so that Germany could invade and defeat France quickly. As part of the plan, the German army attacked on the French–German border and also invaded Belgium. The Belgians, the British Expeditionary Force (BEF) and the French stopped the attack. The war in France (the Western Front) became a war fought mostly from trenches, moving to and fro over the same few miles.

The BEF was joined by more and more soldiers, from Britain and all over the British Empire. New weapons such as tanks and gas were used. But still the war on the Western Front produced huge numbers of dead and no progress. There was also fighting in other parts of the world, on the Eastern Front, where Russia fought Germany and the Allies fought Turkey. The war at sea was mainly concerned with stopping supplies reaching the enemy. Both sides had successes; the German use of submarines almost starved Britain to defeat. The USA joined the war in 1917, after German attacks on US shipping. This tipped the balance in favour of the Allies.

The First World War had a great impact on Britain. Conscription was introduced – men were forced to join the armed forces. Women had to take over the jobs left by the men being sent to war. Almost every family in the country lost a loved one. The government censored the news and used propaganda to keep up morale. Air and sea attacks, as well as the shipping blockades, meant the war affected people at home, as well as the troops away fighting.

1914
- BEF sent to France
- DORA introduced in Britain
- Battle of the Marne
- Failure of Schlieffen Plan
- Battle of Ypres
- German ships shell east Britain
- Battle of the Falkland Islands

1915
- Zeppelin attacks on Britain
- Gas used on the Western Front
- Sinking of *Lusitania* by German U Boat

1916
- Introduction of conscription in Britain
- Battle of Verdun
- Battle of Jutland
- Battle of the Somme
- First use of tanks

1917
- German aircraft bomb south Britain
- Unrestricted submarine warfare introduced
- USA enters war
- Battle of Passchendaele

1918
- Britain introduces convoys
- Rationing of food in Britain
- Mutiny of German fleet
- Defeat of German army

2.1 What was the part played by Britain in the defeat of Germany in the First World War?

The Schlieffen Plan

Germany had been preparing for war for some time before 1914.

- The problem Germany faced was that it would have to fight on two fronts, France in the west and Russia in the east.

- The aim of the Schlieffen Plan was to attack France first and fast, defeating it and moving back across to Russia before Russian troops were **mobilised**.

- Germany attacked France on the French–German border and through Belgium, despite the fact that it had signed a treaty not to attack Belgium. The German attack on Belgium pulled Britain into the war.

The BEF

Britain had only a small army with fighting experience: the **British Expeditionary Force (BEF)** of about 100,000 men. They were sent to France at once. The Germans had not expected them to move so fast. They were also surprised by the BEF's skill. In the **Battle of Le Cateau**, on 26 August, the Germans reported the BEF had 28 machine-guns in each battalion. They really had only two each, but were expert at using them.

The BEF, combined with French and Belgian forces, stopped the German advance at the **Battle of the Marne**. The Germans had to retreat to the River Aisne and dug the first trenches of the war. The German attempt to capture the Channel ports was defeated at the **Battle of Ypres**, a battle that dragged out from 12 October to 11 November. Casualties (deaths) were high: 50,000 Allies and at least 100,000 Germans. The Schlieffen Plan had failed and this meant that Germany had to fight a war on two fronts.

Source A   German troops 'digging in' at the end of 1914.

The 'long slog'

Both sides had lost a lot of men and were forced to concentrate on defence and dig trenches.

The war on the Western Front did not move more than ten miles in any direction for the next four years.

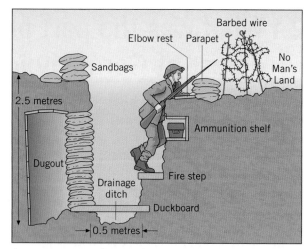

A cross-section of a trench.

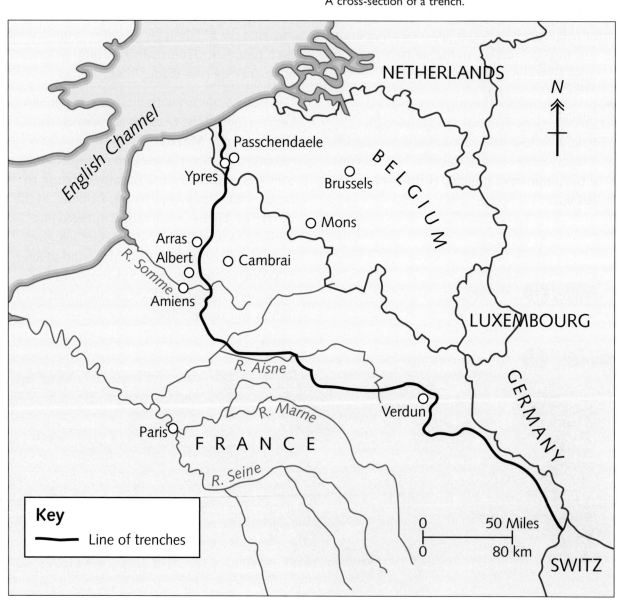

The Western Front, 1914–18.

Trenches, weapons and strategy

Before the First World War, most battles had been fought in the open by **cavalry** (men on horses) and **infantry** (foot soldiers). Several things made the First World War different:

- The trenches fixed the positions of the armies in a long line that stretched almost right across France. This made winning a war with one battle impossible.

- A new weapon, the **machine-gun**, meant that people (or horses) out in the open could be killed very quickly. Once **trenches** were dug, machines-guns could be used to pin people down in the opposite trench.

- Bigger guns, such as the **howitzer**, could fire **shells** quite accurately over long distances.

The Germans were quicker to adapt to this new kind of war. They dug more permanent trenches and built concrete machine-gun posts. They also had many more machine-guns in use. However, this was not enough for them to drive the Allied troops out of their trenches. The war became a **stalemate**. Neither side seemed able to win the war.

THINGS TO DO

1. (a) What was the Schlieffen Plan?
   (b) Why did the Schlieffen Plan fail?

2. Why did digging trenches turn the war into a 'long slog'?

3. What weapon kept both sides pinned down in the trenches?

 British soldiers defending their trench with a Vickers machine-gun.

Britain in the First World War

The nature of trench warfare

As soon as both sides began digging trenches, it seemed to their generals that the first step to victory had to be to drive the other side out of its trenches. The land between the enemy trenches was called 'No Man's Land'. Each side defended the part of No Man's Land nearest to its trenches with coils of barbed wire. They both used the same method to try to capture the enemy's trenches.

- They bombed the trenches and No Man's Land with **heavy artillery** (such as howitzers). This could go on for days. They hoped to break down barbed wire defences and destroy machine-gun posts and trenches.

- Once the other side had been heavily bombed, the soldiers in the trenches were ordered to go '**over the top**'. They climbed out of the trenches into No Man's Land to attack the enemy trenches. No Man's Land very quickly became very muddy and was covered with water-filled holes from the bombardment. Some unexploded bombs lay there, as did ripped up barbed wire.

The use of gas, 1915

In April 1915, the Germans broke through the Allies' front line for the first time. They used a new weapon – **poison gas**. The gas made it hard to see and hard to breathe (many died from suffocation).

- That first gas attack showed the weakness of gas. The wind changed direction. The Germans were caught by their own gas and had to retreat. Even so, soon both sides began using gas.

- The Germans later used **phosgene** (mustard gas). This caused temporary blindness, burned skin and poisoned lungs; it could cause a long, slow death.

Soldiers on both sides hated the gas. Both sides quickly began using gas masks and it became less effective at killing people. But gas was still used all through the war to panic enemy trenches.

One side's First World War trench system. The other side had a similar system on the other side of No Man's Land.

artillery

machine-gun post

officers in a dugout

trenches

barbed wire

No Man's Land

attacking forces

Verdun, 1916

It soon became clear that the only way to win the war was to wear the enemy down by **attrition**. This means both sides went on bombing and attacking each other's trenches. They used a great deal of **ammunition**. Many thousands of soldiers died. Yet neither side gave in, they waited for the other side to run out of men and ammunition.

In 1916, both sides built up their ammunition supplies to launch one huge attack on the enemy lines. The British and French prepared to attack at the River Somme. Meanwhile, the Germans attacked Verdun, a French fortress.

Verdun was important to the French people. It was a fortress that had never been captured by attackers. The French Prime Minister said he would sack all the generals if they did not save the fort. General Petain was determined to keep the Germans out of Verdun, announcing to the soldiers: 'Ils ne passeront pas' (They shall not pass). The French urged the British to start their planned attack on the Somme, to draw German troops away from Verdun.

Source C

Kitchener is convinced we are wasting ammunition. I told him he and his advisers have no idea what a modern war is like. The enemy trenches and wire must be broken down. His machine-gun posts must be destroyed or the gunners pinned down by constant fire.

Part of the diary of Sir John French, commander of the BEF until December 1915.

Source D

A British field gun used in the First World War.

Source E

I wish those who call this a holy war could see our heaps of gassed cases. They are burned and blistered all over with blind eyes all glued together. They fight for breath all the time, whispering that they are choking.

Written by a British officer in the trenches.

THINGS TO DO

1 Draw a diagram explaining the steps of a trench attack.

2 Why was 'No Man's Land' so dangerous?

3 Why do you think the soldiers hated gas attacks?

The Somme, 1916: a battle of attrition

The German attack on Verdun changed the Allied generals' battle plan for the Somme:

- The attack on the Somme, planned as a joint British and French attack, had only half the French soldiers originally promised.

- It had to start sooner than planned.

- It was planned as a push to break through enemy lines. But now it was aimed at helping the French at Verdun by killing as many Germans as possible.

The battle

On 26 June 1916, the British began bombarding the Germans. On 1 July, the British soldiers were ordered to go 'over the top'. By this time, General Haig said, 'not even a rat' would be alive. Haig did not know that the Germans had dug very deep **dugouts**, which they had gone into as soon as the bombardment began.

When it stopped they came out and went back to the trenches, which were not as damaged as expected. The Germans gunned down 20,000 British soldiers on 1 July. 40,000 more were injured. The British retreated.

Source F

Our men climbed up the steep shafts from the dugouts and ran to the nearest shell craters. We quickly put the machine-guns in position.

We could see the British moving forwards from their trenches. There were four lines stretching out of sight in each direction. The soldiers advanced as if they expected to find nothing alive in our trenches.

A German soldier describing, in a later interview, the view from the German trenches as the British advanced on 1 July. German machine-gunners killed thousands of British soldiers as they crossed No Man's Land.

Source G British troops going 'over the top' at the Somme, a scene from the British government's film, *The Battle of the Somme*, released in August 1916.

A battle lasting months

When the British troops did not break through the German lines on 1 July, Haig told them to keep up 'a steady pressure on the Somme battle'. They were to wear down the enemy troops (a plan called 'attrition'). The troops did their best, but the Somme, like the whole war on the Western Front, killed thousands on both sides, while getting nowhere.

The British army rushed a new weapon into action – the **tank**. The designers said tanks needed more work; but Haig needed them at once. On 15 September, tanks were used for the first time. They went in front, giving the troops cover, and crushing barbed wire and machine-gun posts. The Germans, taken by surprise, retreated. But, by the end of the day, troops from each side were back in their own trenches. The tanks had either broken down, stuck in the mud or been blown up.

Source

When the Germans came out of the dugout in the morning to look for the English, their blood chilled.

Strange monsters were crawling towards them over the craters through the mist. Nothing could stop them. Someone said 'The devil is coming.'

A German war correspondent describing the effect of British tanks when first used at the Somme. The tanks may have had a lot of disadvantages but they terrified the enemy.

Tanks

Advantages:

- soldiers protected
- well armed
- terrified the enemy
- moved well over the mud and craters of No Man's Land.

Disadvantages:

- needed eight men to work them; were very cramped
- noisy and hot inside; if a crew stayed in a tank for more than eight hours they could die from the heat and the lack of air
- very hard to manoeuvre and see out of
- got stuck in deep craters.

Source I

Tanks and infantry advance at Cambrai, 1917. The tanks are carrying 'fascines' – which made bridges across trenches for them.

Britain in the First World War

Effects of the Somme

At the end of September in 1916, it rained so hard that the area of the Somme became a huge mass of mud. No one could advance in such conditions, so the Battle of the Somme ended, without either side winning. Did it have any effect at all?

- Haig's revised aim, to kill a lot of Germans, was met. 500,000 German soldiers were killed. But so were 420,000 British and 200,000 French soldiers.

- No one gained any land.

- Verdun was saved. This was not just because Germans were pulled out to fight at the Somme. There was also a Russian attack, launched on 4 June 1916, on the Eastern Front that took German troops away from Verdun.

- Tanks were used for the first time, as was **aerial photography** to plan an advance.

Source J

The fighting on the Somme completely exhausted our army. We began to feel that if the fighting went on like that, we were bound to lose. Looking back, I do not see how we could have gained control, if the Allies had kept up the attacks of 1916.

From the memoirs of the German general, Ludendorff.

Losses in the major battles of 1916.

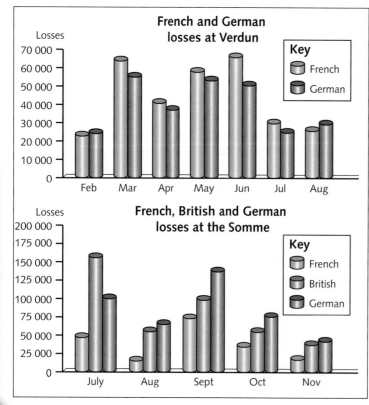

THINGS TO DO

1 (a) What was the plan for the Battle of the Somme?
   (b) How did the plan change and why?
   (c) How long did the battle last?
   (d) Who won the battle?

2 Look at the chart of deaths on this page. Do you think the aim of the battle was enough to justify the number of soldiers killed?

The war at sea

The British navy had three main aims in the war:

- To keep the British coastline safe and keep the Channel clear so troops could be ferried to France.

- To keep supplies coming to Britain by sea from the Empire and the USA.

- To blockade the German coast so they couldn't move supplies by sea. This would starve Germany into defeat.

There were only a few early sea battles, in the North Sea and the South Atlantic. There were two battles at **Dogger Bank** in January 1915 (see page 105).

When war broke out in 1914 a small British fleet was defeated by the Germans at Coronel, near Chile, on 1 November. This defeat was embarrassing for the British. At the **Battle of the Falkland Islands** on 8 December 1914 the British got their revenge and beat the Germans.

By 1915, the Allies controlled the sea. They stopped ships going to Germany, including ships using ports in Holland (despite the fact that Holland was not involved in the war). The ships were searched. Forbidden goods were seized by the British navy. **Neutral countries**, including the USA, complained that this was theft. The British navy ignored complaints. Soon their actions looked mild compared to German action against suspicious ships – sinking them with submarines (see page 104).

By 1916, Germany was suffering. Some people were starving, most were underfed. This led to them catching diseases more easily. The death rate in Germany rose in 1917 and 1918 because of this. The lowered morale and the increasing hunger and ill-health of the German people were partly why the Germans surrendered in 1918.

THINGS TO DO

1 What were the main aims of the British navy during the war?

2 Why were blockades important on both sides?

3 What were the effects of the blockade on Germany?

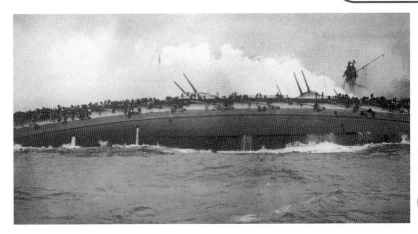

The German cruiser *Blücher* sinking at the Dogger Bank in January 1915.

Source K

Submarine warfare

The British navy controlled the sea from July 1915 onwards. German war boats could not beat the British ships. But the Germans made increasing use of **U-boats** (submarines) to attack supply ships coming to Britain. In February 1915, the Germans declared the seas around Britain a war zone. They would sink all ships in this zone, even if they belonged to neutral countries.

The *Lusitania* is sunk

U-boats had not been used in war before. They terrified people, because they were invisible. There was no warning, so no time to evacuate the ship. In 1915, the British liner, the *Lusitania*, was sunk by a single **torpedo** from a U-boat. It took just 18 minutes to sink. Over 1000 passengers were killed, including 128 Americans.

- The Germans said the *Lusitania* was in the war zone, and had been carrying weapons. The sinking was therefore not a crime but a victory.

- The British said the *Lusitania* was a passenger ship, carrying innocent people, many of them American.

Britain hoped the sinking would make the USA join the war. The sinking of the *Lusitania* horrified neutral countries. The USA did not join the war at once, but it made Americans consider the idea far more seriously than they had before. The Germans had to call off their policy of '**unrestricted warfare**' in the war zone around Britain. They only attacked British ships that were clearly carrying supplies or were navy ships.

Source L

The sinking of the *Lusitania* is a success. We are proud of our navy. It will not be the last of its brave deeds.

A report from a German newspaper in 1915.

Source M · An artist's impression of the sinking of the *Lusitania*, 1915.

The Battle of Jutland

On 31 May and 1 June 1916, the only big sea battle of the war took place, the **Battle of Jutland**. The British fleet trapped the German fleet. The British ships fired on the Germans, but their ammunition was faulty and broke up as it came into contact with the German ships. The German fleet fled back to port and never left again. When they were ordered to do so in 1918, the sailors **mutinied**. Both sides claimed a victory at Jutland.

Who won?

- The Germans said they won. They had sunk fourteen ships and killed 6000 sailors. The British had only sunk eleven ships and killed 2500 sailors. Their ships and weapons were better made and more reliable.

- The British said they won because the German ships did not leave port again.

Really, no one won. The British had driven the German fleet back to port, but had to keep guarding it there. If they had destroyed the German fleet, they could have tried to fight the U-boats. The Germans had survived, but never went to sea again.

Source N · Jellicoe's flagship at Jutland.

Source O · Beatty's flagship firing the first shots in the battle.

The British blockade of the German fleet.

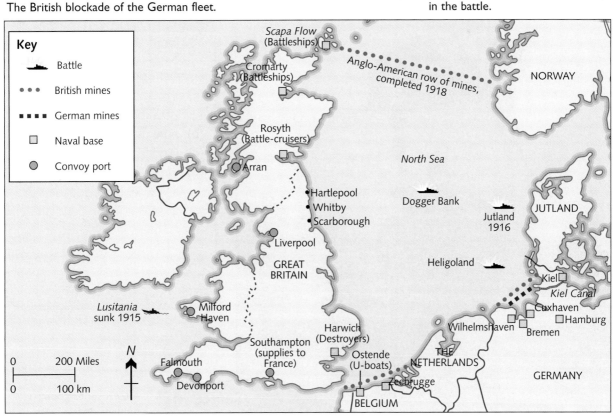

Key

- Battle
- British mines
- German mines
- Naval base
- Convoy port

Scapa Flow (Battleships)

Anglo-American row of mines, completed 1918

NORWAY

Cromarty (Battleships)

Rosyth (Battle-cruisers)

Arran

North Sea

Hartlepool
Whitby
Scarborough

Dogger Bank

JUTLAND

Jutland 1916

Liverpool

GREAT BRITAIN

Heligoland

Kiel
Kiel Canal
Cuxhaven
Hamburg
Bremen

Lusitania sunk 1915

Milford Haven

Wilhelmshaven

Harwich (Destroyers)

Southampton (supplies to France)

Ostende (U-boats)

THE NETHERLANDS

GERMANY

Falmouth
Devonport

Zeebrugge

BELGIUM

0 — 200 Miles
0 — 100 km

N

Renewal of unrestricted submarine warfare, 1917

After Jutland, the Germans began a policy of unrestricted warfare in the seas around Britain. They had many more U-boats by now.

- In January 1917, 386,000 tons of shipping of various sizes were sunk. By April, this had risen to 881,000 tons.

- In April 1917, there was only enough food left to feed the British for another six weeks.

The British had to do something – fast.

THINGS TO DO

1 What is a U-boat?

2 Why were U-boat attacks so frightening?

3 Why did the British condemn the sinking of the *Lusitania*?

4 How did the Germans justify the attack on the *Lusitania*?

5 List the ways the British tackled the U-boat threat.

6 Was the German policy of 'unrestricted warfare' a good policy for Germany or not?

THINGS TO DO

Look at **Source P**.
(a) What does 'splendid isolation' mean?
(b) How is Britain isolated?
(c) How are U-boats shown?
(d) How useful is this cartoon as evidence about the war at sea?

Source A German cartoon showing Britain in its 'splendid isolation'.

Defeat of the U-boats

The British were already taking measures against U-boats.

- **Q ships**, armed ships designed to look like ordinary ships, sailed the Atlantic to lure the U-boats into attacking.

- **Nets** and **mines** were placed in the Dover Straits to catch U-boats. If the U-boats wanted to get into the English Channel they had to waste time and fuel sailing around Scotland.

- Mines were also placed at other points around the coast of Britain.

The convoy system

In May 1917, the British introduced the **convoy system**. How did this work?

Ships that wanted to cross the Atlantic had to sail in groups, called convoys. In this way they made a single target, rather than a lot of scattered targets. Warships guarded each convoy. The warships carried **depth charges** (underwater bombs) to sink the U-boats. So, while the convoy was easier to find, it was far more dangerous to attack.

Did the convoy system work?

From 1917 to 1918, 132 U-boats were destroyed. Mines were the most successful method against them. The Germans were producing U-boats almost as fast as they were being sunk.

However, the British were building more supply ships than they were losing. And, thanks to the convoy system, more ships were getting through with supplies. **Rationing** was introduced in 1918, but the British people did not starve.

Eventually, damage to American ships caused by Germany's unrestricted warfare led to the USA joining the war on the side of the Allies.

Source **Q** A German cartoon that shows the U-boat as Germany's new hope, its 'baby'.

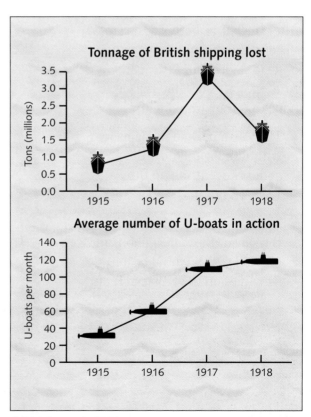

British losses and U-boats in action.

The Battle of Passchendaele, 1917 – attrition continues

In 1917, the British attacked heavily again, this time at **Ypres**. They began on 31 July with a two-week bombardment. The infantry then advanced, at about the same time as heavy rain set in.

The fighting centred on the village of **Passchendaele**, which was soon a sea of mud. Conditions were so bad that fighting stopped in November. Once again, there were no winners.

Effects of Passchendaele

- 200,000 German soldiers were killed. But so were 250,000 British soldiers.

- The Allies had gained between five and seven miles of mud.

After the battle, both sides were sickened by the many thousands of dead soldiers for little gain. And yet both sides had reason to hope that they would win.

- The Germans had made peace with Russia, and now they could concentrate on the Western Front.

- The USA had joined the war on the side of the Allies. Thousands of fresh troops would be joining the Allies on the Western Front.

The defeat of Germany, 1918

The Germans knew they had to win the war before great numbers of US troops arrived. The general in charge, Ludendorff, launched a huge attack in 1918, at St Quentin. At first, moving through fog, the Germans pushed the Allies back. They gained 1200 square miles of land. This was, in Western Front terms, a significant advance.

However, with the help of the newly arrived US troops, the Allies then stopped the German advance. The Allies advanced on the German front in waves, attack after attack. The German army began to surrender in large numbers, sometimes whole companies surrendered to a single tank.

The Germans were forced to admit defeat. The **Armistice** (ceasefire) was signed on 11 November 1918.

Source **R**   The town of Ypres after the Passchendaele campaign

Life in the trenches and its effects

Men usually spent four days at a time in the front line trench – although this could stretch to several weeks. They then moved back to the secondary trenches. After this, they went behind 'the lines' to rest, if things were quiet enough. Then the cycle began again. What was life like in the trenches?

- Food was army rations – tinned beef, a biscuit and jam.

- There was not much washing water, so many people had lice. The toilets overran and stank. Rats fed on the dead.

- There was little shelter from the weather. Rain filled the trench with water and mud. The water got into soldiers' boots and caused their feet to swell – '**trench foot**'. Over 75,000 soldiers had trench foot during the war. Often toes had to be **amputated**.

- Men on **sentry duty**, repairing trenches or getting the wounded out of No Man's Land were shot if the Germans spotted them.

- It was boring if fighting stopped. It was cramped, even sleeping was difficult.

- There were so many ways to die – gas attacks, shelling, **snipers**, falling into a shell hole in No Man's Land or being shot 'going over the top'.

- Sometimes the fighting was so fierce that there wasn't even time to clear the dead bodies out of the trenches.

Living in such constant fear gave some men '**shell shock**'. They shook uncontrollably, stammered or cried. At first, the army refused to accept there was such a thing as shell shock.

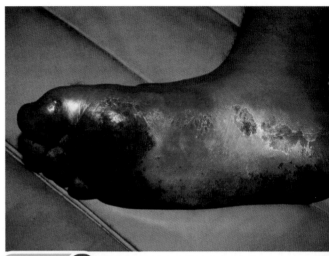

Source **S** Feet swollen from trench foot.

Source **T** British soldiers in a trench during the Battle of the Somme, 1916.

Views of the Front

Soldiers quickly came to hate the Front. Yet their families at home in Britain had no real idea what it was like. News of any kind – newspaper reports, letters home, photographs and so on – were all **censored** (checked).

- Officers read their soldiers' mail and crossed out anything too bad.

- Newspapers were told of pretend victories and not told of defeats.

- Only official war photographers and artists went to the Front. There were lists of things they could not show (artists could not paint dead bodies, for instance).

Source U

Forward Joe Soap's Army, marching without fear

With our own commander, safely in the rear.

He boasts and strikes from morn till night and thinks he's very brave,

But the men who really did the job are dead and in their grave.

An extract from a popular song sung by soldiers in the trenches.

Source V

There is an awful, sour smell of corpses that gets everywhere. Men killed last October lie half in swamp and half in beet fields. The corpse of an Englishman has been built into the parapet. The legs stick out into the trench and a soldier hangs his rifle on them.

Part of a letter written by a German soldier in April 1915.

Source W

The Harvest of Battle, a painting by a war artist of the effects of battle on the Western Front, completed in 1921. The artist will have made sketches of the battle and used his sketches to complete the painting later.

X A painting showing men blinded by gas, queuing for treatment between the heaps of dead and wounded. It was painted after the war.

The contribution of Empire troops to the war

Over a quarter of the soldiers who fought for Britain came from countries that had been part of the British Empire. These countries now governed themselves, although they had various links with Britain. They could have refused to join the war. They did not. Most of them fought on the Western Front.

- **New Zealand**, a country with a small population, sent 100,000 soldiers. 58,000 died or were wounded.

- **Canada** had 365,000 volunteers serving in Europe by March 1918 when service became compulsory.

- **Australia** sent 332,000 soldiers. 318,000 died or were wounded.

- **India** sent one million soldiers, despite the fact that, at the beginning of the war in 1914, it had only 160,000 soldiers in its army.

THINGS TO DO

1 Draw a diagram or cartoon to show the many different problems that affected people in the trenches.

2 Who sang the song in **Source U**?
   - What was their feeling about their commander?
   - Why do you think their officers let them sing songs like this?

3 Would the censor have allowed **Source V** to be sent home? Explain your answer.

4 'Source W is only a painting, done after the war – it's not a useful source'. Explain whether you agree with this or not.

2.2 How did the war change life in Britain?

Recruitment

When war broke out in August 1914 most people supported it. Britain had only a small army – more soldiers were needed, and fast. Lord Kitchener was put in charge of recruiting the extra troops.

- Posters were put up in all big towns, urging men to volunteer.

- Men who were fit enough to fight who did not join up were treated as cowards. In some places, women handed out white feathers, the symbol of cowardice, to men who looked like '**shirkers**'.

During August 1914, the first month of the war, 500,000 men volunteered. Everyone was sure the war would be over by Christmas.

Source **A**

We volunteered. Call it patriotism.

I was bored with shop work.

Other chaps joined, so I did too.

I wanted a change.

Some recruits explaining why they joined up in 1914.

Source **B** Recruitment poster using women to persuade men to enlist for the war.

Source **C**

Oh we don't want to lose you,
But we think you ought to go,
For your King and your country
Both need you so.
We shall want you and miss you,
But with all our might and main,
We shall cheer you, thank you, kiss you,
When you come back again.

A recruitment song from 1914.

"A SCRAP OF PAPER"

Source D   Propaganda postcard showing the British attitude to Germany's invasion of Belgium.

Changing attitudes

The war wasn't over by Christmas. People grew less keen to volunteer. In September 1914, there were 436,000 volunteers. By December 1915 there were only 55,000. People had stopped supporting the war. Why?

- People in Britain were not told everything, but even the reported death toll was awful.

- People had expected the war to end by Christmas. As it dragged on people suffered shortages, while knowing their loved ones were being killed or injured at the Front.

The high death rate meant that Britain needed more soldiers. So, in January 1916, the government set up **conscription**.

- All fit, single, men aged 18–41 could be made to join the army.

- From March 1916, married men could be conscripted, too.

- Some industries, such as farming and mining, were too important for their workers to be conscripted.

Some people refused to join the army, even under conscription. These **conscientious objectors** (COs) were against the war on moral or religious grounds. Some COs agreed to work in hospitals or act as stretcher-bearers. Those who refused to go were put in prison.

Propaganda

All through the war the government used posters, newspapers and even the new entertainment – cinema – to convince people that the Germans were evil and that the war had to be fought and won.

> ### THINGS TO DO
>
> (a) Why did people join up in 1914?
> (b) Draw a diagram of recruitment in August and September 1914 and December 1915.
> (c) Why did the army need more volunteers?
> (d) How did the government get more troops?

DORA

In August 1914, the British government introduced the **Defence of the Realm Act** (DORA).

This gave the government more power than it had in peacetime.

Censorship

- News reports, photos and paintings from the Western Front all had to follow rules. British heroism and German brutality could be shown, but not the terrible conditions at the Front.

- Letters home were read first, and anything that might 'affect morale' was crossed out.

- Even discussing the war in a public place was forbidden.

Government control of everyday life

- The government took over factories and farms to make weapons and grow certain foods.

- Women were expected to work and everyone was expected to work longer hours than before the war.

- British Summer Time was brought in. The clocks were moved forward to get an extra hour of daylight working.

- Pub opening hours were cut and beer was watered down.

- As food shortages increased, public parks could be used to grow vegetables. Even feeding bread to pigeons was forbidden because it was wasting food.

- In 1918, the government had to bring in rationing for foods such as sugar, butter and beef. People were given ration books with coupons in them that could be exchanged for limited amounts of these things.

Source   E

> I can't tell you where I am. The General is afraid you might tell someone at school, who might tell the German teacher, who might tell the Kaiser, who would send aeroplanes to drop bombs on us.
>
> *Part of a soldier's letter home to his children, 1914.*

Women and the war

Before the First World War, women were treated differently from men:

- Most women, unless they were very poor were expected not to work, but to marry and raise families instead.

- They were not allowed to vote.

The First World War changed all that. The government needed women on their side during the war. They needed women to encourage men to join the armed forces. They also needed women to take over the jobs that men left to go to war.

Women who took over men's jobs proved that they could do these jobs as well as or even better than men. Arguments about not letting women work, or vote, because they were not up to it looked foolish by the end of the war.

During the war:

- About 23,000 women worked as nurses on the front line. 15,000 more worked in VADs (**Voluntary Aid Detachments**), nursing in hospitals behind the front line.

- In 1917, the WAAC (**Women's Army Auxiliary Corps**) was formed. Members took over office and driving jobs in the army, to free men to fight.

- Over 100,000 women joined the Women's Land Army, working on farms.

- Thousands of others worked in mines, factories and shipyards. They also took over the necessary everyday jobs of delivering the post, driving buses and fighting fires.

Edith Cavell

When Belgium was invaded in August 1914, Edith Cavell was running a nursing school there. Rather than returning to England, Cavell turned the school into a Red Cross hospital. Thousands of Allied soldiers who had been captured by the Germans were nursed there.

Edith Cavell did more than nurse the soldiers. She also helped soldiers to escape. In 1915, the Germans arrested her as a spy and executed her. She became a heroine in Britain. Her death was used in the propaganda war against Germany.

Women and munitions work

By the end of the war, over 900,000 women worked in **munitions** (weapons) factories. This was about 60 per cent of the workforce. The work was difficult and dangerous.

When the working day was extended by DORA, many women worked twelve-hour shifts. Because they worked with dangerous explosives, explosions and fires were common.

Working with TNT could cause 'toxic jaundice'. This showed itself in yellow skin, and the women were nicknamed 'canary girls'. The condition could be fatal.

Women were proud to be earning their own wages and to be helping the 'war effort'. They were glad to show that they could do the same work as men.

So what happened after the war?

- In 1918 women aged 30 and over were given the vote, partly because of their work in the war.

- It was now more generally accepted that women could work as well as men.

But:

- As the men came back from the war, women lost their jobs to men.

- Women were still expected to be wives and mothers first, and workers second.

Source G

Mabel Lethbridge volunteered to work in the danger zone, where high explosives were packed into shells. She and four other girls packed huge shells with TNT and amatol, hauling on a rope with a huge weight on the end, to pound the explosives down hard into the shell case.

One woman's job in a munitions factory.

Source H Women in a munitions factory in 1916.

Danger of invasion

The First World War brought fighting to Britain, too. There were fears of invasion, which the government used in its **propaganda** war against Germany.

In December 1914, German ships shelled Hartlepool, Whitby and Scarborough on the east coast. Over 500 people were killed. Even when the navy had made the coast safe, there was still a danger at sea. German U-boats cut off British food supplies by sinking shipping in the waters around Britain (see Section 2.1 of this chapter).

Zeppelins

Zeppelins were airships, carried by huge balloons filled with **helium**. In January 1915, Zeppelins bombed Great Yarmouth and King's Lynn. There were attacks on London all through 1915 and 1916, but by 1917 they stopped because of British defences.

Barrage balloons were flown on cables, to confuse the Zeppelins and tangle them up. Searchlights could pinpoint Zeppelins for a fighter plane or ground artillery to fire at. If hit, the helium caused a huge explosion.

THINGS TO DO

1 How did DORA change life in Britain? Give examples in your answer.

2 What work did women do during the war?

3 Would it have mattered if women had not gone to work during the war?

4 Did things change for women after the war?

Source A Zeppelin.

Aeroplane warfare

Aeroplanes were a new invention in 1914. They were made of wood and canvas, and held together with piano wire. The pilots had:

- no radio
- no parachutes
- few navigational instruments
- an open cockpit
- unreliable engines.

At first planes were used to photograph enemy positions. This led to **dogfights** between planes from either side. The first of these were carried out with handguns!

Both sides saw the need to develop planes. Despite the changes that were made, planes were not very safe. In 1917, a front-line pilot could expect to live for two weeks.

- Machine-guns were fixed to the cockpit to replace handguns. Unfortunately, the pilot couldn't fire them without hitting the propeller.

- Then, the machine-gun was attached to the propeller and fired between the propeller blades.

- Planes became faster and engines more reliable.

- Planes that could carry bombs were developed.

- From 1917, the Germans bombed towns on the south coast of Britain.

- Over 1500 people were killed in these attacks and many homes and shops were damaged.

A big impact?

Compared to the loss of life on the Western Front, the damage and loss of life in Britain cause by air attacks was small. But it had a huge effect on morale. People had seen Britain as safe from invasion, once the seas were secured. Now it was not. This led to the Royal Air Force being set up in 1918.

Source J

The whole street seemed to explode, smoke and flames all over. Worst of all were the screams of the wounded and dying and mothers looking for their kids.

An eyewitness describes an air raid on Folkestone in May 1917.

Source K Air raid damage in London during the First World War.

Exam-style assessment

This question follows the pattern of questions to be set by AQA for Paper 1, **Section B**, of its new Modern World History specification.

Study **Sources A**, **B**, **C** and **D** and then answer all parts of the Question which follows.

Source A: Problems with food supplies

By 1917 food supply in Britain had become quite desperate. In April German U-boats were sinking one in every four British merchant ships. In April 1917 Britain had only six weeks' supply of wheat left. As food supplies ran short, so prices rose.

From *Modern World History* (1996) by BEN WALSH

Source B: Eat less bread!

A government poster of 1917.

Source C: A cross-section of a trench

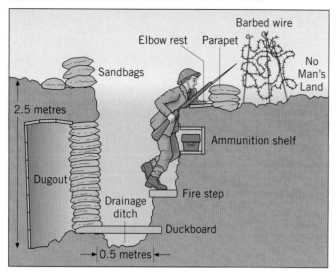

From *Modern World History* (2000) by
D. FERRIBY, D. HANSOM and S. WAUGH

Source D: Civilian attitudes in Britain to the war

At the beginning of the war, cheering crowds had gathered in the streets of London, and young men had eagerly enlisted 'to fight for King and Country'. But the mood of the people quickly changed from cheerful optimism to grim acceptance of the horrors of trench warfare.

From *Britain Since 1700* (1968) by R. J. Cootes

Questions

(a) What can you learn from **Source A** about food supplies in Britain in 1917? **(3 marks)**

(b) How useful is **Source B** for studying about food shortages in Britain in the First World War? Use **Source B** and your own knowledge to explain your answer. **(8 marks)**

(c) Use **Source C** and your own knowledge to explain what conditions were like for soldiers in the trenches during the First World War. **(6 marks)**

(d) Is **Source D** a fair interpretation of how attitudes towards the war changed in Britain in the years 1914–18? Explain your answer by using **Source D** and your own knowledge. **(8 marks)**

3 Britain in the Second World War

INTRODUCTION

The Second World War was very different from the First World War. The development of better aircraft, tanks and transport meant that attacks could be quicker. It also meant that civilians were more at risk than they had ever been before. At the beginning of the war, Hitler used the new technology to develop new tactics which were called *Blitzkrieg*. This involved using aircraft and tanks to attack with speed and surprise. He used these tactics against Poland and the West.

Britain declared war against Germany after the invasion of Poland. Hitler tried to use *Blitzkrieg* tactics against Britain. To do this he had to control the skies. This led to the Battle of Britain. When this didn't work Hitler began the bombing of British cities. The bombing of London was called 'the Blitz'.

Life for civilians changed. Children were evacuated from the cities; air raid shelters were built; gas masks were issued to everyone and Civil Defence Forces were set up. There was also a shortage of food due to the sinking of supply ships by German U-boats. This also changed people's lives. Rationing was introduced; propaganda encouraged people to grow their own food; women helped on the land, took civil defence jobs or joined the armed forces.

The final defeat of Germany began with the D-Day landings in Normandy in 1944. Britain and the USA attacked in the west while Russia attacked in the east. This eventually led to the surrender of Germany in 1945.

1939	Conscription
	Evacuation
	Poland attacked
	Convoys introduced
	BEF sent to France
	Poland defeated
	Phoney War
1940	Rationing in Britain
	Blitzkrieg in West
	Defeat of Norway
	Defeat of Netherlands, Belgium and France
	Dunkirk
	Home Guard formed
	Battle of Britain
	Blitz
	Bombing of Germany
1941	USA entered war
1942	Bombing of Germany intensified
1943	Turning point in battle of the Atlantic
1944	Britain and USA gain control of air over Germany
	D-Day – advance into Germany
1945	Bombing of Dresden
	Defeat of Germany

3.1 How did Britain resist and contribute to the defeat of Germany in the Second World War?

The Phoney War, 1939–40

The Germans attacked Poland from the west on 17 September 1939. Russia attacked at the same time from the east. In less than two weeks Poland no longer existed. Britain and France had been unable to do anything about it. Between the end of September and April 1940 little seemed to happen in the war. This became known as the **Phoney War** (pretend war).

Hitler hoped that Britain and France would now back down over Poland. He did not want a war with them because he did not have the resources to fight a long, drawn-out war.

Britain and France used this time to prepare for a war with Germany. Britain sent some forces to help the French, but the French did not take the preparations too seriously because they thought Germany could not attack them because of the **Maginot Line**.

The Maginot Line was a line of forts linked by underground tunnels that stretched along the French–German border from Belgium to Switzerland. The French had built these forts in the 1930s and thought no one could get through them.

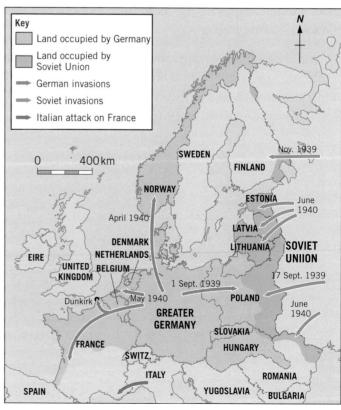

Source Ⓐ German tanks rest during the invasion of France.

This map shows land taken over by Germany and the USSR, 1939–40.

Modern World History for AQA

The German invasion of Norway, April 1940

The Phoney War ended in April 1940 when the Germans invaded the neutral country of Norway.

The British Prime Minister, Neville Chamberlain, had thought about stopping German supplies of iron ore coming from Norway. But he was frightened about what the rest of the world would think. In the end he was too late. Hitler ordered a *Blitzkrieg* attack on Norway. Britain and France did not provide enough help quickly enough and, as a result, Norway was defeated.

Neville Chamberlain took responsibility and resigned. Winston Churchill was chosen to lead the government for the rest of the war.

Source B

I have nothing to offer but blood, toil, tears and sweat. You ask, what is our policy? I will say: It is to wage war, by sea, land and air, with all our might. You ask, what is our aim? I can answer in one word: Victory – victory at all costs, victory, however long and hard the road may be.

Winston Churchill speaking in the House of Commons, 13 May 1940.

Source C
A British poster from May 1940.

"LET US GO FORWARD TOGETHER"

THINGS TO DO

1 What was the Phoney War?

2 How did this time help Britain and France?

3 Read **Source B**. Why do you think Churchill made this speech?

The defeat of France, 1940

Blitzkrieg warfare

Blitzkrieg means 'lighting war' in German. It was very important to German successes in the early part of the Second World War. They used the new technology, tanks and planes, to take the enemy by surprise.

Firstly key targets were bombed. At the same time parachutists were dropped behind enemy lines. Then tanks and foot soldiers carried out the main attack, attacking weak points first. They would then encircle the enemy while more **reinforcements** arrived.

The invasion of France, May 1940

The French did not expect the Germans to attack them through the Maginot Line. It was too well defended. They thought the Germans would attack through the lowlands of Belgium in the way they had in the First World War. Instead, on 10 May 1940 the Germans decided to attack through the forests of the Ardennes beyond the end of the Maginot line. They caught the French by surprise, using tanks and trucks to spearhead their attacks and capture important enemy positions. The British and the French still thought that the infantry should be at the front with the tanks backing them up. They quickly realised that tactics had changed. The French and British armies were soon in retreat and heading for the beaches of Dunkirk.

THINGS TO DO

1. Explain why *Blitzkrieg* (lightning war) was only possible in the Second World War.
2. Why did the French think the Maginot Line was going to save them from a German invasion?
3. Why was the Maginot Line of no use to the French in the end?
4. Why did Neville Chamberlain resign after the Germans invaded Norway?

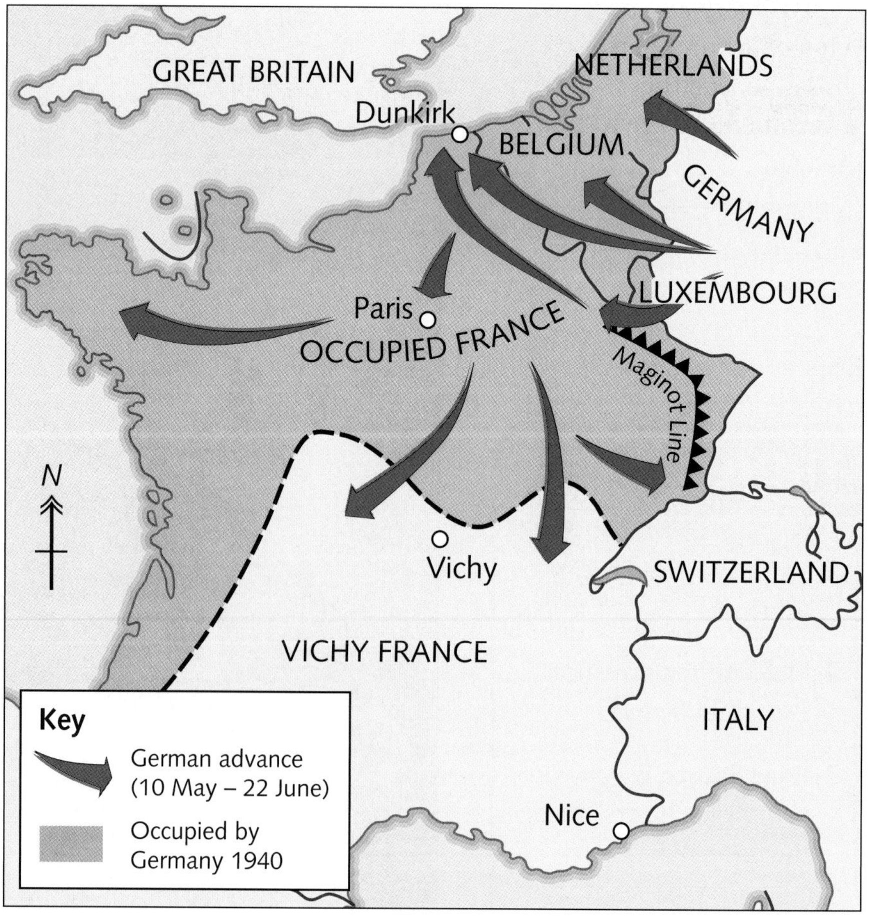

GREAT BRITAIN
NETHERLANDS
Dunkirk
BELGIUM
GERMANY
LUXEMBOURG
Paris
OCCUPIED FRANCE
Maginot Line
N
Vichy
SWITZERLAND
VICHY FRANCE
ITALY
Nice
Key
German advance (10 May – 22 June)
Occupied by Germany 1940

The path of the German *Blitzkrieg* in 1940.

The evacuation from Dunkirk

Source **D** A contemporary painting by Charles Cundall showing British troops being rescued from the beaches of Dunkirk.

In May 1940, the British Expeditionary Force had been placed under the overall control of the French commander. It soon became clear that the French were going to be defeated. The British commander, Lord Gort, was told to stop co-operation with the French and try to save as much of the BEF as he could. This was called **Operation Dynamo**.

- 10 May 1940: German invasion of France.

- 27 May 1940: Operation Dynamo, 7000 BEF troops evacuated.

- 28 May 1940: Belgium surrenders; the Germans take Calais.

- 27 May–4 June: 338,000 men rescued (139,000 were French) from the beaches of Dunkirk.

- 22 June: France surrenders to Hitler.

Operation Dynamo: a victory out of defeat?
Operation Dynamo was a greater success than expected. Royal Navy destroyers, helped by hundreds of privately owned vessels, pleasure boats, river ferries and fishing boats, brought more than 338,000 men back to Britain.

Fine weather and Hitler's decision not to press home the attack at Dunkirk helped Britain and France. However, the beaches at Dunkirk were attacked by the German airforce, causing many casualties: 68,000 men were lost. Those saved were to form the basis of the new army.

Britain in the Second World War

Was the Dunkirk retreat a German victory?

Hitler claimed that Operation Dynamo was a victory for the Germans because:

- 1200 field guns captured
- 68,000 British casualties
- 1250 anti-aircraft guns captured
- 11,000 machine-guns captured
- 75,000 vehicles captured
- 474 aircraft shot down.

Men had abandoned their rifles as they swam out to the waiting small ships. Uniforms were damaged. Personal possessions were lost. Morale was low. Men returned home not knowing what would happen next.

And within a month of the Dunkirk evacuation Paris had been captured and the French had surrendered to Germany. Germany occupied the northern half of France and allowed General Petain to set up a government for southern France in the town of Vichy. The Vichy government was really controlled by the Germans.

Britain was now alone.

Source **E** Dunkirk, 1940.

THINGS TO DO

1 Why did the British government claim that Operation Dynamo was a victory?

2 Why did Hitler also claim that Dunkirk was a victory?

3 What does **Source E** show us about
   (a) the number of soldiers involved
   (b) the organisation of Operation Dynamo?

Battle of Britain and the Blitz

The Battle of Britain

After the defeat of France Hitler planned to invade Britain. This plan was called **Operation Sealion**. To do this the *Luftwaffe* (German airforce) needed to control the skies over the English Channel and Britain. They attacked British airfields, ports and radar stations. Using the famous Spitfire and Hurricane fighters the RAF (Royal Air Force) fought hard against the *Luftwaffe*. This was the **Battle of Britain**. The RAF came very close to defeat. In the first week of September 1940, the British lost 185 aircraft and 300 airmen.

The Blitz

Hitler soon changed his tactics and decided to start the bombing of British cities. He hoped to break the morale of the British people. On 7 September 1940, German bombers attacked London. This was the start of the **Blitz**.

Civilians were now the main targets. This change in tactics gave the fighter pilots a rest and allowed the RAF time to train new pilots and industry time to build new aircraft.

Over a period of 77 days London was bombed almost every night. Many ports (such as Southampton, Bristol, Liverpool and Plymouth) and industrial centres (such as Manchester, Birmingham, Coventry and Glasgow) were also bombed.

The bombing of Coventry

The bombing of Coventry in November 1940 destroyed a motor works and an aero-engine factory. The raid lasted ten hours and over 4000 people were killed. Despite this it proved to be less effective than the Germans had hoped:

- The government used the destruction of the city's cathedral as propaganda against the Germans.

- People were frightened but pulled together.

- Industrial production actually went up after the attack.

By the time the Blitz ended in the summer of 1941 about 43,000 people had been killed and over two million were homeless. Hitler thought Britain was no longer a threat.

Source **F** The ruins of Coventry Cathedral after the German bombing of the city in 1940.

The Battle of the Atlantic

In the First World War, the Germans had almost defeated the British by using U-boats.

They thought that U-boats would help them win the Second World War. Within hours of the war starting they sank a British passenger liner, the *Athenia*.

Why did the Germans want to sink ships? The aim was to sink any ship bringing oil, food or raw materials to Britain.

German tactics were to:

- Use French ports as bases to attack British merchant ships.

- Hunt in '**wolfpacks**' (groups of up to 40 U-boats).

- Attack from the surface.

- Attack at night.

British tactics were to:

- Keep ships together in convoys.

- Use warships to protect convoys.

- Use warships to attack U-boats.

- Use radar to detect U-boats on the surface.

- Use **sonic** (sound) techniques to detect U-boats under water.

- Use aircraft to bomb submarines with depth charges.

Allied shipping losses were high at the start of the war but the convoy system started to work, especially after the USA joined the war in 1941. By 1943, the **Battle of the Atlantic** was being won. For the first time the Allies were building more ships than the U-boats could destroy and in 1943 and 1944 more than 200 U-boats were destroyed each year.

THINGS TO DO

1 Why did the Germans want to attack merchant ships?

2 Which years were the best for the Germans and which for the Allies?

3 Why did the Allies win the Battle of the Atlantic?

Source G

Britain's ability to maintain her supply lines is the decisive factor for the outcome of the war.

Admiral Raeder, Chief of German Naval Staff, speaking in 1940.

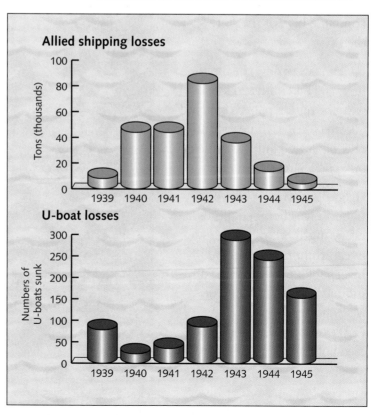

These charts show the amount of allied shipping losses and corresponding losses of U-boats in 1939–45.

The bombing of Germany

Britain began bombing German cities in 1940. The RAF bombed military targets, but by 1942 the decision was made to attack entire cities.

The first 'Thousand Bomber' raid was on Cologne in May 1942. It killed about 400 German civilians. In 1943, there were 43 raids on the industrial Ruhr, 33 on Hamburg and 16 on Berlin.

These bombing raids took place at night. The aircraft pilots could not accurately pinpoint military or industrial targets and many civilian areas were hit.

Civilians in Britain and Germany were now in the front line of war.

The British war effort was helped by the bombing of Germany.

- German industry and transport were badly damaged.

- It raised British morale.

- It seemed to help the USSR, Britain's new ally in the fight against Hitler.

However, the bombing of Germany had advantages for Germany:

- The German government used it in its own propaganda war against the British.

- RAF losses were high.

Source **H**   A British cartoon published after the bombing of German cities in 1943.

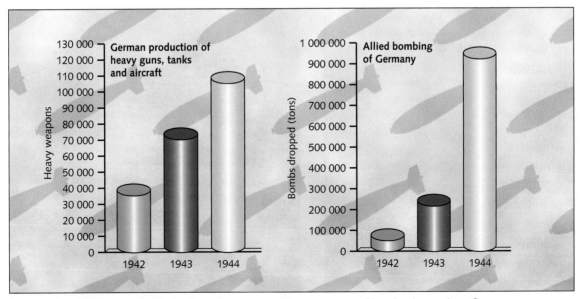

A comparison of Germany's production of weapons with the amount of bombs dropped on Germany.

Victory in the air

American bombing raids on Germany began in August 1942. These new attacks were in daylight. The pilots could hit the military and industrial targets they wanted to. However, this raised the number of aircraft and crew lost.

In 1944, new bombing techniques made the bombing even more accurate. By the end of the year, the Allies controlled the skies over Germany and its main roads, railways and bridges became targets too.

In February 1945, three months before the end of the war, British aircraft destroyed the city of **Dresden** killing 25,000 people. Even Churchill described the attacks on Dresden as 'mere acts of terror and wanton destruction'. By the end of the war, over 600,000 German civilians had been killed.

However, German morale did not break. Just like the British during the Blitz, people kept going despite everything that was happening around them.

THINGS TO DO

1 Look at all the information on this page. How bad was the destruction of Dresden?

2 Do you think the photographer who took this photo (**Source 1**) was German? Why?

3 What are the arguments for bombing cities and killing ordinary people?

4 Why did the Allies bomb Dresden when they were close to defeating Germany?

Percentage of German cities destroyed by Allied air attacks.

Bonn	83%
Bochum (Ruhr)	83%
Bremerhaven	79%
Hamburg	75%
Kiel	69%
Kassell	69%
Hagen (Ruhr)	67%
Munster	65%
Dusseldorf	64%
Mainz	61%
Cologne	61%
Hanover	60%
Bremen	60%
Dresden	59%
Aachen	59%
Koblenz	58%
Emden	56%
Dortmund	54%
Munich	54%
Stettin	53%
Frankfurt	52%
Nuremberg	51%
Essen	50%

Source Dresden after being bombed by the British, February 1945.

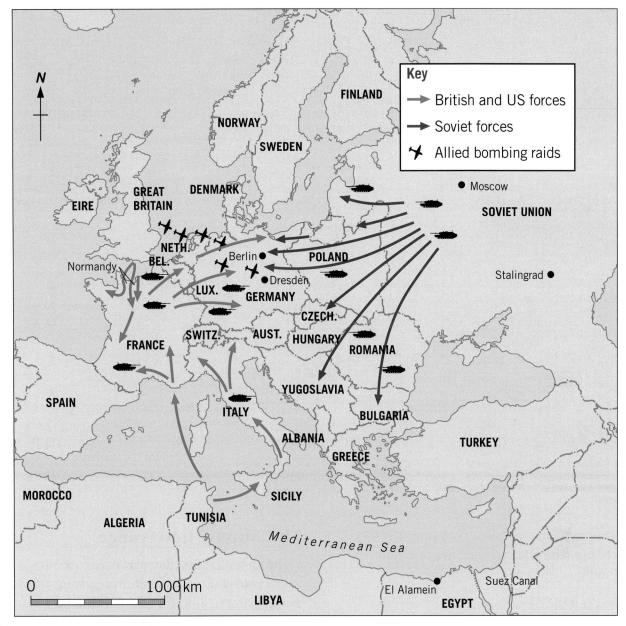

The defeat of Germany 1944–5.

The defeat of Germany

In 1941, the Germans invaded the Soviet Union. This was a bloody war that cost both sides thousands of lives. Stalin, the leader of the USSR, had asked Britain and the USA to attack Germany so that some of the German troops fighting on the Eastern Front would have to be transferred to the Western Front. At first, Britain concentrated on fighting in North Africa. This did little to help the USSR.

D-Day landings, June 1944

By 1944, Britain and the USA were prepared to attack Germany. **Operation Overlord** was planned. As part of that plan, Calais was bombed and dummy (fake) military camps were set up on the Kent coast. This was all done to fool the Germans into thinking the invasion would come via the shortest sea crossing, Dover to Calais. Few Germans thought the invasion would be in Normandy.

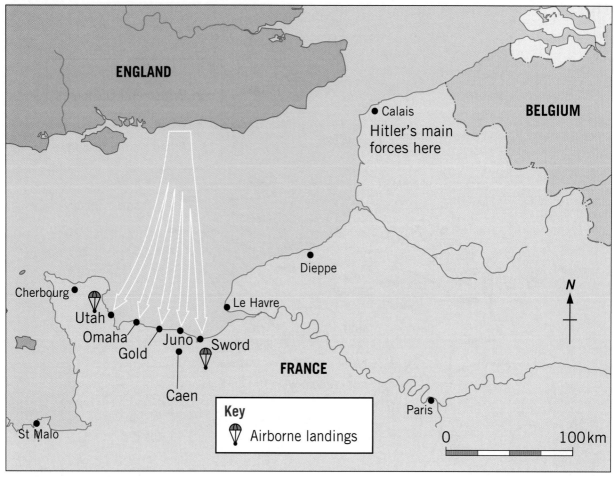

Key

🪂 Airborne landings

0   100 km

D-Day landings in France, June 1944.

The invasion took place on 6 June 1944 – **D-Day**. The plan involved five separate landings. They were code named:

- Utah (USA)

- Omaha (USA)

- Gold (Britain and Canada)

- Juno (Britain and Canada)

- Sword (Britain and Canada).

When the attacks began, Hitler still did not believe that the invasion would only take place in Normandy. He thought there would be another attack in Calais and so he kept many of his troops there.

The advance into France

Fighting on the first day was fierce. About 3600 British and Canadian troops were killed. For the Americans on Utah and Omaha beaches it was worse. They lost 6000 men. However, by the end of the first day there were 150,000 Allied troops in northern France.

By 12 June 1944, there were 325,000 Allied troops in France, moving inland to liberate (free) the French from Nazi rule. The Germans fought hard. It took nearly a month to free the port of Cherbourg. On 25 August, Paris was freed and **Charles de Gaulle** became the new French leader. The Germans began to retreat towards their own border.

The advance into Germany

In September 1944 the Allies reached the River Rhine. They began to capture the bridges leading into Germany. In December 1944 the Germans fought back in the Ardennes but by January 1945 they were in retreat once again. Soviet troops started moving in from the east. By April 1945, the Allies were fighting in Berlin. On 30 April 1945, **Hitler's suicide** signalled the final defeat of Nazi Germany.

THINGS TO DO

Why do you think the D-Day landings were successful?

Source Troops going ashore on D-Day.

Recruitment

Hitler invaded Czechoslovakia in March 1939. The British government realised that war might happen, so it introduced conscription. This meant that all men between 18 and 40 could be forced to join the army, navy or airforce. Britain declared war on 3 September 1939 and men started to 'join up'. Certain workers, such as coalminers, fire-fighters and doctors, remained in their jobs as they were important to the country's security. In May 1940, the **Emergency Powers Act** gave the government control over 'person and property'.

Attack from the air

When the war started the government thought the country would be attacked from the air so it appointed air-raid wardens to make sure that all lights were covered at night. They checked gas masks and helped people to the air-raid shelters. During the Blitz, they organised the clearing up of damage.

In May 1940, the Local Defence Volunteers (LDV) were formed. The LDV became known as the **Home Guard**. All men between 17 and 65 could volunteer. On the first day alone, 250,000 did so. In fact, there were so many volunteers that they were short of real weapons. The Home Guard (now referred to as 'Dad's Army') met in the evenings after work. They were trained in unarmed combat and anti-tank warfare. They acted as lookouts, removed local signposts which might help invading forces, guarded important buildings and manned road blocks.

ARP

SERVE TO SAVE

Source A A wartime poster calling on men to volunteer for the job of air-raid warden.

Source B

Such a force is of the highest value and importance. A country where every street and every village bristles with resolute, armed men is a country against which the tactics which destroyed the Dutch resistance would not succeed.

Winston Churchill speaking in Parliament about the Home Guard, November 1940.

Women and the war

The Second World War affected women much more than the First World War.

- They were at much greater danger from being bombed than in the First World War.

- They and their children were evacuated from cities.

- They had to deal with rationing.

- Many had to take on jobs in factories.

- Some joined the armed forces.

- Some joined the Women's Land Army to boost food production.

Conscription meant that many men went off to fight. As in the First World War, many women volunteered to do the jobs they left behind. By 1941, the government began to conscript unmarried women into jobs to help the war effort. By 1943, 57 per cent of workers were female.

New munitions (weapons) factories were often built in the countryside to stop them being bombed. Some women were forced to go and live in hostels so that they could work there. Many of the jobs needed skills like welding. Women built aircraft and ships. People soon realised how skilled many of the women were. For others the jobs were boring, so posters were put up to try to show how exciting it could be.

Source **E**

> This work the women are performing in munitions factories has to be seen to be believed. Precision engineering jobs ... are performed with deadly accuracy by girls who had no industrial experience.
>
> *Clement Attlee, the Deputy Prime Minister, writing about the work women did during the war.*

Source **C** — A poster encouraging men to volunteer for the Home Guard.

Source **D** — A poster advertising for women to help the war effort by working in factories.

Women in service

Each of the armed forces developed its own force for women during the Second World War:

- Army: ATS (**Auxiliary Territorial Service**)

- Air Force: WAAF (**Women's Auxiliary Air Force**)

- Navy: WRNS (**Women's Royal Naval Service**).

Women worked alongside men. The women did the 'backroom' jobs but also faced the same dangers as the men. They operated searchlights, filled sandbags, acted as radar controllers. They repaired planes and some women even flew the planes from one airfield to another. Some acted as nurses. Others worked in the intelligence service, and some were even spies in foreign countries.

The Women's Land Army

Food shortages grew as the U-boat campaign sank hundreds of British and Allied ships.

Rationing was not enough so the government began the campaign called '**Dig for Victory**'. The Women's Land Army was re-formed in 1939 and by 1944 had 80,000 women working on the land. They did all the jobs that the men had previously done. By 1943, production in Britain had almost doubled.

The 'Grow your Own' campaign

Farms provided the basic foods like grain, potatoes, milk and meat. It was up to the '**Grow your Own**' campaign to persuade people to grow all their own vegetables. Cartoon characters like Potato Pete and Dr Carrot (see Source H) were very successful. People grew food in window boxes, in public parks and even on golf courses. The Tower of London moat was even turned into **allotments**.

Source A poster calling for women to join the Women's Land Army.

Rationing

The government introduced rationing in January 1940. Each person had a ration book filled with coupons, which they had to hand over when buying food each week. If you did not have the coupons you could not buy the food. Later, a points system was introduced to give people more choice in what they bought.

Recipe books were issued to show people how to make meals using what food was available. Some foods, such as powdered egg and milk and Spam (**Supply Pressed American Meat**), came from America.

Things that were rationed during the war included butter, meat, bacon, tea, sugar, clothes and fuel

The government also asked people to mend old clothes and, when they needed to buy new things, to buy more cheaply. These items were given a **utility mark** to show buyers that they were helping the war effort.

Source G Mending your own clothes to save on materials needed for the war was encouraged by government posters like this one.

Source H These cartoon characters were part of the campaign to encourage people to eat healthy food.

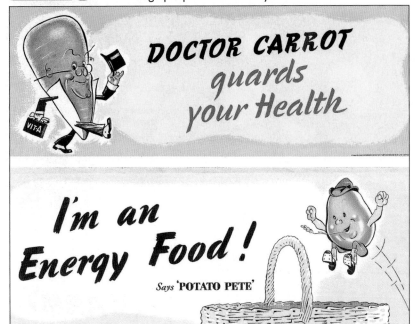

The 'black market'

Some people did not like rationing and they bought items on the 'black market'. Traders and shopkeepers sold goods that were rationed for high prices. This was illegal, and the government said it was unpatriotic. But many people used the black market if they could afford to.

Britain in the Second World War

How were civilians protected by the government?

Evacuation

The government expected the Germans to attack the cities from the air. To protect children, it was decided to **evacuate** them from the cities to the countryside. Many parents did not want to be separated from their children but accepted it would be safer.

- 31 August 1939: the government announced the evacuation of children.

- 1 September 1939: Hitler invaded Poland and evacuation began.

Schools were closed because many teachers went with their pupils to the countryside.

The local children bullied some evacuees because they did not want them in their school. Many of the foster families were

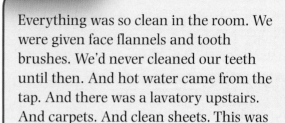

Source I

Everything was so clean in the room. We were given face flannels and tooth brushes. We'd never cleaned our teeth until then. And hot water came from the tap. And there was a lavatory upstairs. And carpets. And clean sheets. This was all very odd. I didn't like it. It was scary.

The memories of a Second World War evacuee.

shocked by how poor some children from the cities really were. It was hard for evacuees and foster families to adjust to each other (see Source I).

When the bombing of the cities did not begin immediately many parents and children decided to return to the cities. The government tried to encourage them to stay, but it did not work.

Source J — Evacuee children on their way from the city to the countryside to escape the danger of German air raids.

THIRD

When the Germans switched tactics after the Battle of Britain and began to bomb London and other major cities during the Blitz, children returned to the countryside, but not in the numbers that went in September 1939.

For many families, staying together and taking risks together was more important than being apart.

Source K

We left feeling sad for our parents and afraid that they would be killed by the bombs. We had no idea where we were going or whom we would live with, but at least we had been told by our parents that we would be safe.

When we arrived in Sandbach, we were chosen for a variety of reasons: for the extra income the family received for us, to help on the farm or with the housework. I was upset because I was separated from my sister.

School was a joke: we shared it with the locals so there was only half a day attendance and not enough teachers. The children whose school it was did not like us being there and made fun of us in the playground. There were many fights.

I was glad when I returned home for Christmas.

A boy, writing about his experiences as an evacuee in September 1939.

Source L

A government poster trying to persuade parents not to take their children back from the countryside.

Source M

Clarence and I used to sleep together and poor Clarence used to wet the bed because he was a very nervous kid. She (the foster mother) could never tell who'd done it so she used to bash the daylights out of the both of us. So, of course, the more Clarence got hit the more he wet the bed. It was then we started to get locked in the cupboard.

The film actor, Michael Caine, remembers his evacuation with his brother.

The Blitz

The government began to prepare for the bombing of British cities before the war began. In fact, the first air-raid shelters were delivered in February 1939 – seven months before the outbreak of the war. The government supplied **Anderson shelters**, **Morrison shelters**, and gas masks. It sent public information leaflets (see Source O) to every house in July 1939 to tell people what to do if there was an air raid. On 1 September the **blackout** came into force. People had to hang dark curtains or paper at the windows to make sure that no light could be seen from outside by enemy bombers.

Sheltering from the bombing

Anderson shelters were dug in the back garden. It was felt that they were safer than staying in the house although some people preferred to stay in their homes protected by the Morrison shelters.

People in London and other towns and cities were encouraged to go to purpose-built brick shelters. The government did not want people to shelter in the underground railway stations in case they were trapped there. But the people forced the authorities to give way and they became popular places to shelter during the Blitz.

Volunteers keep the towns and cities moving

The Air Raid Precaution Act of 1937 required local authorities to draw up civil defence plans which involved air-raid wardens, the Auxiliary Fire Service, the Auxiliary Police Corps, the Red Cross, St John's Ambulance Brigade and the Women's Voluntary Service. The volunteers and emergency services worked together to deal with the air raids.

Despite this some people did not cope. People in the East End became angry that they were bombed night after night and there were even examples of looting and stealing from bomb damaged shops and homes.

Air-raid wardens check on civilians in an Anderson shelter after a bombing raid.

Source
A public information leaflet telling people what to do to protect themselves against gas attacks.

Air-raid precautions

At first there was little that could be done against air raids. Radar helped spot planes crossing the east and south coasts only. Searchlights were not powerful enough because the Germans simply flew above them.

Air-raid wardens did their bit by checking that the blackout worked and that people carried their gas masks.

Source **P** Damage in the centre of Canterbury, Kent, after heavy bombing in 1942.

Source **Q**

Lighting restrictions

All windows, sky-lights, glazed doors, or other openings which would show a light, will have to be screened in war time with dark blinds or blankets, or brown paper pasted on the glass, so that no light is visible on the outside.

No outside lights will be allowed, and all street lighting will be put out.

Instructions will be issued about the dimming of lights on vehicles.

Fire precautions

An air attack may bring large numbers of small incendiary bombs, which might start up so many fires that the Fire Brigades could not be expected to deal with them all. Everyone should be prepared to do all he can to tackle a fire started in his own house. Most large fires start as small ones.

Clearing the top floor of all inflammable materials will lessen the danger of fire, and prevent a fire from spreading. See that you can reach your attic or roof space easily.

Water is the best means of putting out a fire started by an incendiary bomb. Have some buckets ready.

Extracts from a civil defence leaflet, issued in July 1939 by the British government.

Source **R**

We shall defend our island, whatever the cost may be, we shall fight on the beaches, we shall fight on the landing grounds, we shall fight in the fields and in the streets, we shall fight in the hills; we shall never surrender.

Churchill speaking in the House of Commons, 4 June 1940.

THINGS TO DO

1 What did the British do to try to reduce the effects of the bombing?

2 Why do you think people were keen to join the Home Guard?

Britain in the Second World War

Propaganda and censorship

The **Ministry of Information** produced posters to encourage people to join the voluntary services and to work hard and save in order to help the war effort. People were told not to talk about the war in public just in case a spy was listening to them. A Ministry of Information poster warned that 'careless talk' could be dangerous (see Source V). An organisation called **Mass Observation** carried out surveys and checked on what people were talking about.

Other propaganda encouraged people not to waste anything. The '**squander bug**' became a regular feature of the propaganda (see Source W).

Newspapers were censored. They were allowed to report on the bombing but were expected to concentrate on heroes and heroines rather than deaths and destruction. The *Daily Worker* newspaper was banned in 1941 because it did not do that.

Radio and film

Special newsreel films were produced to try to show how well the war was going.

These were watched each week in the local cinema. The Germans used a British citizen living in Hamburg to broadcast on Radio Hamburg and attempt to break the morale of the British people. These 'Lord Haw Haw' broadcasts did worry many people, while others ignored or laughed at them. Britain did the same with its broadcasts to Germany, which were also a mixture of truth and rumour.

Source

Everybody is worried about the feeling in the East End, where there is much bitterness. It is said that even the King and Queen were booed the other day when they visited the destroyed areas.

From the diary of Harold Nicolson, a minister in the Ministry of Information, 17 September 1940.

Source

There were more signs of terror and panic observed than during the whole of the previous two months together in all areas. The overwhelming feeling on Friday was the feeling of helplessness. The huge impact of the previous night had left people almost speechless in many cases. On Friday evening (15 November), there were several signs of panic as darkness approached.

A Mass Observation report on the bombing of Coventry in 1940.

THINGS TO DO

1 Why did some children like being evacuated?

2 How did the government persuade people to stop wasting anything?

3 How did the government know what was going on in the country at any time?

4 How did the government try to keep people happy during the war?

Internment

The worry about spies led to the **internment** (imprisonment) of German and Italian citizens. They were arrested and put in prisoner-of-war camps. Some of them were in Britain because they had escaped from Hitler and Mussolini. By the summer of 1941, all but 5000 were released because the government realised that they were no longer any sort of threat.

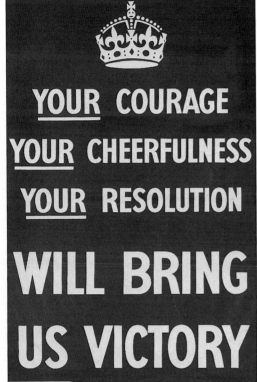

YOUR COURAGE YOUR CHEERFULNESS YOUR RESOLUTION WILL BRING US VICTORY

Source **U** A Ministry of Information poster from early in the war. Some people thought this reinforced a 'them and us' attitude. The workers would win the war; the upper classes would benefit from the victory.

You never know who's listening!

CARELESS TALK COSTS LIVES

Source One of a series of posters intended to stop people carelessly giving away secret information to enemy spies.

DON'T TAKE THE SQUANDER BUG WHEN YOU GO SHOPPING

Source The intention of this poster was to make people think twice about spending money unnecessarily.

THINGS TO DO

1 List ways in which women helped with the war effort in Britain.

2 Find two pieces of propaganda. Try to explain why you have chosen each one and how each tries to influence what people thought.

Exam-style assessment

This question follows the pattern of questions to be set by AQA in Paper 1, Section B, of its new Modern World History specification.

Study **Sources A**, **B**, **C** and **D**, and then answer all parts of the question which follow.

Source A: Work for women in the army, servicing a 6-ton truck

Source B: Changes in numbers of women employed, 1939–43

Changes in numbers of women employed, 1939–43	
Distribution	−6,000
Services	+58,000
Textiles	−165,000
Clothing	−149,000
Admin/clerical	+480,000
Engineering/aircraft/ships	+1,197,000
Manufacturing	−48,000
Food	−18,000
Chemicals	+220,000
Agriculture	+102,000
Transport	+147,000
Other	+531,000

From *Life in Wartime Britain* (1993) by RICHARD TAMES

Source C: Be careful about giving away secret information!

A government poster during the Second World War.

Source D: The importance of the Battle of Britain

> The Battle of Britain was an attempt by Hitler to destroy the fighters of the Royal Air Force so as to clear the way for an invasion of Britain in the autumn of 1940. The attempt failed. The failure was decisive for the future direction of the war.

From *The World at War* (1973) by MARK ARNOLD-FORSTER

Questions

(a) What can you learn from **Source B** about the numbers of employed women in the Second World War? **(3 marks)**

(b) Use **Source A** and your own knowledge to explain how attitudes towards women in the armed forces changed during the Second World War. **(6 marks)**

(c) How useful is **Source C** for studying propaganda and censorship during the Second World War? Explain your answer by using **Source C** and your own knowledge. **(8 marks)**

(d) How accurate is the interpretation in **Source D** of the importance of the Battle of Britain within Britain's role in the Second World War? Use **Source D** and your own knowledge to explain your answer. **(8 marks)**

Russia/USSR, 1914–41

INTRODUCTION

In the early 1900s, Russia was the most backward country in Europe. Its ruler, the Tsar, had complete power. The First World War led to the collapse of Tsarist rule. The Provisional Government that took over lasted just eight months before the Bolshevik Revolution put the Bolsheviks (Communists), led by Lenin, in power.

Lenin had to deal with severe economic problems and civil war, for not everyone accepted Communist rule. However, the Bolsheviks won the civil war and introduced policies to make the economy work better. Stalin followed Lenin as leader. He made Communist Russia (the USSR, the Union of Soviet Socialist Republics) stronger with collectivisation on farms and Five-Year Plans for industry. But this was done by ignoring people's needs and concentrating on the good of the state.

Stalin may have led the Communist Party, but he took over more and more power until he ruled the USSR almost as completely as the Tsar had in 1914. While he 'purged' many people he saw as opponents, including many innocent people, his reforms did help the USSR to get through the Second World War.

1894	Nicholas II becomes Tsar
1904	Russo-Japanese War
1905	Revolution
1914	Russia enters the First World War
1917	Two revolutions in March and November
1918	Treaty of Brest-Litovsk with Germany
1921	New Economic Policy (NEP) introduced
1924	Death of Lenin
1928	Stalin introduces collectivisation and first Five-Year Plan
1934	Assassination of Kirov
1936	New constitution introduced
1940	Assassination of Trotsky
1941	Germany invades the Soviet Union

4.1 The end of Tsarism, 1914–17

How strong was the Tsarist regime in 1914?

Source (A) Tsar Nicholas II and Tsarina Alexandra in 1903.

The Tsar, Nicholas II

Nicholas II believed that God had made him **Tsar**, to rule Russia alone. He wanted to rule Russia well. However, he did not know how people lived in most of the country. He lived surrounded by his court and depended on others to tell him what was going on.

Government

Only the Tsar could make laws. He had ministers to help him run the country, but they had no power. There was no elected parliament; the idea of a parliament was dismissed by Nicholas II as a 'senseless dream'. Local councils (*zemstva*) ran things like schools and hospitals.

Policing people

The **Okhrana** (secret police) made sure people obeyed the Tsar.

- They stamped out any opposition.
- They **censored** newspapers and books and imprisoned opponents.

The Church and the Tsar

The Russian Orthodox Church also supported the Tsar and it preached to the people over and over that God had chosen him as leader and that opposition was a sin.

Modern World History for AQA

The countryside

Over 90 per cent of Russians were **peasant** farmers. Their lives were hard:

- Most of them did not own their land; they worked for rich landowners who lived on huge estates.

- They only had old-fashioned tools.

- They farmed inefficiently, working on small strips of land.

- They had to obey the decisions of the *zemstva* (local council), which was controlled by the landowners. So they had no way to complain about bad treatment, because the *zemstva* would not support them against the powerful landlords.

The towns

Russia was just beginning to become **industrialised**. Large factories were built and industries were developed. Coal mining, iron and steel working and cloth-making were all operating on a far larger scale than before. This had several effects:

- Towns grew.

- Many peasants went to the towns to look for work and a better life.

- The industrial workers (the **proletariat**) lived crammed together in slum areas of the cities.

- The proletariat were badly paid and their working conditions were terrible.

- They could not form trade unions. The police crushed protests or strikes.

Russia in 1914. It covered one-sixth of world's surface.

Russia/USSR, 1914–41

Source B

Often the peasants do not have enough land to feed and clothe their families. They cannot heat their homes, buy seed for sowing or pay their taxes.

From a police report on conditions in the countryside, written in 1905.

Source C

Every minute of the day we are in danger. When there are accidents, they accuse us of carelessness. The greed of the bosses, the long hours, the bad wages – these cause accidents.

From a Russian trade union leaflet, written in 1898.

Opposition to Tsarist rule

Various groups opposed Tsarist rule:

- **The Liberals:** wanted to keep the Tsar but have him share power with an elected parliament. There were various Liberal groups. Most members were middle-class people such as doctors and lawyers.

- **The Social Revolutionaries:** wanted the peasants to overthrow the Tsar, take over the land and farm together in 'communes'. They knew this would mean violence.

- **The Social Democrats:** wanted the proletariat to overthrow the Tsar. The Social Democrats followed the teachings of **Karl Marx**, but were split into two groups:

- **The Bolsheviks,** led by **Lenin**, who believed that the revolution had to be organised. A small group would lead the revolution and set up a system so the people could rule.

- **The Mensheviks,** led by **Trotsky**, who believed that the revolution had to be an organised mass movement.

Because opposition to the Tsar was crushed by the Okhrana, it was hard for these groups to organise. Social Revolutionaries and Social Democrats spent a lot of their time abroad, in exile. It was hard to believe that they could really organise a revolution under these circumstances.

Source D

How long have you been a member of the Communist Party?

Since 1894.

Have you ever belonged to any other parties?

No.

What sentences were you given for revolutionary activities?

1887 prison;
1898-1900 Siberia;
1900 prison.

How long did you spend in prison?

Several days and 14 months.

How long at hard labour?

None.

How long in exile?

Three years.

How long a political refugee?

9-10 years.

Extract from Lenin's answers to a Communist Party questionnaire.

THINGS TO DO

1 Why was Russia hard to rule in 1914? Think about:
   - how it was ruled
   - how much the ruler knew about Russia and its people.

2 (a) What proportion of Russians lived in the countryside?
   (b) What jobs did these people do?
   (c) Who did they work for?
   (d) What were their working conditions like?
   (e) What were their living conditions like?

3 Why might you distrust the information in **Source C**?

Modern World History for AQA

150

The causes of the 1905 Revolution

People were unhappy with Tsarist rule. From 1902 onwards, a series of events made matters worse:

- There were many bad harvests.

- There had been an economic depression.

- These led to demonstrations, strikes and violence. The army crushed them, brutally.

- In 1904, the minister in charge of the secret police, Plehve, was assassinated.

- In 1904, a war broke out between Russia and Japan; Russian troops were defeated.

Source Bloody Sunday: the marchers' path to the Winter Palace is blocked by troops.

Bloody Sunday, January 1905

On 22 January 1905, about 200,000 people marched through St Petersburg to the Tsar's Winter Palace. The marchers wanted the Tsar to make reforms. They were led by a priest, **Father Gapon**, and sang hymns and waved pictures of the Tsar to show that they were peaceful and loyal.

Even though the Tsar was not in St Petersburg, troops blocked the marchers' way and opened fire. Hundreds of marchers were killed.

The 1905 Revolution

People were horrified by the massacre and blamed the Tsar. Strikes and riots broke out in towns all over Russia. Peasants took over the landowners' estates. There was even a mutiny (revolt) by sailors on the battleship *Potemkin*. Things looked bad for the Tsar.

Russia was in uproar. The Tsar had lost the war with Japan and was forced to give up land in the peace treaty. This made people even angrier. From 10 October on, workers began to form **soviets** (workers' councils) and take control of the towns.

The October Manifesto and the end of the 1905 Revolution

The Tsar did not want to give in to demands for reform. But his advisers convinced him that he had to. So, he issued the **October Manifesto**, which said:

- People were allowed **freedom of speech**.

- They could form **political parties**.

- There was to be a **Duma** (parliament) elected by the people, to help the Tsar rule.

The Liberals were pleased by the October Manifesto. The more revolutionary groups were not – they wanted to get rid of the Tsar.

The Tsar had regained control of the army. He crushed the revolutionary opposition and left the October Manifesto in place, to keep the Liberals happy.

Meanwhile, the Okhrana were hunting revolutionaries to send to labour camps as a punishment. Those who could, including Lenin, fled. They thought they had missed their chance for revolution.

The Dumas

In April 1906, the first Duma was elected. By now, the Tsar felt he had complete control of Russia again. He now regretted the October Manifesto. He issued the **Fundamental Laws**, *before* the election. These laws left any Duma powerless. They said:

- the Tsar could dismiss a Duma at any time

- only the Tsar could appoint ministers

- in 'emergencies' he could rule without the Duma.

Source **F**

Sire, we the workers of St Petersburg come to you with our wives, children and elderly relatives to ask you for protection and justice. We do not ask much: to reduce the working day to eight hours, to provide a minimum wage. Do not refuse to help your people.

The Workers' Petition, 1905.

Source **G**

The riots in our Empire fill us with grief. We allow people freedom of speech, of conscience and of assembly. All men will be allowed to vote for a Duma. Laws cannot be passed unless the Duma accepts them.

Part of the October Manifesto.

Source **H**

I set up the Duma to advise, not instruct, me.

Said by the Tsar in 1908.

Military defeat

In 1914, Russia joined Britain and France in their war against Germany and Austria–Hungary. People were enthusiastic at first. St Petersburg (a German-sounding name) was renamed **Petrograd**. Suddenly the Tsar had a lot of support.

Unfortunately, the Russian army suffered defeats. Why?

- It was large, but badly equipped (almost one-third of soldiers did not even have a rifle).

- Officers were chosen because they were rich, not because they had military skills.

The Germans beat the Russians at the battles of **Tannenburg** and the **Masurian Lakes** and invaded Russia.

Effects of war on the Russians

- Millions of peasants were forced into the army. It was hard to grow enough food to feed everyone. Prices rose rapidly.

- Food did not often reach the cities – the railways were used by the army.

- While food prices shot up, wages stayed the same.

- Refugees from land taken over by the Germans moved into towns. The towns became more overcrowded and food was in even shorter supply.

- Factories shut down because there were not enough raw materials, like coal, to run them. Unemployment rose.

- Cold and starvation were killing thousands of people. Meanwhile the army was losing the war.

Source

Thousands of workers and students marched to the Winter Palace, carrying pictures of the Tsar and singing hymns and the national anthem. When they arrived they fell on their knees and cried 'God save the Tsar'. The Tsar has never been so popular.

A Russian eyewitness to scenes in St Petersburg when war broke out in 1914.

Source Russian prisoners of war under guard in May 1915.

The Tsar and the war

The defeats of the Russian army made the Tsar unpopular. In 1915, he decided to take personal command of the army. This had two important consequences:

- He was now seen as personally to blame for the Russian army's defeats by the Germans. It was no longer possible to blame his generals, as it was the Tsar who was making the decisions.

- He left the government of the country to his wife, the **Tsarina Alexandra**, who was German. People were suspicious of her because of this. She did not rule wisely, refusing to listen to the Duma, and relying more and more on **Rasputin** (see the Case Study).

Source (K) The Tsar blesses his troops.

THINGS TO DO

Look at the evidence in the case study and the sources. Why do you think Rasputin's relations with the royal family helped to weaken the Tsar's rule?

Case Study: Rasputin

Rasputin was a Russian peasant who came to the court at St Petersburg saying he was a holy man. He gave advice and 'healed' people. He was asked to heal the Tsarina's eldest son, Alexis, who had a disease that made it hard for his blood to clot (even small cuts and bruises threatened his health).

The Tsar and Tsarina felt Rasputin had saved Alexis's life. They thought he was sent by God. They trusted him and asked his advice more and more, even on choosing ministers.

When the Tsar went to war the Tsarina depended on Rasputin. She chose and sacked ministers on his advice and she gave his friends important jobs. She even sent letters to the Tsar, giving him Rasputin's advice on how to run the war.

Rasputin's power made him many enemies; the nobles at court did not like a peasant having power over them. A group of nobles eventually assassinated Rasputin. Unfortunately, he had already badly damaged the reputation of the royal family and people no longer trusted them.

The move towards revolution

By 1917, Russia was in chaos:

- The German army had invaded.

- Food was expensive and in short supply.

- A harsh winter meant it was more difficult than ever to move food and fuel around. More and more people died of starvation and cold.

- The government was unpopular and was not coping with the problems.

Russia was ready for **revolution**. There were two of them within nine months. The first, in March 1917, ended the rule of the Tsars.

Source L

A Russian cartoon of Rasputin with the Tsar and Tsarina. By showing the Tsar and Tsarina as puppets it is criticising Rasputin's power over them.

SUMMARY

Effects of the First World War

- Russian army beaten, Germany invaded Russia.

- Economic disruption.

- Starvation.

- Weak government.

- Tsar and Tsarina more and more unpopular.

- Revolution and collapse of Tsarist rule.

Source M A queue of hungry people outside a bread shop in 1917.

The March Revolution and the abdication of the Tsar

The severe winter, food and fuel shortages and the defeats of the war caused unrest, which turned to revolution:

- On 4 March 1917, workers at an engineering works in Petrograd went on strike. The factory was forced to close.

- The strike spread. Several workers were killed in clashes with the army.

- The Tsar, who was away at war, was warned of the problem. He ignored it.

- On 12 March 1917, soldiers refused to fire on strikers. They joined the strikers and marched on the Duma to demand a new government.

- The Tsar tried to get back to Petrograd. It was too late. His train was stopped outside the city and he was advised to **abdicate** (give up his rule). He did, on 15 March. He and his family were arrested and were taken to Siberia.

Source

Petrograd is out of control. The government cannot act. Food and fuel supplies are breaking down. Everywhere there is rising discontent. There is shooting on the streets. Troops are firing at each other.

Telegram to the Tsar from the Duma, 11 March 1917.

THINGS TO DO

Look at **Sources K** and **L**.
(a) What does each one suggest were the feelings of Russians towards the Tsar?
(b) Why do you think they are so different?

4.2 The Provisional Government and the Bolshevik Revolution

Why did the Provisional Government last for only eight months?

The Provisional Government and the Petrograd Soviet

When the Tsar abdicated, the Duma set up the **Provisional Government**, to run things until elections were held for a new government. At the same time, the **Petrograd Soviet** (a council of workers' and soldiers' representatives) met. Other soviets were set up in Russia too. The Petrograd Soviet organised food and housing and rail services. It also took over the army.

The weaknesses of the Provisional Government

The Provisional Government was popular at first. It granted people basic rights, such as free speech. But it had many weaknesses:

- It was made up of too many political groups – it was hard for them to agree on policies.

- It wanted to leave most decisions until the new government was elected, even the redistribution of land that the peasants wanted. This made the Provisional Government look even weaker. Many peasants took the land anyway.

- It decided to go on fighting the war. Soldiers were deserting (leaving the army); people were desperate for the war to end. But the Provisional Government thought a peace treaty at this time would be too hard on Russia.

- The Petrograd Soviet, which had many Bolshevik members, was well organised and had clear aims. It seemed to be running the city. More and more people came to see the Bolsheviks as the answer.

Source A

The Soviet of Workers and Soldiers' Deputies has decided:

- All military units must have a committee.
- The Provisional Government will only be obeyed if it does not go against Soviet decisions.
- Military committees will keep all weapons and not give them to the former officers.
- Everyone will be equal in rank.

  Order No. 1 of the Petrograd Soviet, 14 March 1917.

THINGS TO DO

1 Draw a flow diagram showing the steps to the Tsar's abdication from March 1917.

2 What made the Provisional Government unpopular?

Lenin's return and the *April Theses*

A painting of Lenin's return to Petrograd in April 1917.

Source B

The various revolutionary groups were unprepared for the speed of the revolution. Many revolutionaries were still in exile in March, including Lenin. Lenin rushed back to Russia. The Germans helped him, thinking the Bolsheviks were likely to agree to end the war. Lenin knew he had to act fast. He reached Petrograd on 16 April and issued his *April Theses* which said:

- The Bolsheviks would no longer work with the Provisional Government, but work to overthrow it.

- The Bolsheviks would end the war.

- The Bolsheviks would give the land to the peasants.

Lenin's points in the *April Theses* were summed up in slogans such as '**Peace, Bread, Land**'.

The July Days

In July, the Provisional Government ordered a big attack on the Germans. It failed.

- On 16 and 17 July, there were huge demonstrations against the government.

- The Bolsheviks joined in, as did the **Red Guard** – a private Bolshevik army.

- Troops loyal to the Provisional Government stopped the rising.

- Many Bolshevik leaders were arrested, although Lenin escaped to Finland.

The Provisional Government had stopped the revolution this time. But it was dependent on the army and still had not solved the problems that set off the demonstrations.

Source C

There was less and less food. The bread ration of 1.5lb a day fell so that by the end of the week there was no bread at all. On the freezing front the army continued to starve and die without enthusiasm.

Written by John Reed, an American who was living in Petrograd in 1917.

The Kornilov Affair

In September, **General Kornilov** tried to take over the government.

He and his troops marched on Petrograd. The Provisional Government panicked. These had once been loyal troops. The Provisional Government asked the Bolshevik Red Guard for help and gave them weapons. The Red Guard went to stop Kornilov's army. Kornilov's troops would not shoot fellow Russians. Kornilov was arrested and put in prison.

The Provisional Government had been shown as weak by asking the Red Guard for help. The Bolsheviks had been shown as strong and the Red Guard kept the weapons the Provisional Government had given them.

Source **D** Leon Trotsky had been a leader of the Mensheviks. He joined the Bolsheviks in 1917 and became a key figure in organising the revolution.

SUMMARY

The Provisional Government failed to survive because:

- It was weak politically. It was not elected and was made up of different parties.
- The Petrograd Soviet did not support it.
- It did not give land to the peasants.
- It continued the war and was blamed for the defeats of the Russian army.
- It failed to solve food shortages and other economic problems.
- Bolshevik policies were more popular.

The Russian calendar

Until February 1918, the Russians used a calendar that was thirteen days behind the rest of Europe.

In February 1918, the Bolsheviks changed the calendar to match Europe.

Dates before this time have alternative dates. So, the first revolution is either the February or March revolution. This book uses the modern dates.

How were the Bolsheviks able to seize power in October/November 1917?

In November 1917, Lenin and Trotsky led a successful Bolshevik revolution. How did they do this?

The Bolsheviks

Lenin had been involved in the failed revolutions and felt it was still possible to organise a successful one. The Bolsheviks gained support because:

- The Provisional Government was losing support.

- Lenin's *April Theses* had a wide appeal.

- It was the Bolshevik Red Guard that had defeated Kornilov.

The Bolsheviks gained support from the people but also, importantly, from the various workers' soviets.

- In September 1917, the Bolsheviks had a majority in the Petrograd and Moscow Soviets.

- Lenin came back from exile in Finland.

- He convinced the Bolshevik leaders it was time for revolution.

- He put Trotsky in charge of planning.

The events of the Bolshevik revolution

The Revolution was planned for the time when the All-Russian Congress of Soviets met in Petrograd.

On 7 November:

- The Red Guard seized rail stations, bridges, power station, waterworks and newspaper offices.

- The Red Guard seized the telephone exchange, the telegraph agency and the state bank.

- **Kerensky**, the leader of the Provisional Government, fled and asked the army at the front for help. The army refused and he left the country.

- The Bolsheviks demanded that the Provisional Government surrender. No reply.

- The Bolshevik-controlled cruiser, the *Aurora*, fired on the Winter Palace. The remaining loyal troops deserted the Provisional Government.

On 8 November:

- Menshevik and Social Revolutionary members of the All-Russian Congress of Soviets protested at the Bolshevik revolution. Most walked out.

On 9 November:

- Lenin announced a new government: the Council of the People's Commissars.

By 15 November:

- The Bolsheviks controlled Petrograd and Moscow; the most powerful cities in Russia. Next they had to win over the rest of Russia.

Reasons for the Bolshevik success

The Bolsheviks later said they won because the masses were on their side. In fact most Russians, even in Petrograd and Moscow, did not even know the revolution was happening. How did it succeed?

- The Provisional Government made mistakes, and the Bolsheviks used these mistakes against it.

- Bolshevik ideas did have a wide appeal, especially the slogan 'Peace, Bread, Land'.

- The Bolsheviks timed the revolution right and planned it carefully. The seizing of key positions at the same time was vital.

Source **E**   A painting from 1937 showing the storming of the Winter Palace.

Source **G**

The November revolution was an armed rising by a small group led by Lenin, a political genius, against a government that had already lost control.

Written by a British historian in 1987.

Source **F**

The Bolshevik party wanted to win over the masses. Its leader, Lenin, spoke at many rallies and meetings. His speeches were clever and well delivered. They inspired workers and soldiers and party membership grew.

Written by a Soviet historian in 1981.

THINGS TO DO

1 How useful is **Source E** as a view of the Bolshevik revolution?

2 How do **Sources F** and **G** differ in their interpretation of the Bolshevik revolution?

Russia/USSR, 1914–41

How did Lenin impose Communist control on Russia?

A communist poster 'Lenin, Father of the Working People.'

Source A

Setting up a Bolshevik government

Most of the **commissars** (ministers) in the Council of the People's Commissars were Bolshevik.

- Lenin was the Chairman.

- Trotsky was the Commissar for Foreign Affairs.

- **Stalin** was the Commissar for nationalities – he dealt with issues concerning non-Russian peoples such as the Slavs who were part of the Russian Empire.

Lenin announced that the war with Germany was at an end and began peace negotiations. He also issued a **land decree** (law) that took land from the Tsar, rich landowners and the Church and gave it to the peasants. These two measures made the Bolsheviks very popular.

The Constituent Assembly

The elections that the Provisional Government had set up still took place. These elections were for a parliament called the **Constituent Assembly**.

- Before the elections Lenin renamed the Bolshevik party the **Communist Party**, and tried to appeal to more voters.

- The Communists won 175 seats out of 700. The Social Revolutionaries won 370 seats. Most of their votes were from the peasants, even though the Bolsheviks had given them the land they wanted.

- Because the Communists could not control the Constituent Assembly, Lenin shut it down after one day. It was the first step to a Communist Party dictatorship.

> When I made my speech in the Assembly I was jeered by the Bolsheviks; many of them waved guns.
>
> Lenin lounged in his chair, looking bored to death.
>
> ***A Social Revolutionary describes the one-day life of the Constituent Assembly.***

This map shows the land that Russia lost in the Treaty of Brest-Litovsk, March 1918. The Ukraine was one of the richest areas in Russia, with good farmland and iron and coal mines.

The communist dictatorship

- In December 1917, Lenin set up a new secret police force, the **Cheka**. They spied in factories and villages and arrested anyone who seemed anti-communist.

- In 1918, there was a plot to assassinate Lenin. He began the '**Red Terror**' campaign. Over 50,000 opponents were arrested and executed.

By 1920, Lenin had as tight a control of Russia as the Tsar had ever had.

Peace: the Treaty of Brest-Litovsk

Lenin wanted to get Russia out of the First World War. It would win him support, while continuing the war might lose him power altogether. There was no way that the Russian army, badly supplied and with thousands of soldiers deserting, could win the war. Besides, the Communists could not fight the Germans and their opponents within Russia. They had to make peace with the Germans.

On 3 March 1918, the **Treaty of Brest-Litovsk** was signed. Russia lost a large amount of land in the west, on the border with Germany.

This area contained:

- one-sixth of the population

- three-quarters of Russia's iron and coal

- one-quarter of the farmland, some of it the best in Russia.

THINGS TO DO

What were the advantages and disadvantages to Russia of the peace treaty with Germany? Do you think that Lenin was right to agree to it?

The Russian civil war, 1918–21

This map shows the main events of the Russian civil war. The Reds faced attack from all sides.

All these groups, the **'Whites'**, joined together to fight the **'Reds'**. The Whites were led by Russians loyal to the Tsar – Admiral Kolchak and Generals Deniken and Wrangel. Foreign armies sent them weapons. Britain, France and Japan all sent troops. These troops landed in various parts of Russia: Murmansk in the north, Vladivostok in the east and in the south.

Causes of the civil war

The Bolsheviks had many different opponents:

- people who wanted a Tsar again

- people who wanted a liberal government, not communism

- landowners who had had lands taken from them by the Bolsheviks (including the Church and its supporters)

- foreign countries, such as Britain and France, who were against communism

- the Czech Legion – a group of Czechs who had supported Russia in the First World War and wanted Russia to stay in the war.

Source C

Of all the tyrannies in history the Bolshevik tyranny is the worst.

Lenin and Trotsky have committed far more atrocities, of a far worse kind, than the Kaiser ever did.

Said by Winston Churchill, Secretary of State for War, in 1919.

The events of the civil war

- **Admiral Kolchak**, in the east, won at first, taking many Red Army prisoners and killing them. When Kolchak's men were defeated in 1919, their leaders were shot.

- **General Yudenich**, helped by British troops, moved in on Petrograd in the north-west. By 1920, he was only a few kilometres away. Trotsky encouraged the Red Army to drive him back.

- In the south-west, **Deniken** marched on Moscow. By 1920, he had been defeated.

- **Wrangel** attacked in the Crimea, but by November 1920 he was defeated, too.

- The **Red Army** also had to fight a Polish invasion. The Poles hoped to take advantage of Russia's civil war to take more land for Poland. The Red Army drove them back to Warsaw, making peace at the Treaty of Riga in 1921.

- The **Czech Legion** took over the Trans-Siberian Railway, an important transport link. Bolshevik supporters drove them off.

Reasons for Bolshevik success

At one point in the civil war the Reds were fighting the Whites and fourteen foreign countries, on seven different fronts. How did they win? It was a combination of weaknesses of the Whites and strengths of the Bolsheviks.

Weaknesses of the Whites

- They did not have a single leader. White generals worked for their own victories, not together.

- They did not have a general cause to unite them.

- Their use of foreign help made them unpopular with the Russian people. The Bolsheviks were seen as the 'patriotic' party.

- White troops behaved badly to people in the areas they controlled. They took food without paying. Deniken's men murdered 100,000 Jews.

- Some White troops gave land back to the landlords. This lost them peasant support.

Strengths of the Reds.

- They controlled the industrial centres and the rail network.

- They controlled less land than the Whites, so they could concentrate their troops.

- They were fighting for a cause, the communist revolution, and their soldiers had good morale.

- Trotsky was a great leader of the Red Army. It was well run and, although discipline was harsh, well motivated.

- Supplies were better organised. They set up **War Communism**, taking in all supplies and handing them out (see page 168).

- The **Cheka** (the new secret police) killed opponents to the Bolsheviks in Bolshevik-controlled land. They also, eventually, executed the Tsar, in case he was rescued to lead the Whites.

- Many Russians supported their ideas. The actions of the Whites (such as giving landlords their land back in some places) boosted Bolshevik support.

ПСЫ АНТАНТЫ.

ДЕНИКIН КОЛЧАК ЮДЕНИЧ

This Bolshevik propaganda poster shows France, the USA and Britain as evil capitalists who were trying to control Russia. The 'dogs' they are using to do this are the White generals.

Source D

The consequences of the civil war

The civil war had a damaging effect on the people of Russia who were already badly hit by the growing economic problems since 1900.

- Between 1914 and 1921, 21 million people were killed in fighting, either in the First World War or the civil war.

- Industry lost workers and supplies.

- Agriculture lost workers; only 50 per cent of the land was being farmed.

- There were many outbreaks of disease. People were badly fed and many were starving. The fuel shortages meant people died of cold, too.

- In 1921, things were made worse by a serious famine. Workers left the towns in the hope of finding more food in the countryside. The famine killed about 5 million people.

- The civil war also affected the Bolshevik attitude to foreign countries. Many had helped the Whites in the civil war. So, the Bolsheviks distrusted foreign countries. They set up **Comintern** in 1919. This was a group to encourage communist revolution in other countries. If other countries were communist, Russia would be safe.

Source E

Sometimes a starving family eats one of its children. Sometimes parents rob graves to feed their children.

From the notes of two doctors working in one of Russia's worst-hit famine areas in 1921.

THINGS TO DO

Why do you think the Bolsheviks won the civil war? Give three reasons in your answer.

Modern World History for AQA

166

Case Study: the assassination of the Tsar, July 1918

In March 1917, the Tsar abdicated (gave up the throne). He and his family were arrested, taken to Siberia and imprisoned in a house in the Red-controlled town of Ekaterinburg. During July 1918, White troops closed in on Ekaterinburg. The Reds knew that the Tsar, if freed as leader of the Whites, would win the Whites more support. They decided they had to kill the Tsar. We do not know exactly what happened at the time. Different people give different versions of the story.

The White story

The Tsar and his family were all shot: the Tsar, his wife, his son, his four daughters, the family doctor and three servants. These eleven people were shot in the basement of the house at Ekaterinburg. Those who did not die at once were slaughtered with bayonets. The bodies were then taken to a nearby mine where they were soaked in acid and burned.

The Red story

The Tsar was executed. The rest of the family were sent away to a Red-controlled area. The Reds never said what happened to the rest of the family later. A woman in the USA, Anna Anderson, has said she was one of the princesses who managed to escape from Russia.

Archaeological evidence

In 1991, some bodies were found near Ekaterinburg. They were examined by forensic scientists, to see if they could be the remains of the Russian royal family. Checks on dental records and DNA tests were made. In 1994, the scientists announced that the bodies belonged to the Tsar, his wife and three daughters. They had been shot and bayoneted. Later, the remains of Alexis and one of his sisters were found nearby, badly burned.

Source

Shortly after 1am they were taken from their rooms. I think they knew what was going to happen, but they didn't make a sound. I heard the shooting and returned to the house. All the members of the Tsar's family were lying on the floor, shot many times. The blood was running in streams. The heir (Alexis) was still alive. A soldier shot him three more times.

A Red Army soldier, describing the shooting of the Tsar's family.

Source G The room where the assassination took place.

THINGS TO DO

Look at the evidence in the case study. What do you think happened to the Tsar and his family? Give reasons for your answer.

How successful was Lenin in creating a new society in Russia?

War Communism

To win the civil war Lenin had to keep the Red Army well fed and supplied. He took over the economy and set up War Communism.

- Food was rationed. Only workers got ration cards.

- Factories were run by the state. Workers could not form trade unions. They had to work long hours.

- The Cheka were sent to take all the grain from the peasants, to feed the army and the workers. The peasants hid their grain, or just grew less, rather than give it away. Grain production fell.

- In 1921, there was a drought and the crop was even worse. There was a famine and over four million Russians starved to death.

The Kronstad Revolt

War Communism made the communist government unpopular. The communists expected support from the peasants and the town workers, but neither group supported War Communism.

In March 1921, sailors at the Kronstadt naval base revolted. Lenin ordered the Red Army to stop the revolt and execute the leaders. Lenin was lucky. The Red Army acted against the sailors.

But Lenin remembered the way the army had refused to obey the Provisional Government. He realised he had to abandon War Communism.

Source **H**

Groups were sent into the countryside to take grain from the peasants by force. They were driven off with pitchforks. Peasants slit open the collectors' bellies, filled them with grain and left them on the road as a warning.

Unrest in the countryside, described by someone living in Russia at the time.

THINGS TO DO

1 What was War Communism?

2 Why do you think War Communism was unpopular?

Source **I** Starving children during the famine of 1921.

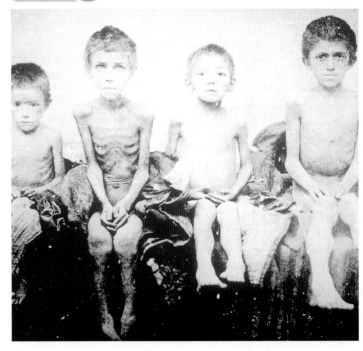

New Economic Policy

Lenin set up the **New Economic Policy** (**NEP**) to replace War Communism. The state still kept control of important industries (coal, steel, railways and banks), but elsewhere there were changes.

- Smaller industries and factories could be privately run.

- The goods from these factories could be sold for profit.

- The peasants had to give a set amount of grain to the state as a tax.

- Any extra grain they grew, they could sell for a profit.

Some communists disliked the NEP, because letting the factories and peasants make a profit was against the ideas of communism. Lenin hoped it would encourage factories and peasants to produce more and boost the economy.

Did the NEP work?

The NEP did improve things.

- Grain production went up. So did the production of small industries.

- The end of the civil war also helped the economy.

But, the NEP created problems.

- Some peasants (**Kulaks**) made a big profit and began to hire less well-off peasants to work for them.

- Some traders in towns (**Nepmen**) began to buy food and goods cheaply and sell them at higher prices.

Both types of behaviour were a move back to the old ways.

The creation of the USSR

By 1921, when the civil war ended, the communists controlled most of the Tsar's old empire. As areas were taken, they became Socialist Republics.

In 1924, Russia became the USSR (**Union of Soviet Socialist Republics**). The USSR had a parliament, with members elected by the people. In fact, the communists were the only party, so they ran the USSR. Lenin died in 1924, leaving the Communist Party firmly in control.

Production in the USSR, 1913–28.

Output (in millions of tons)			
	1913	**1921**	**1928**
Coal	29.0	9.0	35.0
Oil	9.2	3.8	11.7
Iron	4.2	0.1	3.3
Steel	4.3	0.2	4.0
Grain	80.0	37.6	73.3

SUMMARY

Communism in Russia, 1918–24

- State control of industry.
- State control of banks.
- Grain taken from peasants (as tax or just taken).
- Russia becomes the USSR.

THINGS TO DO

1 What was the New Economic Policy?

2 How successful was it?

How far did Stalin set up a personal dictatorship in Communist Russia?

The struggle for power with Trotsky

When Lenin died in 1924 no one had been chosen to take over after him, although Lenin had already warned the Party against Stalin (Source B). Trotsky and Stalin seemed to be the most likely people.

- **Trotsky** had Lenin's approval, but some Party members distrusted him because he had only joined the Party in 1917. He was also arrogant.

- **Stalin** was a loyal Party member. He was General Secretary of the Party, which meant he appointed people to Party jobs. So he could make sure there were plenty of his supporters in the administration.

Different views on spreading communism

One of the biggest disagreements that Stalin and Trotsky had was over the future of communism.

- Trotsky believed that communism would survive only if it spread to other countries by '**permanent revolution**'.

- Stalin believed that the USSR had to become a powerful state, able to compete with other countries, before spreading communism. This policy was called '**socialism in one country**'.

Source **A** Joseph Stalin.

Source **B**

Comrade Stalin, as General Secretary, is very powerful. I am not sure he knows how to use this power. I suggest to the comrades that a way is found to remove him.

An extract from Lenin's Political Testament, 1923.

The removal of Trotsky

Stalin became leader, by building up support in the Central Committee; he also got rid of Trotsky.

- 1924: the Party Congress elected Stalin as leader.

- 1925: Trotsky dismissed as Commissar for War.

- 1926: Trotsky dismissed from the Central Committee.

- 1927: Trotsky expelled from the Communist Party.

- 1929: Trotsky exiled from the USSR (went to Mexico).

- 1940: Trotsky assassinated on Stalin's orders.

The removal of other communist leaders

Stalin was just as harsh with anyone else he thought might be a threat to his total control. Only his supporters stayed on the Central Committee.

- 1926: Kamenev and Zinoviev (on the left wing of the Party) dismissed from the Central Committee.

- 1929: Bukharin (on the right wing) dismissed from the Central Committee.

Stalin's control of the USSR

In 1936, a new constitution set up two chambers of parliament, elected every four years. But there was only one political party – the Communist Party. The Central Committee of the Communist Party ran things.

The most powerful member of the Central Committee was the Chairman – Stalin – who also controlled:

- **religion:** services of any kind were banned, priests were sent to labour camps

- **art, music and literature:** were censored (controlled) and had to support the Communists

- **news:** was censored.

The cult of personality

The USSR had become a totalitarian state – one party controlled every aspect of people's lives. Added to this, there was the '**cult of personality**' surrounding Stalin.

Posters, radio programmes, even films and paintings, were used to spread the message that Stalin was a hero and that he was looking after the Russian people.

History books were rewritten to show Stalin as Lenin's most trusted adviser. Trotsky did not appear at all in histories of the communist revolution.

Source

Stalin's face is everywhere. Every speech praises him. Every room has his picture on the wall. Love or fear? I do not know.

Said by a foreign visitor to the USSR in the 1930s.

THINGS TO DO

List the steps that Stalin took to power under the headings: 'Removal of opposition', 'Control of the state' and 'Personal power'.

Case Study: the Purges and Great Terror

Purges

By 1934, Stalin was in total control of the USSR. But he did not trust some of the people around him. Between 1934 and 1938 he purged (got rid of) traitors (enemies) of the Communist Party:

- He arrested people he feared, such as Kamenev and Zinoviev in 1936.

- They were tortured until they confessed to crimes they had not done.

- Important Party members had big public '**show trials**'.

- The accused were always found guilty of treason (disloyalty to the state).

- Less important communists that Stalin wanted to get rid of were expelled from the Party. They were often sent to labour camps in Siberia or the Arctic.

The Great Terror

Stalin also purged the armed forces and millions of ordinary Russians in the same way as he purged the Communist Party. This was called the **Great Terror**. It was carried out by the **NKVD** (the secret police that replaced Lenin's Cheka).

Almost 90 per cent of the top officers in the army and all the admirals of the navy were purged. No one could feel safe. Everyone was encouraged to report 'suspicious' behaviour by colleagues, friends, even family. If there was no evidence, the NKVD would invent it.

The Terror ends

By 1939, it was clear even to Stalin that the Terror was destroying the USSR. About 20 million people were sent to the labour camps; over half of them died there. The country lost many of its scientists, doctors, teachers, engineers and military officers.

Stalin realised he was damaging the Soviet Union and the Terror eased off; although the NKVD still watched for real opposition to Stalin and stamped it out.

A French cartoon of the 1930s showing a poor Russian with a banner saying 'We are really happy'.

Source

Prisoners were charged with many crimes: treason, murder, spying and all kinds of sabotage. They signed written confessions and accused other innocent people. What they said was not true.

It became clear that the show trials were used to turn political opponents into common criminals.

Said by a British eyewitness to the show trials.

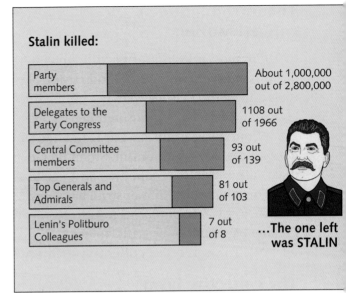

Stalin killed:

Party members	About 1,000,000 out of 2,800,000
Delegates to the Party Congress	1108 out of 1966
Central Committee members	93 out of 139
Top Generals and Admirals	81 out of 103
Lenin's Politburo Colleagues	7 out of 8

...The one left was STALIN

The purge of the Communist Party.

THINGS TO DO

1 Read **Source C**. List the ways it shows Stalin spreading his cult of personality.

2 How did the purges and the Great Terror affect:
   (a) the Communist Party
   (b) the armed forces
   (c) Russia's industry
   (d) the way people behaved towards each other?

SUMMARY

Stalin set up a personal dictatorship by

- removing Trotsky
- purging the Communist Party
- removing opposition through the Great Terror
- censoring information and the arts
- setting up a cult of personality.

To what extent did Stalin make the USSR a great economic power?

The need for economic growth

By 1928, Russia's economy was much stronger than it had been in 1900, thanks to Lenin's New Economic Policy (NEP). But it still had a long way to go to catch up with other industrial countries, such as Britain.

Stalin wanted to build up the USSR's industry so it was strong enough to resist invasion.

Stalin wanted to:

- build new factories and industrial towns, using modern machinery bought from the West

- create more jobs in industry, especially coal, steel and oil

- increase grain production, to feed the workers and their families and to export to the West to pay for western machinery.

Russia/USSR, 1914–41

The introduction of collectivisation

In 1928, most peasants farmed the small farms handed out in the revolution using old tools and methods. They were not producing enough food. In bad years Stalin had to take grain from the peasants, just as Lenin had done under War Communism. Stalin had to make farming more productive – fast – to feed the growing number of industrial workers. The answer was to put farms together, making big farms for peasants to work on together. This was called **collectivisation**.

The collective farm

How did the collective farm, called the *Kolkhoz*, work?

- All the land and animals from several farms were put together.

- The peasants ran it by committee and shared the work and the profit.

- The peasants had to give a set amount of grain to the state. Any extra could be sold at a profit.

- The state provided tractors and other machines to modernise the farms.

The process of collectivisation

Stalin enforced collectivisation step by step.

- First, he got rid of the 'greedy capitalist Kulaks' whose power had grown under the NEP. He turned their farms into collectives.

- The remaining peasants were told to form collectives. Some did.

- Some destroyed their crops, homes and animals rather than give them to the state. The state still took the land. By 1930, over half the farmland was collectivised.

- Stalin was worried by the peasant resistance, so he changed the system. Peasants could keep their homes and a small plot of land, but they worked on collectives. By 1937, almost all the USSR was collectivised.

All through history Russia has been beaten back, over and over, because of our backwardness. We are 50–100 years behind the advanced countries. We must make up that gap in ten years. Either we do it or they crush us.

From a speech made by Stalin in 1931.

Source G

Every night the peasants killed their animals. Bulls, sheep, pigs, even cows were slaughtered.

'Kill, it's not ours any more ... Kill, they'll take it for meat anyway ... Kill, eat, you won't get meat on the collective.' So they killed and ate until they could eat no more.

From a Russian novel written at the time of collectivisation.

Source H

Collectivisation met its main aims. The government could take food from the peasants at very low prices. The use of machines, especially tractors, cut the number of farm workers. These workers could go to industry.

Written by a modern British historian.

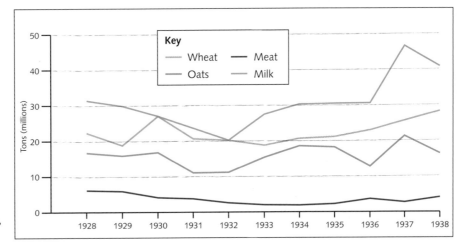

Russian agricultural production, 1928–38.

Results of collectivisation

- In the years 1929–33 food production fell. Bad harvests, plus the peasants' destruction of crops and animals, caused famine in 1932–3. Millions starved to death.

THINGS TO DO

1 What was collectivisation?

2 How did Stalin set it up?

3 Did collectivisation work? Explain your answer.

- From 1933, the peasants were getting used to collectives. The organisation of the collectives, and the growing use of machinery, meant that grain production began to rise.

The production of milk and oats also rose though less steadily. Meat production rose much more slowly and by 1938 had still not reached 1928 levels.

- Over five million Kulaks were killed or sent to labour camps. Over 13 million peasants died during collectivisation, many of them during the famine.

Industry: the Five-Year Plans

Stalin knew he had to modernise the USSR's industry to make it strong.

- The state took over industrial production.

- **Gosplan** (the state planning agency) was set up to plan a series of **Five-Year Plans** that set production targets for every factory.

- Factories and workers that met their targets were rewarded. Those that failed were punished.

The first Five-Year Plan (1928–32) set targets for coal, iron, steel, oil and electricity. Production increased hugely, but the targets were too high.

The second Five-Year Plan (1933–7) set more realistic targets for coal, iron, steel, oil and electricity. It also focused on war goods.

The third Five-Year Plan (1938–) aimed to increase production and improve the quality of consumer goods. It was disrupted by the Second World War.

The growth of industry

The Five-Year Plans.

- Modernised and increased the production of old industries.

- Set up new industrial areas, well away from any land Germany might attack.

- Set up new towns, like Magnitogorsk, in the Ural Mountains.

- Built dams, improved roads and railways. The hydro-electric dam on the River Dneiper produced more electricity than the whole of Russia when the Tsar ruled.

Results of the Five-Year Plans

Achievements
- By 1938, the USSR was a major industrial producer of oil, coal, steel, iron and electricity.

- It was still behind the western powers, but was more able to face a threat from Germany.

- The state built new towns and provided schools and hospitals, as well as setting up insurance schemes.

Source J Magnitogorsk, a new industrial city in Russia.

Problems

- Forced labour killed millions of workers; the hours were long and working conditions were bad.

- New workers from the countryside caused overcrowding and food shortages in towns and cities.

- There was a greater demand for all state services than could be met.

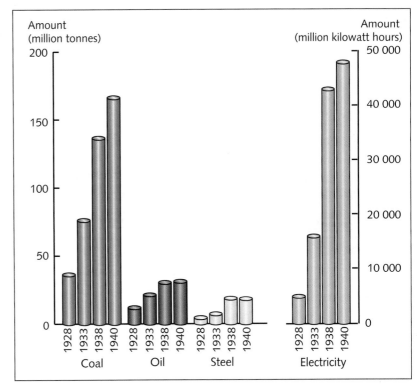

Industrial production, 1928–40.

Source K

250,000 people – communists, Kulaks, foreigners, convicts and a mass of peasants – built the largest steelworks in Europe in **Magnitogorsk**.

Here men froze, went hungry and suffered. The work went on, disregarding individual suffering.

Written by J. Scott, an American engineer who worked in Magnitogorsk and other places in the USSR in the 1930s.

THINGS TO DO

1 What did Stalin want to achieve with the Five-Year Plans?

2 Study the graph on this page. What were the effects on the four industries of the Five-Year Plans?

SUMMARY

Stalin's economic achievements

- All farms collectivised.

- More grain produced, enough to export.

- Industrial production rose.

- New industries set up.

Cost of these achievements

- Kulaks killed and deported.

- Peasant resistance caused famine.

- Bad conditions in the cities and towns.

- Starvation and overwork killed millions of Russians.

Exam-style assessment

These questions follow the pattern of questions to be set by AQA for Paper 2 of its new Modern World History specification.

SECTION A: Industrialisation and Collectivisation under Stalin

Study **Sources A** to **E** and then answer all parts of Question 1 which follow.

Source A: Estimated figures for the First Five-Year Plan

Industry	1927-8 production	Target for 1932	1932 production
Electricity (milliard kWh)	5.05	17.0	13.4
Coal (million tonnes)	35.4	68.0	64.3
Oil (million tonnes)	11.7	19.0	21.4
Steel (million tonnes)	4.0	8.3	5.9

From *Russia and the USSR, 1900-1995* (1996) by R. RADWAY

Source B: A Soviet poster from 1931

The poster says 'We strike down lazy workers'.

Source C: Building the Moscow Underground in the 1930s

We got so dirty and we were such young things – small, slender, fragile. But we had our orders to build the metro and we wanted to do it more than anything else. We wore our miners' overalls with such style. My feet were size four and the boots were size eleven. But there was such enthusiasm.

From an interview with Tatyana Fyodorova in 1990 when she was 90 years old

Source D: The effects of industrialisation

Beginning with 1928 Soviet national economic development was based on five-year plans. The working people sought to implement them as soon as possible. Nationwide campaigns were launched for the speedy fulfilment of planned targets. By 1936 Russia had been transformed from an economically backward country into a mighty industrial state.

From *History of the Soviet Union* (1974) published by the Novosti Press Agency, an official Soviet government publisher

Source E: Another view of the effects of industrialisation

The Five Year Plans resulted in hunger, shortages and inefficiency. It is necessary to dwell on these many negative features. Even though there were achievements, they must be seen against a background of appalling difficulties.

From *An Economic History of the USSR* (1969) by ALEC NOVE, a British historian

Question 1

(a) What can you learn from **Source A** about Stalin's Five-Year Plans? **(5 marks)**

(b) Are **Source B** and **Source C** agreeing about the responses of the Russian people towards industrialisation? Explain your answer. **(6 marks)**

(c) How reliable is **Source C** for studying Russian attitudes towards industrialisation in the 1930s? Explain your answer using **Source C** and your own knowledge. **(9 marks)**

(d) Why do you think **Source D** and **Source E** give different interpretations of the Five-Year Plans? Explain your answer using **Sources D** and **E** and your own knowledge. **(10 marks)**

(e) In the same period, Stalin ordered the collectivisation of agriculture. Use your own knowledge to explain whether you think this policy was a success. **(15 marks)**

SECTION B: Russia 1917–28

Study **Sources F** and **G** and then answer parts **(a)**, **(b)**, **(c)**, and **either (d) or (e)** of Question 5 which follows.

Source F: Discipline in the Red Army

- Every scoundrel who incites anyone to retreat or to desert will be shot.
- Every soldier who throws away his rifle will be shot.

From Orders to the Red Army by TROTSKY *during the Civil War*

Source G: Russia in the Civil War, 1918–21

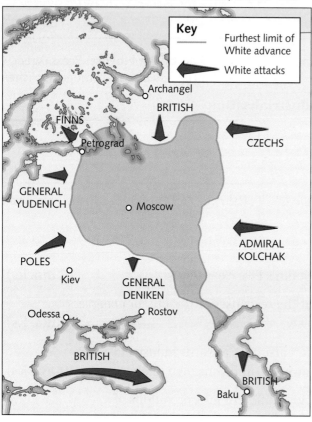

Question 5

(a) What can you learn from **Source F** about how Trotsky controlled the Red Army during the Civil War? **(3 marks)**

(b) Describe Lenin's policy of War Communism. **(5 marks)**

(c) Using the map (**Source G**) and your own knowledge, explain why the Reds were able to win the Civil War by 1921. **(7 marks)**

EITHER

(d) Explain why the Bolsheviks had been able to seize power in Russia in October/November 1917. **(15 marks)**

OR

(e) Why was Stalin able to defeat Trotsky in the struggle for power after Lenin's death? **(15 marks)**

5 Germany, 1918–39

INTRODUCTION

In 1918, Germany lost the First World War. Germany was not allowed to take part in making the Treaty of Versailles, which ended the war. The Treaty was very hard on Germany. It added to the problems of the new Weimar government. As well as rebuilding Germany, it had to make huge payments to cover war damage. The German people resented the Treaty.

In the later 1920s there was an economic recovery under Gustav Stresemann. However, the recovery did not last. When it became clear after 1929 that the new government was not dealing with the worsening economic problems, extremist groups gained more and more public support. One of these groups, the Nazi Party, took over in 1933.

Hitler and his Nazis were voted into power. As soon as they gained power they got rid of democratic elections and turned Germany into a fascist state. The Nazis controlled all aspects of German life, such as education, religion, the media and the law. They persecuted 'undesirables' – these groups included political opponents, homosexuals, and all non-Germans, especially Jewish people.

Under Hitler's rule unemployment dropped and the standard of living rose. But the Germans paid a high price for this, which finally led to war.

1918	Kaiser Wilhelm II abdicates New republic set up
1919	Weimar constitution set up Germany signs the Treaty of Versailles
1920	Kapp *Putsch*
1923	French occupation of the Ruhr Munich *Putsch*
1924	Dawes Plan
1925	Germany signs the Locarno Pact
1929	Death of Gustav Stresemann Wall Street Crash
1930	Brüning becomes Chancellor
1932	Nazis win 230 seats in Reichstag elections
1933	30 January: Hitler becomes Chancellor
1934	30 June: 'Night of the Long Knives'
1936	Olympics held in Berlin
1938	9 November: *Kristallnacht*
1939	1 September: Germany invades Poland

How far do the early problems of the Weimar Republic suggest that it was doomed from the start?

The abdication of the Kaiser

The **Kaiser** (emperor) had led Germany to war in 1914. By 1918, the German people were exhausted by the war. Many were starving. Germany's enemies, the Allies, were winning. Soldiers, sailors and workers were all going on strike. Even the army leaders no longer supported the Kaiser.

On 9 November 1918, he **abdicated** and fled to Holland. His sudden departure left Germany without a government.

A new government

Friedrich Ebert, leader of the largest political party in the **Reichstag** (parliament), took over. Two days later, Germany signed an **armistice** (an agreement to stop fighting) with the Allies to end the war. Ebert declared a new republic and announced elections for a new government. But not all Germans accepted the new republic.

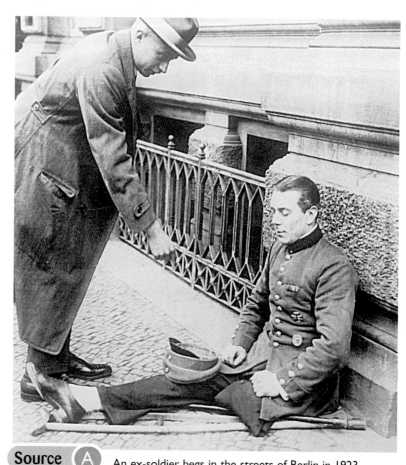

Source (A) An ex-soldier begs in the streets of Berlin in 1923.

The Spartacist Revolt

Cause: political opposition

- The Spartacists were a communist group, so they opposed Ebert's party, the Social Democratic Party.

- In the November risings in Germany some people had formed communist soviets. The Spartacists renamed themselves the **German Communist Party** and planned to seize power.

Events

- The Spartacists tried to seize power on 5 January 1919.

- They occupied public buildings, organised a general strike and formed a revolutionary committee to take control.

- The **Free Corps** army (an army made up of ex-soldiers) did a deal with Ebert. Ebert promised that they would not be replaced by an army that supported Ebert's government. In return this army would crush the Spartacists.

- The Free Corps did crush the Spartacists. Thousands were killed, including the leaders Rosa Luxemburg and Karl Liebknecht.

Results

- Ebert's government was saved.

- Elections could take place.

- The army was not one that was loyal to the government.

- The communists now saw the Social Democrats as their enemies, and would not help them politically.

The creation of the Weimar Republic

On 19 January 1919, there was an election for a new Reichstag. The Social Democrats won the most seats and Ebert became the first President of the new republic. The government felt that Berlin was unsafe, so it moved to the town of Weimar. This is why the government became called the **Weimar Republic**.

Revolts in Berlin and Bavaria

The government had been elected by the German people, but almost at once it faced two revolts.

- In March 1919, the communists had organised themselves again and set off riots and strikes in Berlin. The army, once again, crushed them.

- In early April, Bavaria (one of the German states) declared itself a Socialist Republic, with its own government and capital city (Munich). The government began to take food, money and houses from the rich and give them to the workers. The army eventually broke up the Republic, killing many of its leaders and supporters.

The Weimar Republic was having to use a lot of force to keep in power and this was losing it support.

The Spartacists want to seize power. The government wants people to choose their future in a free election.

The Spartacists do not allow people safety or freedom. They have suppressed newspapers.

There have been bloody battles in parts of Berlin. Some places have no water or light. Food warehouses have been attacked. The government is going to do whatever is needed to destroy this rule of terror.

Part of an article published by the Ebert government in January 1919.

THINGS TO DO

1 How did the Weimar Republic prevent communist risings and revolts?

2 Explain why this was a problem.

The problems of the Weimar Republic

German reactions to defeat

- Some people felt the Weimar government gave in when Germany could still have won the war. They called the government 'the **November Criminals**'.

- Many people could not forget that members of the Weimar government had been in the government when the **Treaty of Versailles** was signed.

- The Weimar government was blamed for the fact that Germany had not taken part in the talks and had been forced to sign the Treaty of Versailles.

The Treaty of Versailles

The Treaty of Versailles was very hard on Germany.

- Germany had a lot of land taken away. It lost all its colonies and over 70,000 square kilometres of land.

- Germany's army and navy were cut back and its air force scrapped. It was not allowed to send any troops into the Rhineland, on the border with France. Allied troops occupied the Rhineland to make sure of this.

- Hardest of all, in many ways, Germany was forced to accept responsibility for the war. This **War Guilt Clause** meant that the Allies could make Germany pay a huge amount in war damages, called '**reparations**'.

- In 1921, the amount of reparations was fixed at £6600 million, to be paid in yearly instalments.

Source C This cartoon was published in a German magazine in 1919. It was called 'Clemenceau the Vampire' and shows the French Prime Minister sucking the blood from Germany.

Reactions to the Treaty of Versailles

Most Germans were shocked by the harshness of the Treaty of Versailles.

- The German press ignored the fact that the government had had very little choice but to sign the treaty. They said it was shameful and that Germans should remember this and get revenge.

- People took to the streets in angry mass demonstrations against the treaty.

- People blamed the government for 'giving in' and the bad feeling did not go away. The government could never be popular while constantly associated with humiliation and defeat.

The Weimar Constitution

In August 1919, the Weimar published its **Constitution**. Many people praised it as one of the most democratic in Europe:

- All men and women over the age of 20 voted for members of the Reichstag.

- Each party was given seats in proportion to the number of votes it had won. This system (**proportional representation**) let small parties get into the Reichstag, as well as large ones.

- The **Chancellor**, who ran the government, had to have the support of a majority of Reichstag members.

- The **President**, the head of state who could make laws without the Chancellor and the Reichstag in a crisis, was elected by the people every seven years.

- As well as a lower house of elected members, there was an upper house of members from each German state (the **Reichsrat**). The German states ran themselves, but had to obey national laws.

- The German people were given important rights, such as **free speech** and **religious freedom**.

Weaknesses of the Constitution

- Prussia was such a big state that it had a majority in the Reichsrat. So, it could block any laws, even if all the other states approved.

- Article 48 allowed the President to act alone in an emergency. This was a power that could be misused.

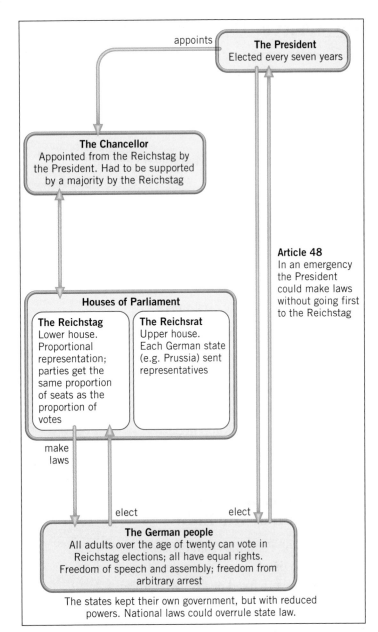

The Weimar Constitution.

- Proportional representation meant that no political party had a majority in the Reichstag. Governments were made up of coalitions (several political groups acting together). This meant they were more likely to argue over policies and not act decisively.

- Proportional representation also allowed small extremist groups, such as the Communists and National Socialists, to enter the Reichstag, have a say and grow.

The Kapp *Putsch*, 1920

The German army was made much smaller by the Treaty of Versailles. Some ex-soldiers joined the Free Corps, a volunteer army, which had helped to defeat early socialist and communist risings.

In early 1920, the Allies tried to get Germany to break up the Free Corps, which then marched on Berlin and attempted a *putsch* – a takeover by force.

By this time, the government had moved from Weimar back to Berlin. It was horrified when the police and the army in Berlin supported Kapp, the leader of the Free Corps.

The government fled to Dresden and asked the workers of Berlin to support the government. The workers organised a general strike. Within days Berlin had no water, gas, electricity or transport. The *putsch* collapsed. Kapp fled to Sweden and the government came back to Berlin.

Reparations and the occupation of the Ruhr

The Treaty of Versailles had ordered Germany to pay for war damage. These reparations were fixed at £6600 million in 1921. The Germans paid the first instalment, but in 1922 said they were unable to pay the next instalment until their economic problems were solved. They said this would take three years. The French reacted at once:

- On 9 January 1923, about 60,000 French and Belgian soldiers invaded the Ruhr industrial area of Germany.

- They took over every mine, factory, steelworks and railway.

- The German government did not have a large enough army to drive them out. It told the workers to use **passive resistance** – not to fight, but not to work for the invaders. The workers went on strike; nothing was working.

- The French reacted by throwing strikers out of their homes, even shooting people who refused to work.

Source **D**

A German poster from 1923. It says 'Hands off the Ruhr!'

Hände weg vom Ruhrgebiet!

Hyperinflation, 1923

One of the government's reactions to Germany's economic problems was to print more money. It hoped this would also help to pay the reparations sooner. Unfortunately, when money is added to an economy in this way its value goes down, because there is more of it. This pushes up prices. The government reacted by printing more money, which pushed up prices even more. This is called **hyperinflation**.

Effects of hyperinflation

- Wages and prices kept rising, even several times a day.

- Everyone struggled to buy food and clothes and heat their homes.

- People who had fixed incomes, such a pensioners, found their money was worthless.

- People who had borrowed money could pay it back easily because wages rose rapidly and loans were a fixed amount.

- The government was blamed for the situation. Printing more money had been its solution to the problem and had caused hyperinflation.

- There were outbreaks of violence against the government. Could it survive?

Source E Children playing with worthless money, 1923.

Source **F**

As soon as I got my day's pay I went shopping. I had just enough for a loaf of bread and a small piece of cheese.
A friend of mine went to buy his baby a pair of shoes. He took a month's pay. By the time he reached Berlin all he could afford was a cup of coffee.

A German woman writing about the effects of hyperinflation.

How far did the Weimar Republic recover under Stresemann?

The role of Stresemann

In November 1923, the Weimar Republic faced its worst crisis. **Gustav Stresemann**, leader of the German People's Party (DVP) helped to save it:

- In 1923, Stresemann was elected Chancellor. He replaced the worthless German mark with a new currency, the *Rentenmark*.

- Stresemann saw that the strikes in the Ruhr were making things worse. He ordered the workers back to work.

He got the French to leave by promising to begin reparation payments. These moves made him so unpopular he lost his job as Chancellor.

- However, Stresemann did a lot as Foreign Minister to improve Germany's reputation in Europe, so much so that Germany was allowed to join the **League of Nations** and trade in Europe again. Stresemann won the Nobel Peace Prize in 1929. Unfortunately, he died four months later.

Economic recovery

- The *Rentenmark* helped to stabilise the German economy.

- In 1924, the **Dawes Plan**, agreed by Stresemann with the USA, Britain and France, arranged that the USA would lend Germany money to rebuild its economy. It also set sensible levels for reparations, tying them to the economy, while making sure they were paid.

- Germany rebuilt its industry, which encouraged other countries to invest in it and trade with it. Exports rose, unemployment fell.

- In 1929, Stresemann fixed another extension of the time set to for the payment of reparations, under a plan called the **Young Plan**.

Source G

Gustav Stresemann.

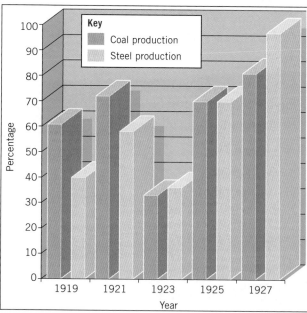

Steel and coal production in Germany, 1919–27. 100 on the Percentage line is the amount produced in 1913. In 1919, only 59 per cent of the 1913 amount of coal and 40 per cent of steel had been produced. You can see the effect of the Ruhr strikes on production.

International relations

Stresemann's work as foreign minister led to Germany becoming more accepted by other countries.

- In 1925, Germany and France signed the **Locarno Pact**, agreeing never to try to change the border between them.

- In 1926, Germany was allowed to join the League of Nations.

- In 1928, Germany was one of 60 countries to sign the **Kellogg–Briand Pact**. The Pact said that these countries would not go to war with each other.

Impact of recovery

- Germany was more prosperous and more welcome in Europe.

- The government gained support, while extreme political parties, like the Communists and the Nazis, lost support.

- People had more money to spend and Berlin became the pleasure capital of Europe.

- The lack of censorship attracted writers and artists to Berlin, so German culture boomed. Artists such as **George Grosz** began to be critical of society.

A golden age?

Although things had undoubtedly improved, Germany still had problems:

- The huge US loans made Germany dependent on aid from the USA.

- The economy needed time to recover fully. It also needed a period of steady growth. However, as early as 1927 both industry and farming were in trouble again.

Source H   A painting by the artist George Grosz, showing a contrast between the 'fat cat' business man, the one-armed war veteran and the labourer.

THINGS TO DO

Look at the chart on page 188.

1 Which were the worst/best years for
   (a) coal production
   (b) steel production in Germany?

2 Does it look as if Stresemann's plans were working?

The Great Depression

In October 1929, Stresemann died and, shortly after, the US stock market collapsed in the **Wall Street Crash**. Germany was hit hard.

- From 1924 on, the USA had lent Germany a lot of money.

- US banks and businesses now wanted Germany to repay the money. They were not able to lend any more money.

- German businesses could not afford to repay the loans and keep running. Many closed down.

- Unemployment shot up. By 1932, there were six million unemployed and millions more were homeless.

Source I

This is a German cartoon, drawn in 1927. It shows the poor being ignored by the rich who are about to have an economic crash but don't realise it.

Unemployment in Germany 1925–33.

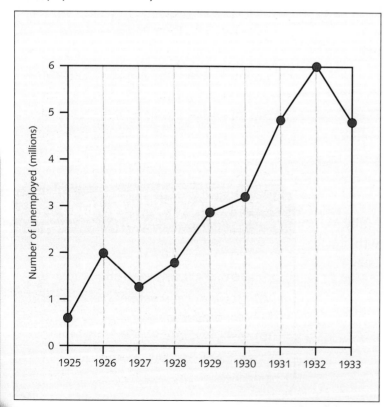

Source J

Men stood hopelessly on the street corners of every industrial town. Families had no food, no heating. Young people had no chance of a job. All these things explain why millions of ordinary Germans were so bitter.

The effects of unemployment in Germany in 1932.

The Weimar government and the Depression

The Weimar government tried to fight the **Depression**. But there was hardly any successful action.

- The government could spend more on helping the poor only if it printed more money. After the hyperinflation of 1923 this was not an option.

- So, the government raised taxes. This gave it more money to help the poor, but was a problem for the businesses and companies being taxed.

- The government reduced the wages of government workers. This gave it more money for the poor, but workers found it hard to live.

- The government reduced unemployment benefit, which was a big problem for the growing numbers of unemployed.

These actions were not popular inside or outside the government.

Source **K** This Nazi election poster of 1932 says 'Our last hope: Hitler!'

SUMMARY

The Great Depression of 1929–33

- Ended Germany's recovery from the 1923 depression.
- Caused by dependence on US loans.
- Brought unemployment and hardship.
- Weimar government blamed for it.
- Increased support for extremist political parties who promised to bring it to an end.

More and more Germans began to listen to extremist political parties that criticised the government and promised to solve the crisis. The communists and the Nazis got more and more support. Political parties left the ruling coalition because they disapproved of government policies. The constitution allowed the President to take control in an emergency: and that is what **President Hindenburg** did, at the age of 84.

THINGS TO DO

List the ways in which the Weimar government tried to fight the Depression.

Hitler and the growth of the Nazi Party to 1933

How did the Nazi Party develop its ideas and organisation up to 1929?

Hitler's life in Vienna

Adolf Hitler was born in Austria in 1889. His father died when he was fourteen, his mother four years later.

Hitler went to Vienna and tried to enrol as an art student, but was turned down. He drifted into poverty and became interested in **extremist politics**. He came to dislike foreigners, especially Jewish people. He blamed Jews for his failure in Vienna.

Hitler and the First World War

Hitler joined the army as soon as the First World War broke out. He was wounded twice and won the Iron Cross, First Class – the highest award for a German soldier. In 1918, he was in hospital recovering from being gassed when he heard that Germany had surrendered. He was angry and blamed the surrender on Jewish and communist plots (see Source B). He returned to Munich and worked for the government spying on extremist groups. One of these groups was the **German Workers Party**.

Source (A) A portrait of Adolf Hitler.

Source (B)

When I heard we were about to surrender I broke down completely. I buried my head in my bedding and cried as I had not cried since the day my mother was buried.

Hitler's description of his feelings when Germany surrendered in 1918.

The foundation of the Nazi Party

The German Workers Party was a small group based in Munich, Bavaria. Hitler joined it as a spy for the government. He had stayed in the army after the war ended and the government was using the army to spy on 'suspect' political groups.

Hitler found he agreed with many of the party's ideas. He soon became its leader and set out to win more support.

- He renamed it the National Socialist German Workers Party – **Nazi Party** for short (from *Nazionale*, the German for 'national').

- In 1920, he drew up a twenty-five-point list of aims for the Nazis (see Source C).

- In 1921, he set up a Nazi army, the **SA** (**Stormtroopers**); they were also called the Brownshirts because of their uniforms. They were supposed to protect Nazi speakers at rallies. In fact, they often beat up opponents.

- He designed a symbol for the Nazis – the **swastika**.

- He set up a Nazi newspaper to spread their ideas.

Hitler and the Nazis soon became well known in Bavaria. Even though they were not well known in the rest of Germany, Hitler thought their ideas would win them support.

As the economic crisis of 1923 swept Germany, Hitler decided the time was right to seize power by force.

Source C

1 All German-speaking lands should be united in a greater Germany.

2 Treaty of Versailles must be abolished.

3 There should be enough land for our people.

4 Only those with German blood may be part of Germany.

5 Germany should have a strong central government.

Some of the Nazi Party's Twenty-five Points.

THINGS TO DO

Read **Source C**.

1 How could Germany be enlarged?

2 What problems would point 4 cause?

The Munich *Putsch*, November 1923

Hitler and his party were not well known outside Bavaria. Why did he try a military *putsch* (takeover)?

- He thought that the economic conditions were so bad that a revolt would suceed.

  He couldn't wait in case the economic conditions improved and the Weimar government became popular again.

- He thought the Bavarian government would support him.

- He thought the German army would support him.

On 8 November 1923, Hitler and 600 Stormtroopers marched into a meeting in Munich led by the Bavarian leader, Gustav Kahr, and tried to force Kahr to support them.

Government troops about to disperse Hitler's supporters in Munich, 9 November 1923.

Kahr agreed but, when freed, called up the army and police.

- The next day the Nazis took control of key buildings in Munich.

- They then marched on the city centre.

- Here they were met by armed police and soldiers.

- The Nazis were defeated in the fight.

- Hitler and other Nazi leaders were arrested.

Was the *putsch* a failure?

- The Nazis did not take over Germany.

- Hitler failed because he had assumed the army would support him and it didn't.

- Hitler was put on trial and arrested.

Did the *putsch* have any good results for Hitler?

- The trial gave Hitler a chance to speak out against the Weimar government. It made him famous.

- Hitler was sent to prison for five years, but was released after just over eight months.

Source E

I am not a criminal. You cannot commit treason against the traitors of 1918. History will show we acted for the good of Germany.

Said by Hitler at his trial in 1923.

Mein Kampf

Hitler used his time in prison to write *Mein Kampf* ('My Struggle') about his life and ideas. It clearly laid out the ideas behind the Nazi Party.

When Hitler came to power all Germans were expected to read the book.

The Nazi Party, 1924–9

When Hitler went to prison the Nazi Party was banned. When he was let out in 1924 it was re-formed.

At first the Nazi Party found it difficult to get support. Germany's economy was recovering and people were less willing to listen to the Nazis. They began to lose seats in the Reichstag.

- 1924 (May)   32 seats
- 1924 (December)   14 seats
- 1928   12 seats

However, Hitler worked hard at gaining the Nazis more support. He set up meetings and **rallies** to increase membership. He wanted as many people as possible to hear him speak because he made rousing speeches. Membership rose from 27,000 in 1925 to 100,000 in 1928.

Even so, the Nazis were not yet a strong political group. Hitler had decided while he was in prison that the best way for the Nazis to seize power was not by a *putsch* but legally, in elections. He needed something to push the voters his way. In 1929 it happened – Germany was hit by a severe **economic depression**.

THINGS TO DO

1 Read 'The Munich *Putsch*' and **Source E**.
  (a) How was the *putsch* a failure for the Nazis?
  (b) How was the *putsch* a success? Explain your answer.

Source

- Germany should be ruled by a strong leader (Führer).
- Germans are from the Aryan race. This is a 'master race'; it is better than any other race.
- Jews and Communists have weakened Germany and must be destroyed.
- The Treaty of Versailles must be destroyed and all land given back to Germany.
- Germany needs *lebensraum* (more land to live in) which can be taken by force.

***The main ideas of* Mein Kampf.**

SUMMARY

The Nazi Party, 1919–28

- **1919:** Hitler joined the German Workers Party.
- **1920:** Hitler became leader of the party. Party changed its name to National Socialist Workers Party (Nazi Party).
- **1921:** SA set up.
- **1923:** Munich *putsch*.
- **1924:** Hitler wrote *Mein Kampf* in prison.
- **1928:** Nazis won twelve Reichstag seats.

How was Hitler able to become Chancellor in January 1933?

The Nazi Party and the Great Depression

The Nazis won support during the Depression because they promised:

- work

- help for businesses

- help for farmers

- to make Germany great again

- to act against Jews and communists who were blamed for all Germany's problems.

Source G

The Nazis were well organised. They knew publicity was important. Their head of propaganda, **Joseph Goebbels**, organised huge rallies. Hitler flew from one rally to another, making exciting speeches. The Nazis also had a poster campaign that targeted all sorts of voters (see Source G).

The SA played an important part in Nazi election campaigns by smashing up opponents' meetings – especially those of the communists, their extremist rivals, who were also gaining support.

Nazi election gains, 1930–2

Reichstag elections:

- 1930   107 seats

- 1932 (July)   230 seats

- 1932 (November)   196 seats; largest party in the Reichstag

1932 presidential election:

- Hitler thirteen million votes.

- Hindenburg nineteen million votes.

A Nazi election poster of 1932 saying 'Women! Millions of men out of work! Millions of children without a future! Save our German families. Vote for Hitler.' The Nazis used a variety of posters targeted at different groups of voters. Notice that, even at this stage, it is Hitler, not the Nazi Party, that people are being asked to vote for.

THINGS TO DO

1 Look at **Source G** and read the caption. What issues do the Nazis think are important to German women?

2 List the reasons for Hitler's rise to Chancellor under the headings 'economic' and 'political'.

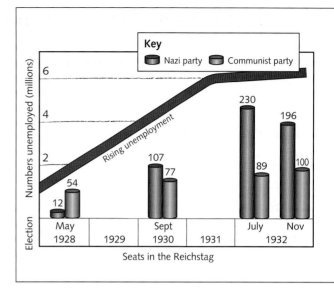

Growth of support for the Nazi Party in Reichstag elections.

Hitler becomes Chancellor

President Hindenburg disliked the Nazi Party. He refused to make Hitler Chancellor in July 1932, even though the Nazis had the most seats in the Reichstag. But, by January 1933, Hitler was Chancellor anyway. How?

- In July 1932, Hindenburg used his powers as President to make the leader of the smaller Centre Party (**Franz von Papen**) Chancellor.

- Hindenburg was warned that the army would not accept von Papen and might act against the government.

- So, in December 1932, Hindenburg made a politician the army favoured, **von Schleicher**, Chancellor.

- Von Schleicher could not get support in the Reichstag.

- So, in January 1933, Hindenburg was forced to make Hitler Chancellor.

Hindenburg tried to control Hitler by making von Papen Vice-Chancellor and putting von Papen's supporters in the government. Hitler accepted this in order to become Chancellor. As soon as he was Chancellor he called an election, hoping to win more seats and take complete control of the Reichstag.

Source H   Hitler as Chancellor being presented to President Hindenburg.

Germany, 1918–39

How did Hitler change Germany from a democracy to a Nazi dictatorship, 1933–4?

Case Study: the Reichstag fire and its results

On 27 February 1933, the Reichstag building was set on fire. The police caught a young Dutch communist, Marinus van der Lubbe, inside the building, with matches in his pocket. He was arrested and confessed. He was quickly tried and executed. Yet there are questions about his guilt:

- Van der Lubbe had limited intelligence and might not have understood what he was confessing to.

- The SA had arrested Van der Lubbe after he had been heard boasting that he would burn the Reichstag.

- The Nazi police force might well have forced a confession.

- There was an underground passage from the Reichstag to the SA offices – the Nazis could have started the fire that way.

The Nazis used the fire to their advantage:

- Hitler claimed that the communists set the fire as a start to a communist uprising (see Source A).

- He persuaded Hindenburg to sign an emergency law: The Law for the Protection of People and the State. It removed all the freedoms of the Weimar constitution – free speech, free assembly, freedom from arrest 'on suspicion' of a crime.

- The police and the SA arrested communist leaders, keeping them locked up without trial. They closed down communist newspapers and broke up communist meetings.

- While stopping the communists from meeting, the Nazis held even more rallies and marches to win support for their party. Nazi propaganda was broadcast more and more over the radio.

Source A

This fire is the worst of all communist outrages in Germany. They started it as the beginning of civil war.

Said by Hitler the day after the Reichstag fire.

At a birthday lunch for the Führer in 1942 people began to talk about the Reichstag fire. Goering interrupted the conversation, shouting: 'The only one who knows about the Reichstag is I, because I set it on fire!'

Said by the Nazi general, Halder, during his trial for war crimes after the war.

THINGS TO DO

From all you have read about the Reichstag fire, work out who you think started it. Give reasons for your answer.

Source C The Reichstag buildings on fire, 27 February 1933.

The 1933 election

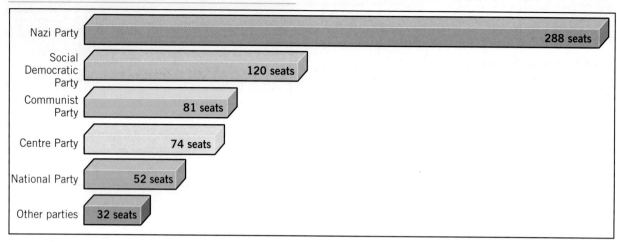

Nazi Party	288 seats
Social Democratic Party	120 seats
Communist Party	81 seats
Centre Party	74 seats
National Party	52 seats
Other parties	32 seats

Results of the March 1933 election.

The Nazis did very well in the March 1933 elections.

- The party won 288 seats.

- It still did not have complete control of the Reichstag.

- If all the smaller parties worked together, they had 359 seats.

- The Nazis persuaded one of the parties, the Nationalist Party, to work with them.

- The extra 52 Nationalist seats gave the Nazis 340 seats against 307.

They had control.

The Enabling Law

On 23 March 1933, Hitler asked the Reichstag to pass the **Enabling Law**. This gave Hitler the power to:

- make laws without the approval of the Reichstag or President.

- make treaties with foreign countries.

The Enabling Law changed the Weimar Constitution, so that it needed to be approved by two-thirds of the Reichstag. The Nazis and Nationalists did not have the support of two-thirds of the Reichstag.

So Hitler set about creating it.

- He used the anti-communist law to ban all 81 communist members.

- The SA then threatened so many other members of the Reichstag that over 100 did not even turn up to vote.

- The Enabling Law was eventually passed by 444 votes to 94.

- In 1933, new elections to the Reichstag were held. Only Nazis could be elected.

Source D

Our leader, Otto Wels, gave our good wishes to all the political opponents of the Nazis who were being imprisoned and put in concentration camps. Hitler was furious. SA and SS officers surrounded us and shouted 'Traitors! You'll all be hanged!'

A Social Democrat's description of what happened in the Reichstag when the Enabling Law was passed.

The removal of opposition

Hitler had already used the law passed after the Reichstag fire to get rid of the communists. He now began to move against the other political parties.

- In June 1933, he banned the Social Democrat Party.

- Then he banned all other parties.

- In July 1933, Hitler passed a law called the Law Against the Formation of New Parties (see Source E). This said the Nazi Party was the only party allowed. Anyone supporting one of the old parties, or setting up a new one, could be arrested. The leaders of the old parties were put in prison.

- In July 1933, Hitler banned **trade unions**. All their leaders were put in prison.

- Because there were no longer any other parties, the Nazis now had all the government jobs.

- Hitler made sure that Nazis, or people who did not oppose the Nazis, got all the important jobs in running the country.

Hitler had dealt quickly and efficiently with opposition outside the Nazi Party. Now he turned on a group that he saw as a danger inside the party – the SA.

Source E

Article I: The National Socialist Party is the only political party in Germany.

Article 2: Anyone keeping an old party going or forming a new one will be imprisoned for at least three years.

From the Law Against the Formation of New Parties, July 1933.

THINGS TO DO

Look at **Sources D** and **E** and the evidence in the section. What methods did Hitler use to remove the opposition to the Nazi Party?

Source F

Stormtroopers arresting suspected communists in 1933. Many of these people ended up in Dachau concentration camp.

Case Study: the Night of the Long Knives

The SA had been important to Hitler during his rise to power. But Hitler was worried about the SA:

- Its leader, Ernst Roehm, wanted the state to take over big businesses and industries. Hitler could not afford to lose the support of big businesses yet.

- The SA was full of thugs. Hitler did not think he could control it. He had a new security force, the SS (*Schutz-Staffel*), which was more controllable.

- Roehm also wanted the SA to take over the German army. This would make him more powerful than Hitler.

- Hitler had been holding talks with army leaders and thought he now had their support. They did not want the SA taking over the army.

- So Hitler had to choose. He could support the SA or the army.

Hitler decided to support the army. On 30 June 1934, Hitler announced that the SA had been plotting to seize control of the government. He sent the SS to arrest its members. Over the next few days hundreds of SA members were arrested. Many, including Roehm, were shot. This night became known as the Night of the Long Knives.

When Hitler explained the events to the Reichstag, he said that he had been defending Germany from dangerous plots. The Reichstag accepted that Hitler had 'saved the nation'. Hitler now felt he had got rid of all opposition, inside and outside the party.

Source G A British cartoon published after the Night of the Long Knives in 1934.

THEY SALUTE WITH BOTH HANDS NOW.

The death of Hindenburg

Hitler was still only Chancellor. Hindenburg was President, although Hitler had managed to take away most of his political power. On 2 August 1934, Hindenburg died. Hitler made himself President and renamed himself **Führer** (leader). On the same day, everyone in the army, the only group that could have removed Hitler, swore an oath of loyalty to him.

Source

The SA was planning a revolution. I had to destroy the SA to save Germany.

Part of Hitler's speech to the Reichstag explaining the removal of the SA.

Source

I swear by God that I will give complete obedience to Adolf Hitler and risk my life for him at any time.

Part of the army oath of loyalty to Hitler.

THINGS TO DO

1 Explain the meaning of:
  • the Enabling Law
  • Führer
  • Law Against the Formation of New Parties
  • Night of the Long Knives.

2 Read 'The Night of the Long Knives' and **Source H.**
  (a) What reason did Hitler give for getting rid of the SA?
  (b) Why do you think he got rid of the SA?

SUMMARY

Setting up a Nazi dictatorship, 1933–4

1933

• **March**   Nazi Party in control of Reichstag. Enabling Law passed.

• **June**   Political parties banned.

• **July**   Law Against the Formation of New Parties: Nazi Party the only legal party.

1934

• **June**   Night of the Long Knives wiped out SA.

• **August**   Hindenburg died. Hitler became Führer. Army oath of loyalty.

Hitler was able to set up a dictatorship because

• politicians like Hindenburg underestimated him at first

• the Nazis wiped out opponents

• Hitler acted quickly against opponents inside and outside the Nazi Party.

5.4 Nazi Rule in Germany, 1934–9

What were the main features of the totalitarian dictatorship in Nazi Germany?

The one-party state: law and order

Germany was controlled by the SS, which had several groups within it:

- The **SS** was set up as a small private bodyguard for Hitler. It was enlarged to wipe out the SA, which it then replaced. By 1934, there were 50,000 SS members, led by **Heinrich Himmler**, who was totally loyal to Hitler.

- The **Death Head Units** were the SS groups that ran the concentration camps. These were prisons for various groups the Nazis saw as 'undesirable' – political opponents, homosexuals, disabled people, gypsies and Jews. Conditions in these camps were harsh and many prisoners died.

By 1939, there were many **concentration camps** in Germany and on land that Germany had taken over. The prisoners were used as slave labour and many were worked and starved to death. During the Second World War some of these camps became death camps just for killing people.

- The SS did not run the courts, but all judges had to take an oath of loyalty to Hitler, so the courts were on Hitler's side, too. There was no longer any hope of a fair trial. If the Nazis wanted you to go to prison, a judge would send you there, wheather there was evidence against you or not.

- The **Gestapo** were the state secret police, formed from the SS. They could spy on and arrest whoever they wanted. They encouraged members of the Nazi Party to report any anti-Nazi behaviour in friends, people they worked with, even their family. They had a tight hold over the ordinary police.

Source Ⓐ Jewish shops were boycotted as part of the Nazi persecution of Jews.

Case Study: Persecution

The Jews

Hitler and the Nazis persecuted many groups of people that they considered 'undesirable' but Jewish people suffered most under the Nazis. Hitler had hated Jews since he was a young man. Why?

- He blamed them for the defeat of Germany in the First World War.

- The Nazis wanted to fill Germany with '**Aryans**' – they said these were people with 'pure' German blood. The perfect Aryan was tall and strong with blonde hair and blue eyes. Jews, along with black people and people from other races, were not Aryan. The Nazis felt that they should be driven out of Germany.

- Jews made up less than one per cent of the German population. But many of them were professional people – bankers, lawyers, doctors and teachers. Hitler said they took jobs from other people.

Once the Nazis were in power they began to persecute the Jews:

- In 1933, Germans were ordered not to use Jewish shops and businesses.

- In 1934, Jewish shops were marked with a yellow star, the Star of David, so Germans knew that they should not shop there.

- Jews who had important government jobs were sacked.

- Jews could not sit in the same seats as Germans on public transport or in parks.

- In 1935, Hitler passed the **Nuremberg Laws**. Jews could not be German citizens. So they could not take any job in government (teaching, the civil service, even cleaning the parks) and were not protected by the law. Jews could not marry non-Jews, or even have sex with them without marrying.

The government was officially anti-Jewish. Many Jewish people decided to leave Germany. For those who stayed, life became more difficult. German shopkeepers would not serve them. They lost their jobs and could not find other work. Jewish doctors, dentists and lawyers could not work for Germans.

Between 1935 and 1938 more and more Jews left Germany. But it became harder for these people to find a country that would let them in.

Germany, 1918–39

205

Violent persecution

In Paris in November 1938, a young Jewish man shot a Nazi official. This gave Hitler a good excuse to turn to violence.

He ordered the SS to act against Jews on *Kristallnacht* (the Night of Broken Glass). The SS:

- looted and destroyed Jewish shops, homes and synagogues

- arrested thousands of Jews, killing about 100

- announced a billion mark fine on all Jews (an excuse to take money)

- forced Jews to do humiliating things, such as scrubbing the streets

- sent about 30,000 Jews to concentration camps.

Once the Second World War broke out in 1939, the Nazis were even harder on Jews. They began openly killing them in greater and greater numbers. They experimented to find the quickest, cheapest way to kill large numbers of people at a time. Their '**Final Solution**', openly adopted in 1943, was to send all Jews to death camps to be killed.

We do not know exactly how many Jews were killed in this Holocaust. It was about six million people.

Other groups

The Nazis believed in the Aryan 'master race'. They persecuted 'undesirables'. This group included gypsies, black people, the disabled, political opponents, the sick and the old. It also included religious groups, such as Jehovah's Witnesses. The Nazis:

- sterilised many of these groups, so they could not have children

- sent them to concentration camps

- took Aryan disabled people into 'care homes' where they were killed.

The Church

Hitler tried to get church support for the Nazis. In 1933, he signed an agreement with the Catholic Church that he would not interfere with it, if its members did not criticise the Nazis.

All Protestant groups had to join the Reich Church, dominated by Nazis. Anyone who objected was sent to the concentration camps.

THINGS TO DO

Look at evidence in the case study. Explain the different ways that Jewish people suffered under the Nazis.

PERIODS	Monday	Tuesday	Wednesday	Thursday	Friday	Saturday
1. 8:00–8:45	German	German	German	German	German	German
2. 8:50–9:35	Geography	History	Singing	Geography	History	Singing
3. 9:40–10:25	Race Study	Race Study	Race Study	Race Study	Party Beliefs	Party Beliefs
4. 10:25–11:00	Break – with sports and special announcements					
5. 11:00–12:05	Domestic Science with Mathematics – Every day					
6. 12:10–12:55	The science of breeding (Eugenics) – Health Biology					
	2:00–6:00 Sport each day					

A 1935 timetable for a girls' school in Nazi Germany. Think of any subjects girls do not study. Notice that Maths is useful only in domestic science.

Source B

Education

Hitler wanted the Nazi rule of Germany to last. He knew that the best way to do this was to turn children into unquestioning Nazis. They had to be soaked in Nazi propaganda, inside and outside school.

- Teachers had to join the **German Teachers' League** (a Nazi organisation) and be happy to teach Nazi ideas.

- The school timetable was changed to put in new subjects the Nazis thought were important, such as **Race Studies** and **Party Beliefs**. Girls were taught domestic science and childcare.

- Even 'normal' sounding subjects, such as history and biology, were taught from a Nazi point of view. So, in history children were taught about the 'betrayal' of the Treaty of Versailles. In biology they were taught 'eugenics'. This told them all about 'breeding' to create healthy, racially pure people.

Hitler Youth Movement

Hitler had set up his '**Hitler Youth Movement**' in 1925, even before the Nazis came to power. It organised activities for young people outside school hours. In 1933, other youth groups were stamped out. After 1935, all children had to join.

There were various sections which all did 'healthy', Nazi-supporting, things together. The sections had different names and did different things, depending on the age and sex of their members.

THINGS TO DO

1 (a) Which subjects in **Source B** do you think were added by the Nazis?
   (b) Which are missing?

Women

The Nazis wanted German women to marry and raise large families. They had several reasons for this:

- The birth rate had been going down in the 1920s and early 1930s. The Nazis wanted the German, **Aryan**, population to grow.

- If women left their jobs to become mothers and homemakers it helped the Nazis to bring down the unemployment rate for men.

- The Nazi ideal world was based on large, stable, happy Aryan families.

How did the Nazis persuade women to behave the way the Nazis wanted them to?

- In 1933, the Nazis passed the **Law for the Encouragement of Marriage**. This lent every newly married couple 1000 marks to set up home. They were supposed to pay the loan back, but were given 250 marks of the loan for every child they had. So, if they had four children they did not need to pay anything back.

- Schools taught girls more domestic skills and 'mothercraft'.

- The Nazis even set up special homes for unmarried Aryan mothers, as long as they had 'racially pure' babies with other Aryans.

- The Nazis did not wait for women to choose to stop work. They sacked them.

- The Nazis produced a lot of radio, newspaper and poster propaganda about the role of women. It advised women about what to cook, what kinds of routines to have with the babies and children, what to wear and what exercise to take.

The Nazi campaign worked, at least to the extent that most women did marry and stay home, however unwillingly. From 1933 onwards, the birth rate steadily rose.

Source C

Age	Boys	Girls
6-10	The Little Fellows	
10-14	The Young Folk	Young Girls
14-18	Hitler Youth	League of German Girls

The organisation of the Hitler Youth Movement.

Source D

A 1930s painting representing the Nazi image of the ideal family.

THINGS TO DO

Look at **Source D**.

1 What are the Nazis saying is the most important job for women?

2 What is the role of the state (the eagle)?

Propaganda

The Nazis realised that one of the best ways to control the German people was not to force them to do things, but to make them believe in Nazi ideas.

To do this they set up a **Ministry of Propaganda and National Enlightenment**, led by **Joseph Goebbels**. This Ministry flooded Germany with information aimed at getting people to accept Nazi ideas. It also made sure that it was harder and harder for German people to hear ideas that criticised the Nazis.

- Newspapers printed only stories that were favourable to the Nazis – or they were closed down.

- Goebbels took control of all radio stations and mass-produced cheap radios that could not pick up foreign radio stations. Soon almost everyone had a radio and all they could listen to on it was what the Nazis wanted them to hear. Loudspeaker pillars were set up in streets and public squares so radio announcements could be played there, too.

- The Nazis took over German film-making. Films were made only if the Nazis had approved the story and the actors. These were shown at cinemas with news films or documentaries.

- The Nazis organised regular rallies for large numbers of people. There were army parades, fireworks displays and, most importantly, mass rallies focusing on speeches by Hitler. The biggest of these was the yearly, week-long rally at **Nuremberg** (see Source E).

- The Nazi control of schools and youth movements gave them a chance to expose children to Nazi propaganda almost every day of their lives.

The Chamber of Culture

Goebbels set up a Reich **Chamber of Culture**. This controlled all music, plays, books and paintings. The people who produced these things had to be approved by the Chamber of Culture (so they could not be Jewish or black, for instance). Each work produced also had to be approved.

Anything the Nazis did not like was banned. In 1933, students were encouraged to burn huge piles of banned books. The radio played the work of the German composer **Wagner**, or traditional folk songs or marching bands. It broadcast only plays with the 'right' message.

Enough to keep in power?

The Nazis rose to power by the clever use of both propaganda and violence. But they wanted to stay in power. They wanted to make Germany great. Propaganda and violence could not make this happen. They had to deal with the economic problems that they had promised to put right when they came to power. Nazi election posters had promised people '**Work and Bread**'. Could the Nazis provide these things?

SUMMARY

Features of Nazi dictatorship

- Police state.

- SS and Gestapo control of law.

- Imprisonment of opponents.

- Persecution of 'undesirables'.

- Control of the Church.

- Indoctrination of young people.

- Propaganda and censorship.

THINGS TO DO

1 Look at **Source F**. What impression does it give of the Nazis?

2 Why do you think the Nazis saw mass rallies as good propaganda?

Modern World History for AQA

To what extent did the German people benefit from Nazi rule in the 1930s?

Economic policy

The Nazis had promised to reverse the depression. **Dr Schacht**, Minister of the Economy 1934–7, devised a 'New Plan' to:

- reduce unemployment

- build up Germany's weapons industry

- make Germany independent of loans or supplies from other countries.

Increasing employment

In 1933, six million Germans were unemployed.

- Schacht set up **National Labour Service** for young men between 18 and 25 years old. These men lived in work camps. They were fed and housed and given a small amount of spending money. They worked on digging ditches, planting forests, building new motorways and public buildings such as hospitals and schools.

- In 1935, Hitler, ignoring the Treaty of Versailles, began to rearm Germany. He introduced **conscription** – men had to serve in the army for a set number of years. From 1935 to 1938 the army employed over one million people. Factories were set up to make weapons and equipment. They employed thousands of men.

- Women were forced out of their jobs. The jobs were given to men. The women did not count as unemployed. The same thing happened to Jews. All the people the Nazis put in labour camps and concentration camps did not count as unemployed, either.

All these measures reduced unemployment rapidly. By 1939, the Nazis were saying that there was a shortage of workers.

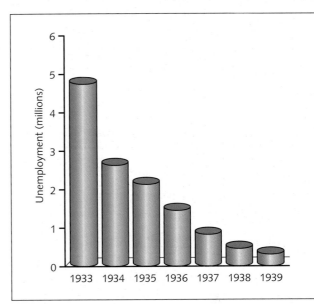

Unemployment in Nazi Germany during 1933–9. It appears to go steadily down. The Nazis sacked women and Jews from their jobs and gave the jobs to the officially unemployed. Women and Jews were not counted as unemployed.

THINGS TO DO

Look at the graph.

1 How many people were unemployed in 1933?

2 How many people were unemployed in 1939?

3 List the ways the Nazis reduced unemployment.

Improving the economy: self-sufficiency

Hitler did not want Germany to depend on other countries for loans, food or raw materials. In 1933, he made a **Four-Year Plan**. By the end of it, Germany was to be self- sufficient (able to produce everything Germany needed).

The Plan was in two parts:

- to produce more raw materials (mine more coal etc)

- to produce more man-made materials (rubber etc).

Both these parts needed more factories and more workers, so unemployment went down. However, they were expensive, because the state had to build factories.

By 1933, Germany still had to buy over one-third of its raw materials from other countries. The only way for the Nazis to become self-sufficient was to use the army to take over land which had raw materials the Nazis could then use.

The German Labour Front and Strength through Joy

All German workers had to join the **German Labour Front**. This replaced earlier trade unions, which were now illegal.

- The Front made strikes and pay negotiations illegal.

- Workers had to accept the wages and working hours that the state set.

- Workers had to have permission to change jobs.

Even workers' free time was organised by the **Strength through Joy** organisation. Workers had to take part in exercise groups and go to lectures. This kept them fit for the army and gave the Nazis another propaganda opportunity.

Strength through Joy also organised yearly holidays for workers. It planned a cheap 'people's car', the **Volkswagen**. Workers paid a small amount of money every week until they had saved the price of the car. Very few workers could save enough, so the plan collapsed.

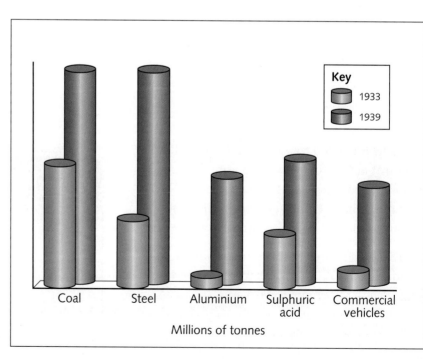

Industrial growth in Nazi Germany.

Nazi rule in the 1930s

Nazi rule was good for some Germans. It:

- reduced unemployment
- built up confidence and pride.

But it also:

- controlled education, work and leisure
- demanded total obedience
- was ruthless with 'undesirables'.

How did Germans feel about Nazi rule? It is hard to say.

Resistance was so quickly stamped on that people were too scared to be critical. As time went on, the Nazis made sure that people had no anti-Nazi information to make judgements from.

On balance, there were probably more people who accepted Nazi rule, even felt better off under it, in the 1930s. Would they still support the Nazis when Hilter took his next step? It was one that would take Germany to war.

Source **G** A poster of 1938 encouraging German workers to 'Save five marks a week and get your own cars'. The Volkswagen ('people's car') was introduced by the Nazis.

THINGS TO DO

How might you feel about Nazi rule in 1938 if you were:

(a) a woman with four children whose husband now had work?

(b) a person with Jewish friends who had been unemployed but now had a job?

(c) a member of the Hitler Youth?

SUMMARY

Nazi economic policy

- Reduced unemployment by public works and rearmament.
- Produced economic plans to make Germany self-sufficient.
- Controlled workers' time off.
- Prepared for war.

Exam-style assessment

These questions follow the pattern of questions to be set by AQA for Paper 2 of its new Modern World History specification.

SECTION A: Germany, 1919–29

Study **Sources A** to **E** and then answer all parts of Question 2 which follow.

Source A: The rising price of a loaf of bread in Berlin

Year	Price
1918	0.63 marks
1922	163 marks
January 1923	250 marks
July 1923	3645 marks
September 1923	1,512,000 marks
November 1923	201,000,000,000 marks

From a British school text-book (1995)

Source B: A German view of the cause of inflation

Germany complains: 'My sons have taken everything away. All they left me is a paper Mark with which to cover my nakedness.'

A German cartoon of 1920 published in a magazine.

Source C: A British view of the German economy

Germany is teeming with wealth. She is humming like a beehive. The comfort and prosperity of her people absolutely astound me. Poverty is practically non-existent.

And yet this is a country that is determined that she will not pay her debts. They are a nation of actors. If it wasn't for the fact that the Germans are without a sense of humour, one might imagine the whole nation was perpetrating an elaborate practical joke.

From *The Times*, 18 April 1922

Source D: A British view of the cause of German inflation

The Weimar Republic was burdened with economic problems arising out of the war.

Defeat left her saddled with a huge internal debt of 144,000 million marks and with a currency which had lost over one-third of its pre-war value.

From *A History of Germany* (1972) by WILLIAM CARR, a British historian

Source E: Another British view

Reparations cost Germany only about 2 per cent of her national output per year.

This suggests that the annual payments were not too harsh and that the Allies were right in claiming that Germany simply did not want to pay.

From *Germany 1815-1939* (1992) by FINLAY McKICHAN, a British historian

Question 2

(a) What can you learn from **Source A** about prices in Germany in the years 1918–23?   **(5 marks)**

(b) Compare the state of the German economy that is suggested in **Source B** with what is suggested in **Source C**.   **(6 marks)**

(c) How useful is **Source C** for studying the state of the German economy in the early 1920s?   **(9 marks)**

(d) **Sources D** and **E** give different interpretations of Germany's ability to pay reparations in the early 1920s. Which do you think is the more accurate interpretation, **Source D** or **Source E**? Explain your answer using **Sources D** and **E** and your own knowledge.   **(10 marks)**

(e) In the period up to 1929, the Nazi Party was regarded as weak and not worth serious consideration. Use your own knowledge to explain how far this was actually true.   **(15 marks)**

SECTION B: Germany, 1929–39

Study **Source F** and then answer parts **(a)**, **(b)**, **(c)** and **either (d) or (e)** of Question 6 which follow.

Source F : Unemployment and Nazi seats gained in elections to the German Parliament, 1928–33

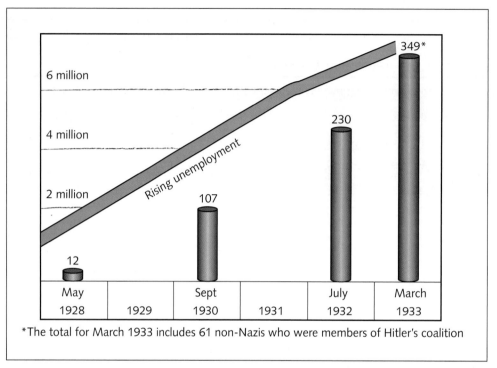

*The total for March 1933 includes 61 non-Nazis who were members of Hitler's coalition

From *The Twentieth Century* (1983) by M. N. DUFFY

This textbook was written for use in British schools.

Question 6

(a) What can you learn from **Source F** about the Nazi Party in the years 1929-33? **(3 marks)**

(b) Using **Source F** and your own knowledge, why did rising unemployment help the Nazi Party in the years 1929–33? **(7 marks)**

(c) Describe how Hitler used the incident of the Reichstag Fire of February 1933 to gain support. **(5 marks)**

EITHER

(d) Did the German people benefit from Nazi rule in the period 1933–9? Explain your answer. **(15 marks)**

OR

(e) Explain how the Nazis treated the Jews in the period 1933–9. **(15 marks)**

6 The USA, 1919–41

INTRODUCTION

The USA joined the First World War in 1917 and took part in the peace settlement that followed. After that, it deliberately cut itself off from European politics; a policy called isolationism. This included cutting the number of immigrants into the USA and cutting back on foreign trade.

In the 1920s and 1930s, the USA had an economic boom. At the same time there was an increase in racism and organised crime. The boom came to an end with the 1929 Wall Street Crash. The Depression that followed brought mass unemployment. During the 1930s, President Roosevelt tried to solve these problems with his 'New Deal'. The New Deal created employment and started to help the economy; but it was the Second World War that ended the Depression in the USA.

1918	End of the First World War
1919	Treaty of Versailles
1920	US Senate votes for America not to join the League of Nations Prohibition introduced
1925	Ku Klux Klan has 5 million members
1927	First 'talkie' at cinema Lindbergh flies solo across the Atlantic
1929	Wall Street Crash starts Great Depression
1932	Election of President F. D. Roosevelt
1933	Beginning of the New Deal
1936	Problems between the New Deal and the Supreme Court
1939	Second World War begins with USA isolationist
1941	(December) USA declares war on Japan and Germany

How did the USA react to the end of the First World War?

The USA in 1919

In 1919, the USA was one of richest and most powerful nations in the world. Many people emigrated from Europe to live there. Between 1850 and 1940 over 40 million **immigrants** had moved to the USA. It was seen as the 'land of opportunity'.

The USA had not joined the First World War until 1917. It played a vital part in defeating Germany and making peace in 1918. The USA had made money out of the war, selling supplies to the Allies.

Source **A**   An immigrant family arriving at Ellis Island in New York in 1905.

US reaction to the end of the First World War

People in the USA had reacted in different ways to the USA's involvement in the First World War.

- The President, **Woodrow Wilson**, had wanted to go to war. When the war ended he had taken part in negotiating the Treaty of Versailles. He was keen to set up the **League of Nations**.

- However, many Americans had not wanted to join in the First World War. It was in Europe, far away. Why should US soldiers die for Europeans? Once the war was over many Americans did not want the USA to be pulled into any more conflicts in other countries.

The mood of isolation grows

President Wilson tried to persuade the USA to join the League of Nations. A majority of Senate members rejected the idea.

When Wilson died in 1920, his party, the **Democrats**, still wanted to join the League. However, the **Republican** opposition party stressed the need for getting back to normal. As their slogan put it, they needed to put 'America First'.

The Republicans got far more support. The USA began to follow a policy of deliberately cutting down contacts with other countries – '**isolationism**'. This included cutting down on trade with other countries. It also meant that the USA grew less and less welcoming to immigrants from other countries.

THINGS TO DO

1 How did the First World War affect the USA?

2 What was 'isolationism'?

3 Why did many people in the USA support the policy of isolationism?

Source B

The First World War showed up the situation among the foreign population in America:

1 Many did not become US citizens.

2 Some were causing political unrest in the trade unions, 'taking their orders from Moscow'.

3 Over 1000 newspapers were in a foreign language.

4 Over 10 per cent could not speak English.

5 Many were used to low wages, so were employed before US workers.

Adapted from a US school textbook from 1961.

How did the policies of the American government encourage isolation?

'Isolationism' meant not becoming involved in the political problems of other countries. It also meant cutting down on foreign trade and restricting the number of immigrants to the USA.

Tariffs against foreign goods

One way to stop people buying foreign goods is to make these goods more expensive. The US government taxed goods from abroad from 1920. Goods from abroad had to pay a **tariff** (fee) to come into the USA. This had several effects:

- It made US goods cheaper.

- This helped to produce an economic boom in the USA.

- Foreign countries put tariffs on US goods, so the USA sold less abroad.

Restricting the flow of immigrants

The USA had been famous for its 'open door' policy to people wanting to move there from other countries. By 1919, Americans were less happy about this policy.

- There was a growing feeling of distrust of foreigners.

- People feared that new immigrants would work for very low wages, so take work away from Americans.

- People were worried about ideas that new immigrants might bring to the USA, such as communism.

So, the government acted to slow the numbers of immigrants.

- The 1917 **Immigration Law** made immigrants prove they could read in English before they were allowed in. This cut down the number of poor Europeans and Asians who could not afford to learn English.

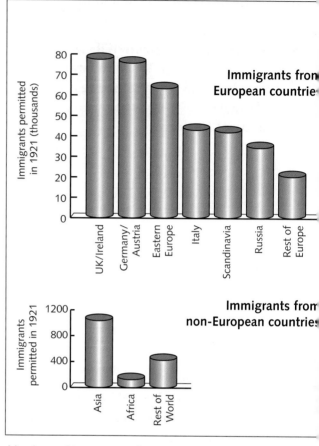

Numbers of immigrants allowed in to the USA, 1921.

- The 1921 **Immigration Quota Act** set a maximum number of 357,000 immigrants for each year. It also set quotas for people from each country. No country could send more than three per cent of the number of people from that country already living in the USA in 1910. This favoured western and northern European immigrants, because they had started arriving in the USA earlier.

- In 1924, the quota was reduced to two per cent of those in the country in 1890.

- In 1929, the maximum number of immigrants for the year was set at 150,000. No Asians were allowed in at all.

More distrust of foreigners

From 1919 on, it was harder to emigrate to the USA. Those 'lucky' enough to be let in often found their troubles were only beginning.

- They could only find low-paid jobs.

- They could only afford poor housing: slum areas divided into **ghettos** of various nationalities.

- Because immigrants in ghettos often spoke their old languages and kept their own customs, Americans distrusted them as foreigners and new immigrants felt unwanted.

- Political distrust grew up about 'foreign ideas' such as communism.

THINGS TO DO

1 What did the US government do to isolate the USA from the rest of the world?

2 What is immigration?

3 List the steps the US government took to reduce immigration.

4 Which groups of immigrants did the government most want to discourage?

Case Study: the Sacco and Vanzetti Case

Nicola Sacco and Bartolomeo Vanzetti were immigrants from Italy. They hated the US system of government. They were anarchists – a political group that believed in no government at all.

In 1920, they were arrested for killing two guards during a robbery.

The evidence against them was:

- They both had loaded guns when arrested.

- The bullets in Sacco's gun matched those that killed the guards.

- There were 61 eyewitnesses who identified them as the killers.

- Vanzetti had already been to jail for armed robbery.

But:

- The eyewitnesses did not agree about the detail of the crime – just who committed it.

- The defence produced 107 people who said Sacco and Vanzetti had been somewhere else at the time.

The jury convicted Sacco and Vanzetti of murder. Appeals and petitions against the verdict failed.

They were executed in 1927.

THINGS TO DO

What does the Sacco and Vanzetti case tell us about the USA in the 1920s?

How far did the USA achieve prosperity in the 1920s?

In the 1920s, the USA enjoyed an economic boom due to the boost to industry provided by:

- the First World War

- the trade policies of isolationism

- the new methods in factories which improved production

- new industries which benefited from new methods and equipment to meet demand for their goods.

Mass production

The mass production system produced more goods more cheaply. How did it work?

- New, large factories were built with moving assembly lines.

- Workers stood or sat beside the **assembly lines**.

- The goods being made, for instance cars, went along the assembly line from worker to worker.

- Each worker had only one job to do on every car.

The car industry

The car industry was one of the first to use mass production. Before the war, cars were expensive. **Henry Ford** mass-produced cheap cars for ordinary people. His cars were all the same, even the same colour – black. In 1911,

Source A

The work is split up. Each man and each machine do just one thing. Everything keeps moving. The work goes to the man.

Henry Ford said this when explaining mass production in 1926.

Source B The assembly line in the Ford Motor Company.

Ford's first mass-produced **Model T** car cost $1,200. By the 1920s, his factories made a Model T every ten seconds. In 1920, a Model T cost $295.

Other industries

Other goods that had been expensive luxuries (radios, telephones, fridges, vacuum cleaners and washing machines) were mass-produced, too. They became cheap enough for many people to buy them.

Cycle of prosperity

The effects of the growth of these new factories were felt right through society.

- A bigger demand for **raw materials** meant more jobs processing these materials.

- The new factories needed thousands of workers.

- High employment meant many people had money to spend. They spent some of it on the new, cheap goods. So there was a big demand for these goods.

- The new factories needed more raw materials and more workers to make more goods. This takes you back to the first point, creating a **cycle of prosperity**.

Government policy

The government encouraged the boom:

- It lowered taxes. This gave people and businesses more money to spend.

- It did not control how banks or businesses were run. This means it did not try to control bank interest rates, for example.

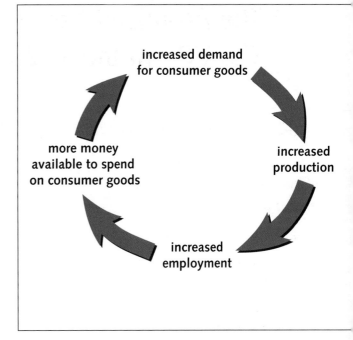

The cycle of prosperity. This diagram shows how once an economic boom started it continued to grow.

Credit facilities

Very few people could buy a new car, or even a fridge, with cash. They had to save up to buy these things. But businesses wanted people to buy straight away and to buy more.

- They used advertising on radio, in cinemas, on billboards, to get people to buy.

- They introduced the **hire purchase** system. People who wanted to buy a car signed an agreement to pay weekly or monthly amounts until they had paid for the car. This encouraged people to spend money they did not have.

	1920	1929
Motor cars on the roads	9 million	26 million
Kilometres of roads	620,000	1 million
Radios	60,000	10 million
Telephones in homes and offices	13 million	20 million

Some changes in the USA during the 1920s.

Confidence

People in the USA were confident in the booming economy:

- They happily signed hire purchase agreements.

- Some bought shares in companies. This gave them a share of the yearly profits. It was even possible to borrow 90 per cent of the price of shares from banks. This was called '**buying on the margin**'.

- Banks also used people's money to buy shares.

Americans who did not share the prosperity

Not all Americans had money to spare. Some were having problems.

- **Farmers** were growing more food than people needed. Food prices fell. Some farmers could no longer pay their mortgages. They lost their farms. Many other farmers had to cut down on workers. These workers then drifted, looking for work.

- **Black people and immigrants** found it hard to find work, except in the lowest paid jobs. Almost one million black farm workers lost their jobs in the 1920s.

- **Workers in older industries** did badly. There was a drop in the demand for coal as new fuels (oil, gas and electricity) were more widely used. Many miners lost their jobs. The cotton industry suffered because high tariffs meant there was less demand for US cotton abroad.

THINGS TO DO

1 Draw a diagram to show how an economic boom works.

2 Explain whether the following people would benefit from the boom:
   - a car factory worker
   - a miner
   - a farmer
   - a banker.

Source C

This cartoon comments on the situation of farmers in the 1920s. They could not afford to run their farms, while the factories made big profits.

'The Roaring Twenties' – is this a good description of the USA in the 1920s?

The economic boom in the USA produced confidence and national pride. But it also produced racial hatred, violence and organised crime.

Ku Klux Klan

The **Ku Klux Klan** was a group that said the only true Americans were White Anglo-Saxon Protestants (WASPs). Any other people (Jews, Catholics, recent immigrants and black people) were not proper Americans. Ku Klux Klan's membership rose from 100,000 in 1920 to five million in 1925.

Who joined the Ku Klux Klan?

The Klan was a secret society. People dressed in white robes and masks. They spoke in secret codes – 'Klonversations'. Who were they?

- poor whites who felt that black people and immigrants were stealing their jobs

- wealthy state politicians

- almost everyone in some southern towns with a history of treating black people badly. Here, black people could not ask the police for help against the Klan – they were all members of the Klan.

Source **D**

1 Are you born in the USA and not Jewish?

2 Are you free of any loyalty to any government other than that of the USA?

3 Are you Christian?

...

8 Will you fight for white supremacy?

Some of the questions asked of someone who wanted to join the Ku Klux Klan.

THINGS TO DO

Look at **Sources D** and **E**. What do they tell us about the Ku Klux Klan?

Source **E**

A Ku Klux Klan parade in 1925.

What did the Ku Klux Klan do?

The Klan tortured, even killed, people who were not WASPs, especially black people. The Klan:

- burned down homes and churches, even with people in them

- beat up or lynched people, for any excuse or none at all

- set up burning crosses, the Klan symbol, to warn or to say 'we did this'.

Lynching is when a group of people take someone and hang them. The people who are lynched are not arrested or tried, simply murdered. Black people in the USA at this time could be lynched for any reason, or none at all. Between 1882 and 1968 there were over 3400 lynchings of black people. Many more went unrecorded.

Was the Klan punished?

In many cases – where police, judges or politicians were Klan members – crimes were not even reported, let alone punished.

However, Klan members were punished in places the Klan did not control. These trials were reported and people reacted against the Klan. After 1925, its numbers fell, although it still exists today in the USA.

Prohibition

In 1920, the US government introduced **Prohibition**. This was the banning of alcohol by law. Alcohol could not be made or sold in the whole of the USA. Alcohol was defined as a drink with more than 0.5 per cent of alcohol in it.

Why did Prohibition happen?

- Alcoholism had been a growing problem in the USA.

Source **F** A poster published by the Anti-Saloon League in 1910.

- Many 'temperance' (anti-alcohol) groups campaigned for a ban because they thought it brought poverty, broke up homes and disrupted work.

- By 1917, eighteen US states had already banned alcohol.

Effects of Prohibition: illegal alcohol and speakeasies

Only the temperance groups were in favour of Prohibition. Most other people thought there was nothing wrong with having a drink. People who would not have dreamed of breaking any other laws broke this one.

- They made their own alcohol, **moonshine**, which often made them ill, even killed some people.

- They went to secret, illegal, drinking clubs, called **speakeasies**, which smuggled in alcohol from the West Indies and Canada. This was called **bootlegging**. By 1930, there were nearly 250,000 of these in the USA, mostly in towns and cities.

Organised crime

Speakeasies made a lot of money. Soon gangsters such as **Al Capone** had taken over the alcohol trade. They then began to deal in drugs, prostitutes and gambling. They fought each other over various 'territories'. In Chicago from 1920 to 1924, 227 gangsters were murdered. The police did nothing. They were either bribed or they left the gangsters to deal with each other.

Reasons for the failure of Prohibition

- Too many people wanted to drink and were prepared to break the law to do it.

- The gangs very quickly became rich and powerful. The only way to enforce Prohibition was to break up the gangs.

- It would take too many police to break up the gangs, especially as many of them took bribes from the gangs.

- In December 1933, **President Roosevelt** repealed (got rid of) the Prohibition Law, saying 'Let's all go out and have a drink.'

THINGS TO DO

Look at **Source F**. What message is the poster presenting about the evils of drink?

Source G

I loved speakeasies. If you knew the right ones the whiskey wouldn't poison you. I'd heard of a girl blinded by bad gin, but I was lucky.

It was like being in a movie and the food was great, even though dreadful things went on in them.

Said by the US songwriter Alex Wilder, who visited speakeasies in the 1920s.

Source H

I was in favour of Prohibition before it was brought in. I am sure it has failed.

The corner bar has gone; but it has just moved to the back of a store and become a speakeasy.

Written by a US journalist in 1928.

Case Study: Al Capone and Organised Crime

Al Capone led the most powerful gang in Chicago. His parents were Italian immigrants to New York. He moved to Chicago as part of 'Terrible Johnny' Torrio's gang and took over in 1925, when Torrio retired.

Capone took control of more and more local gangs; soon his gang had 700 men, armed with sawn-off shotguns and sub-machine-guns. Anyone who opposed Capone was 'rubbed out' (killed).

Despite this, Capone was seen as glamorous and mixed with businessmen and movie stars. Although he had bribed many police and judges, others tried to punish him in the law courts.

Capone avoided being convicted for the murders he ordered, but was eventually sent to prison for eleven years for failing to pay his taxes.

Source **I**

Al Capone on the front cover of *Time* magazine, 1930.

Source J

> I call myself a businessman. I make my money by supplying a popular demand. If I break the law, my customers are as guilty as I am.
>
> ***This was Al Capone's attitude to Prohibition.***

	1921	**1925**	**1929**
Illegal distilleries seized	9746	12,023	15,794
Gallons of distilled spirit seized	414,000	1,103,000	1,186,000
Arrests	34,175	62,747	66,878

Attempts by the authorities to enforce Prohibition, 1921–9. Despite the rise in the number of arrests Prohibition still failed.

THINGS TO DO

1 What was Prohibition?

2 Why did Prohibition fail?

3 What bad effects did Prohibition cause?

4 Read the Case Study on Al Capone.
   (a) How could you use the evidence there to call him a criminal?
   (b) How did he see himself?

Developments in entertainment

In the 1920s, young people wanted to forget the First World War and have a good time. Those who had wages and could enjoy the economic boom did so, ignoring the problems of the poor and unemployed. The 1920s were called the 'Roaring Twenties' because of the speed at which things grew and changed.

The jazz age

Jazz was a new kind of music that grew out of black music. It was played in nightclubs, mainly by black performers, like Duke Ellington and Louis Armstrong. It became the music played in speakeasies that sold illegal alcohol, so was seen as wild music for illegal places.

Radio

Cheap radios brought all kinds of entertainment to people, including jazz. In 1920, only 2 per cent of homes had a radio. By 1930, it was 60 per cent. Local and national radio stations were set up and many made their money by advertising new consumer goods.

New fashions

Young people wanted new things: new dances (the Charleston), new entertainment (the movies). 'Modern' was a word used a lot. Young people used it approvingly. Older people used it critically. 'Modern' young women were 'flappers'. They had short hair and short skirts. They wore make-up, smoked and drove cars. 'Modern' young men wore the same sorts of clothes as each other, smoked, dated flappers and got caught up in various crazes.

A flapper.

Crazes

The speed of the 'Roaring Twenties' was shown by crazes that swept the USA. Something, such as the dance marathon, became very fashionable for a short time; then was dropped. There were crazes for people too – the pilot Charles Lindbergh, after he flew the Atlantic solo in 1929, or the boxer Jack Dempsey.

Source K

The parties were bigger, the pace was faster, the buildings were higher, the morals were looser and the alcohol was cheaper.

The author F. Scott Fitzgerald wrote this about the 1920s.

This is the great picture upon which the famous comedian has worked a whole year.

6 reels of Joy.

Charles Chaplin in "THE KID"

Source L A poster of the film star Charlie Chaplin in *The Kid*.

Film and Hollywood

The movie industry took off after the First World War. By 1929, over 110 million Americans were going to the cinema each week. The film industry grew rapidly, with movie companies like MGM and Paramount making hundreds of films each year. Early films had no sound and were in black and white. Some cinemas had piano players to play the right kind of music.

Actors like Charlie Chaplin and Mary Pickford were early film stars. After the first 'talkie' (a film with sound) was made, in 1927, everyone made them. Some stars, who looked good but had poor voices, found themselves out of work. By the mid-1930s, colour films were being made and Walt Disney had made Mickey Mouse famous across the whole country.

Why did the USA fall into depression in 1929?

The boom years had built-in problems which
would lead to a depression sooner or later.
These were the long-term causes of the
Depression.

Overproduction

Mass production was making lots of goods
cheaply. At first it was a good thing. It created
jobs and boosted the economy. It also
improved the lives of the people who could
afford to buy the new, cheap consumer goods.

But the producers did not slow down. Once
people had a washing machine, however, they
did not need another. So, the factories were
making more goods than people needed.

By 1928, factories were beginning to cut
down production and cut down their
workforce. Unemployment began to go up
again.

Unequal distribution of wealth

Some Americans were well off. But the gap
between rich and poor had been there all
through the 1920s. A survey in 1928 showed
that 60 per cent of Americans earned less
than $2000 a year – the minimum needed to
survive. Most of these were:

- farmers and farm workers
- people who worked in the old industries
- new immigrants
- black people.

THINGS TO DO

Read pages 231 and 232.

1 What problems did the USA have, even
in the boom years, which meant there
would be a depression?

2 What event sparked off the Depression?

The USA, 1919–41

Tariff policy

The government taxes on foreign goods (see page 220) helped US businesses to begin with, because Americans were less likely to buy more expensive foreign goods. But, once Americans had bought all they were going to, it was harder for US businesses to sell goods abroad, because foreign countries had put tariffs on US goods. They did this to balance the US tariffs on their goods. This caused a **cycle of depression**. As there was less demand for goods, less were made. This caused some people to lose their jobs. This meant that less people had money to spend on goods, so the demand was even less.

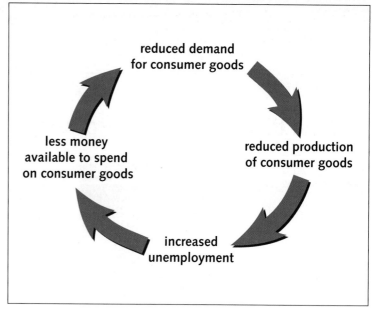

The cycle of depression. This diagram shows that once an economic downturn starts it can quickly turn into a depression.

Financial crisis: speculation

During the 1920s, more and more Americans had bought shares in companies. These shares were bought and sold on the stock market, based in **Wall Street**, New York.

- People expected shares to go on rising in price. They bought shares to sell at a profit a few months later. This is called **speculation**. Many people borrowed money from banks to do this. Some banks were using their customers' money to speculate themselves.

- Shares rose in price, rapidly. Because there were only a certain number of shares and everyone wanted to buy, prices were driven up far more than their real value.

- In 1928, the rapid rise in share prices slowed as companies sold fewer goods.

- Some people began to sell their shares, thinking the price of shares might actually begin to fall. This put more shares on the stock market, so prices did fall.

- More and more people sold their shares. The more people who tried to sell shares, the more prices fell. Panic set in.

The Wall Street Crash, 1929

What happened in the Wall Street Crash?

- On Thursday 24 October 1929 – Black Thursday – nearly 13 million shares were sold.

- Prices dived.

- A group of banks tried to buy shares to stop prices falling.

- This settled prices down for a while.

- The following Monday panic selling broke out again.

- Tuesday was the worst single day – people lost $8,000 million.

- Prices carried on falling until mid-November, when they bottomed out (stopped falling).

- By then, the damage was done.

Effects of the Wall Street Crash

- Many rich Americans lost all their money.

- Many companies lost all their money. They had to close. People lost their jobs.

- Many ordinary people who had been speculating on the stock market also lost everything.

- Many banks lost not only their money, but their customers' money too. So even people who had not been speculating in shares found the money they had saved in the bank was gone. People lost confidence in the banks. In 1929, nearly 700 banks had to close. Banks tried to save themselves by making people who had borrowed from them repay their loans. Many people could not do this and so the banks took their homes and possessions.

SUMMARY

The causes of the Depression

- Too many goods produced.

- Many Americans below poverty line during 1920s.

- Not enough foreign trade.

- Share speculation.

- Panic selling.

- Wall Street Crash.

Share prices of some leading US companies in 1929.

Company	Share Prices	
	3 September	13 November
Anaconda Copper	131.5	70
General Electric	396	168
Radio	101	28
United States Steel	261	150
Woolworth	100	52
Electric Bond & Share	186	50

THINGS TO DO

1 Look at the table of share prices. If you owned shares in any of these companies, what would you have done when you found out the 13 November prices?

2 Why would this make things worse? Explain your answer.

Source B Unemployed workers in New York queuing for free bread in 1930.

The USA, 1919–41

What were the effects of the Depression on the American people?

Unemployment

So many companies had to shut down after the Wall Street Crash that unemployment shot up. The industrial North was hardest hit. In Chicago, for example, nearly 50 per cent of workers were unemployed.

Many people began to travel the country looking for work. They walked, or sneaked rides on goods trains. There were thousands of these **hobos** (tramps). The longer they were unemployed the harder it became for them to find work because:

- the number of unemployed kept rising – they had more competition for jobs

- it was hard to keep clean, so they got dirtier and shabbier as time went on

- it was hard to stay hopeful and keep looking for work.

Homelessness

In 1932 alone, 250,000 people became homeless, for various reasons.

- People who could not repay bank loans had their homes taken to pay the loans.

- People who lost their jobs and could not pay their mortgages had their homes taken away.

- People who lived in rented homes were thrown out if they could not pay the rent.

Some of the homeless became hobos. Some slept on benches or in doorways. Many moved to the edges of towns and built homes from cardboard, wood, scrap metal – whatever they could find. These shanty towns were called **Hoovervilles** as an insult to the President at the time, **Herbert Hoover** (see Source C).

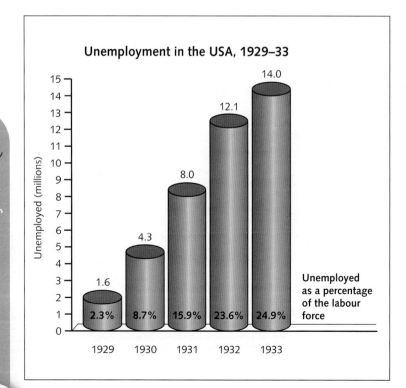

Unemployment in the USA, 1929–33

Year	Unemployed (millions)	Unemployed as a percentage of the labour force
1929	1.6	2.3%
1930	4.3	8.7%
1931	8.0	15.9%
1932	12.1	23.6%
1933	14.0	24.9%

THINGS TO DO

Look at **Source C**. List some of the factors that led to these people having to live in a Hooverville.

Farmers

Farmers had not had a good time during the economic boom of the 1920s. They suffered even more in the Depression. There were two main reasons why farmers ended up homeless and looking for work, often drifting to the fruit farms of California.

- The price of food fell so sharply that many farmers went bankrupt. In 1932, one in ten farmers were evicted because they could not pay their mortgages.

- During the First World War farmers in the South and Mid-West changed from cattle farming to crop farming. They over-farmed the land, so the soil had all its nutrients sucked out of it. A series of dry years in the 1930s meant that strong winds and no rain turned the soil to dust. Their farms became a desert-like **'dust bowl'**.

Source C A 'Hooverville' in the centre of New York.

Help from charities

The USA did not have a welfare system like Britain to help the unemployed. So, who did help?

- charities

- wealthy people (even the gangster Al Capone)

- some government organisations, at a local level.

The most common help these groups provided were free bread and soup, blankets, clothes, places to sleep and, for a lucky few, temporary homes.

The help provided was never enough for the rising numbers of people in need. Long queues formed at food centres.

Source D

In the state of Washington, farmers started forest fires just to earn a few dollars as fire-fighters.

In Oregon, the apples rotted on the trees and sheep farmers fed their sheep to the buzzards.

Written by an American journalist in 1932.

The Republican government and the Depression

Hoover's Republican government believed in '**rugged individualism**' – that is, people should help themselves and the government should not get involved. It waited for the Depression to sort itself out.

As things worsened, the government did act to help people, though as little as possible:

- In 1930, it cut taxes, to encourage spending.

- It provided over $4000 million for public building works. One of these was Hoover Dam on the Colorado River, begun in 1931.

- The 1932 **Emergency Relief Act** gave $300 million to various states to provide relief for the poor in their state.

- In 1932, the **Reconstruction Finance Corporation** was set up to lend money to businesses. In all, the government lent businesses over $1500 million.

These actions were not enough. People blamed Hoover and the government for the Depression; there were many demonstrations and marches that often turned into riots. A common slogan of the time was: 'In Hoover we trusted, now we are busted.'

Case Study: the Bonus Army

At the end of the First World War, the government had promised soldiers a 'bonus' (pension) to be paid by 1945.

The Depression threw many of these veterans (ex-soldiers) out of work. They wanted their bonus at once. In the summer of 1932, about 15–20,000 of them marched to Washington and set up a Hooverville opposite the White House. Congress refused to pay the bonuses.

The veterans refused to leave. The police tried to move them on, but failed. Hoover sent in the army, with tanks and tear gas, to clear the Hooverville.

In the fighting that followed thousands of veterans were injured, two were killed. Hoover became even more unpopular.

Source Fighting between the police and the Bonus Army in 1932.

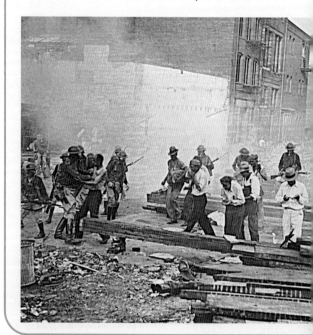

What measures did Roosevelt introduce to deal with the Depression?

The 1932 Presidential election

In 1928, Hoover and the Republicans promised to keep the economic boom of the 1920s going. The Depression hit the USA instead. The American people thought Hoover did not do enough to help. Hoover did not seem to want to change his policies, either. He simply said that he thought the USA had 'turned the corner', that is that it was beginning to recover.

By the time they came to elect a new President, in 1932, they wanted a change. They elected **F. D. Roosevelt** who promised a '**New Deal**' including policies to help the unemployed, farmers, banks and businesses. Roosevelt won the biggest presidential victory ever – 42 of the 48 US states.

Source **A** F. D. Roosevelt.

Source **B**

A cartoon, dated 3 March 1933, showing President Roosevelt throwing out the policies of the previous government, which are shown as rubbish.

The New Deal

In the USA, there is always a gap between the time when a President is elected and the time when the President takes over. Roosevelt used this gap (from November 1932 to March 1933) to work on his New Deal ideas. Roosevelt knew he had to replace 'rugged individualism' with a lot of government involvement. The government had to take control of the economy to set it right, not let it sort itself out.

The New Deal relied on the government spending a lot of money to create new jobs. Roosevelt hoped that this would stop the cycle of depression (see diagram on page 232) and set up a cycle of recovery.

The Hundred Days

As soon as he came to power, Roosevelt asked Congress to give him 'emergency powers' – the sort of control Presidents usually have only if the USA is at war. Roosevelt knew he would have to act fast and set himself targets for his first hundred days in office.

- He had to get the New Deal under way by setting up government agencies to run various parts of the economy. There were a lot of these agencies and they became known as the **Alphabet Agencies** – because people remembered them by their initials, not their full names. So, the Agricultural Adjustment Administration was always called the AAA, for instance.

- He had to get people to understand what made the Depression happen and to understand what he was doing and how it would put things right. He wanted people to have confidence in him. So, he used the radio to reach out to as many Americans as possible. He gave a series of **fireside chats** where he explained all this very simply. He came over as calm, capable and confident when he assured people that 'The only thing we have to fear is fear itself.' People did come to trust him.

The cycle of recovery. Roosevelt hoped that a big enough government investment would re-start the cycle.

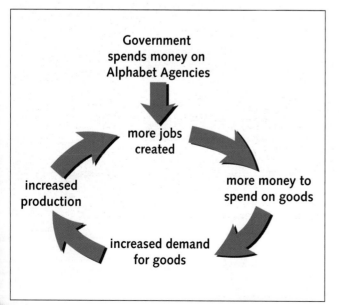

THINGS TO DO

1 Why did the Americans elect Roosevelt in 1932?

2 How was the New Deal different from Hoover's policies?

3 What were Roosevelt's two targets for his first hundred days?

4 Why were these targets were so important?

The banking crisis

During the Depression people had lost confidence in the banks. Some banks had lost their customers' savings in the Wall Street Crash. So, Roosevelt passed the **Emergency Banking Act** in March 1933, as soon as he came to power:

- All banks were closed for four days.
- They were inspected by the government.
- Only properly managed banks could reopen.
- Banks which reopened could have government loans.

All this was explained in Roosevelt's first 'fireside chat'. When the banks re-opened people began to use them again.

Agriculture: the AAA

The Agriculture Adjustment Administration (AAA) was set up in May 1933 to help farmers. It paid farmers to grow fewer crops and keep less livestock. Why?

- Farmers had problems because they could not get good prices for their food.
- If they grew less food, this would push up food prices.
- Farmers would be able to make more money from the food they produced (*and* they had the government grant).

This policy helped farmers who still had farms, but it did not help farm workers or farmers who had already lost their farms. It also made food more expensive.

Source C Roosevelt meeting a farmer in Georgia in 1932.

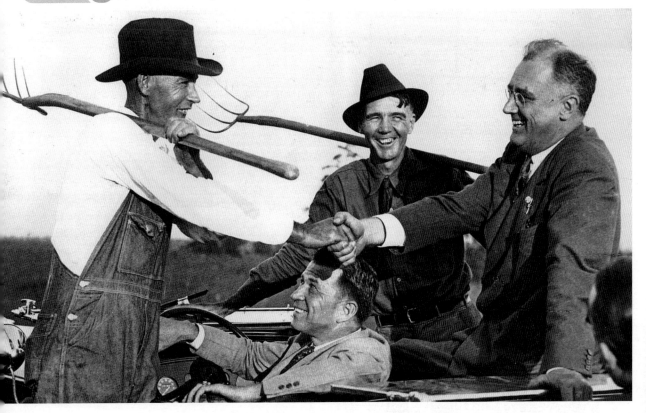

Dealing with unemployment: FERA, CWA, PWA, WPA

The most important part of the New Deal was to create more jobs to cut unemployment. Several different agencies dealt with this problem.

- **FERA** (the Federal Emergency Relief Administration) gave instant help to the poor and unemployed. $500 million dollars were spent providing food, clothing and work.

- **CWA** (the Civil Works Administration) provided short-term work. The work was to see people through the winter of 1933–4. Over four million jobs were created, from building roads to cleaning up parks. Once the winter was over, the CWA shut down. The jobs went.

- **PWA** (the Public Works Administration) organised long-term work, to take over where the CWA left off. These jobs included building hospitals and schools, improving sewers and drains and other jobs that would improve life in the USA. Many of these jobs needed trained people.

- **WPA** (the Works Progress Administration), set up in 1935, provided work on a smaller scale for less skilled people, or for people with specific skills that were not helped by the PWA. These included writers (who wrote guidebooks for visitors), actors (12,000 of them were paid to tour the USA performing plays) and photographers (who took photos for government projects, such as showing how the New Deal was working).

These agencies provided million of jobs for the unemployed. So, people had wages again. They could pay rent and mortgages, buy food and clothes and other goods. This helped the economy; but the government also set up more alphabet agencies.

Source **D** 'Yes, you remembered me,' a cartoon of 1933.

THINGS TO DO

1 What point was the cartoonist making in **Source D**?

2 Outline the work carried out by:
   (a) CWA, (b) PWA, (c) WPA.

Helping the young: CCC

The CCC (Civilian Conservation Corps) gave temporary work to single, unemployed young men aged 18–25. They lived in camps and worked in the countryside, planting trees, clearing land and making reservoirs. They were given food, clothes and $1 a day. Some people criticised it as getting cheap labour but the scheme:

- provided work and training
- helped the environment.

Helping industry: NRA

The NRA (National Recovery Administration) wanted to help businesses and workers. Businesses that joined had to agree to:

- hold talks with workers to fix a fair minimum wage, fair working hours and fair prices
- not use child labour or cheap, sweated labour (they could not make people work long hours in poor conditions).

Businesses did not have to join the NRA, but if they did they could display the 'Blue Eagle' symbol. Americans were encouraged to buy Blue Eagle goods. By the end of 1933, two million businesses had joined.

Other measures of the New Deal

- HOLC (the **Home Owners Loan Corporation**) lent government money at low interest rates to people who were having problems paying their mortgages.

- The **Social Security Act** (1935) set up state pensions for those over 65, widows and the disabled. It also set up state-run unemployment benefits.

- The **National Labour Relations Act** (1935) said workers could form trade unions and could not be sacked for doing so.

Case Study: The Tennessee Valley Authority (TVA)

The Tennessee River ran through seven different states. Roosevelt called it 'the nation's number one economic problem'. Why?

- In the spring it flooded, washing away the soil.
- In the summer it dried up, causing drought.
- People who lived nearby were very poor.
- It was hard to solve the problems, because seven states had to agree about what to do.

Roosevelt set up the Tennessee Valley Authority (TVA). It drew up plans to solve the problems and carried them out. The states were not involved. The TVA:

- planted trees (to improve the soil)
- built dams (to prevent flooding and provide cheap electricity)
- used the dams to create lakes (linked to other rivers, these gave cheap water transport).

The problems of flooding and drought were solved. The cheap electricity and good water transport drew industries to the area, too, and provided more work. The lakes could be used for watersports, so a tourist industry grew up.

THINGS TO DO

1 What problems did the Tennessee Valley have before the TVA was set up?
2 What effects did the TVA have?

Source **E** A dam being built by workers employed by the TVA.

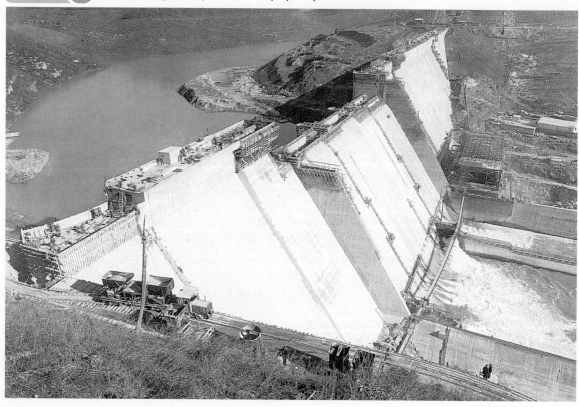

How far was the New Deal successful in ending the Depression in the USA?

In 1932, Roosevelt was voted in by 42 out of 48 US states. In the 1936 election, he won the votes of 46 states. The American people certainly thought the New Deal was working.

Opposition to the New Deal

Roosevelt still had his opponents.

- Republicans who still believed in 'rugged individualism'.

- People who thought Roosevelt was behaving like a dictator.

- Business people who did not like the NRA's restrictions on businesses.

- People who thought that many of the jobs the government created were 'worthless'.

- Those who thought the government was still not doing enough for people, such as Senator **Huey Long** of Louisiana. Long said that anyone who had more than $3 million should have it taken away and shared among everyone.

Source **F**

In this 1933 cartoon Roosevelt said he was 'priming the pump' of the American economy. Priming a pump is getting it started with a flow of water. Here Roosevelt is putting the priming water down the pump. The water is really government spending, as you can see from the '$' signs on the buckets.

THINGS TO DO

Is **Source F** in favour of the New Deal? Explain your answer.

The Supreme Court

The **Supreme Court** makes sure that no President does anything against the American constitution. It can declare an action illegal and stop it. In 1932, there were more Republicans than Democrats in the Supreme Court. They opposed the New Deal.

- In 1935, it shut down the NRA and cancelled all its regulations.

- In 1936, it shut down the AAA.

- In eleven more cases it did not shut down alphabet agencies, but it did stop some of their activities.

Roosevelt was angry. After he was re-elected in 1936, he tried to get six Democrats into the Supreme Court (to give the Democrats a majority). This looked like dictatorship. Many people, even Democrats, objected. Roosevelt backed down. But he had scared the Supreme Court. It stopped blocking New Deal measures.

Was the New Deal a success?

The New Deal helped a lot of people.

- It created jobs.

- It boosted confidence.

- It helped certain groups – the old, the disabled, people who were having trouble paying their mortgages, farmers.

However, the New Deal was not completely successful:

- Farm labourers were still very badly off.

- Black workers tended to do less well out of the New Deal than white workers.

- Certain areas, like the dust bowl, were still in trouble.

Source G In this 1936 cartoon Roosevelt shows 'Uncle Sam' (the USA) the achievements of the New Deal. The cartoonist is clearly in favour of New Deal. He is suggesting that people have jobs, homes and security in their old age thanks to the New Deal.

The New Deal and employment

The New Deal provided a big employment boost to begin with:

- In 1933, fourteen million people were unemployed.

- In 1937, the number had fallen to eight million. Roosevelt, hoping he had done enough to boost the economy, began to cut back on government spending.

- In 1938, unemployment had risen to eleven million and Roosevelt had to spend more again.

- This time, unemployment fell more slowly. In 1939, it was nine million. Had the New Deal done all it could?

The Second World War

The Second World War ended the Depression. The USA did not join the war until 1941, but from 1939 it was affected by it. The USA sold more goods, including war supplies, to Britain and France whose economies were crippled by war.

Once the USA joined the war, it needed to make more war supplies and also needed more people in the armed forces. Many unemployed people joined the armed forces or went to work in the new factories, so unemployment fell.

The verdict?

The New Deal may not have completely beaten the Depression. It made big improvements. It also changed the way the government worked – people now expected the government to care for the old, the unemployed, the homeless and the poor.

Source H

> The New Deal did not get the USA out of the Depression. Even in 1941 there were still six million unemployed. It was not until the war that the army of unemployed disappeared.
>
> ***Written by a historian in 1963.***

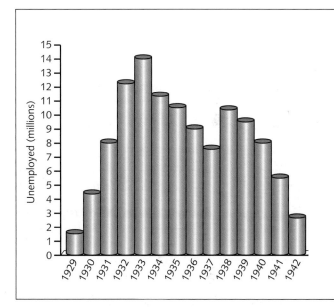

Unemployment in the USA, 1929–42.

THINGS TO DO

1 What does the historian in **Source H** think about the New Deal ?

2 Looking at the unemployment figures in the chart, do you think the historian has been fair to the New Deal?

3 What finally ended the Depression, and why?

Exam-style assessment

These questions follow the pattern of questions to be set by AQA for Paper 2 of its new Modern World History specification.

SECTION A: The USA, 1929–33

Study **Sources A** to **E** and then answer all parts of Question 3 which follow.

Source A: Roosevelt's pledge for a New Deal

> I pledge you, I pledge myself, to a New Deal for the American people. This is a political campaign; it is a call to arms. Give me your help, not to win votes alone, but to win in this crusade to restore America.

From a pre-election speech by F. D. ROOSEVELT in 1932

Source B: Why Hoover lost the 1932 election

> Millions of Americans blamed Hoover for the Depression and all the problems that came with it. With bitterness they said: "In Hoover we trusted, now we are busted".
>
> They were looking for a more positive approach in dealing with the Depression.

From Modern World History (1999) by T. HEWITT, J. McCABE and A. MENDUM

Source C: New York during the Depression

> The visitor would be surprised to discover that, at first and even at second glance, New York City is much the same as it was in pre-depression days. Wandering about the city looking for disaster, the visitor will very likely find no more than he would have in New York in any other winter.

From the American magazine Fortune, in the winter of 1931

Source D: One view of the New Deal

An American cartoon of 1933.

Source E : Another view of the New Deal

A cartoon in an American newspaper, 1933.

Question 3

(a) How does **Source A** help to explain why many people voted for F. D. Roosevelt in the 1932 election? **(5 marks)**

(b) What are the strengths and weaknesses of **Source B** as an interpretation of why Hoover lost the 1932 election? **(10 marks)**

(c) How useful is **Source C** for describing the effects of the Depression on New York in late 1931? Explain your answer using **Source C** and your own knowledge **(9 marks)**

(d) Compare what the two cartoons (**Sources D** and **E**) are saying about the likely effects of the New Deal. **(6 marks)**

(e) Using your own knowledge, what were the causes of America's Great Depression that started in 1929? **(15 marks)**

SECTION B: The USA, 1919–29

Study **Sources F** and **G** and then answer parts **(a)**, **(b)**, **(c)** and **either (d) or (e)** of Question 7 which follow.

Source F: Bootleg liquor being dumped

From a photograph of the 1920s.

Source G: The beliefs of the Ku Klux Klan

There are three great racial instincts which must be used to build a great America: loyalty to the white race, to the traditions of America and to the spirit of Protestantism.

The pioneer must be kept pure. The white race must be supreme.

From a speech in the 1920s by HIRAM WESLEY EVANS, the Imperial Wizard (leader) of the Ku Klux Klan

Question 7

(a) What can you learn from **Source F** about Prohibition in the USA in the 1920s? **(3 marks)**

(b) Describe the effects of Prohibition in the USA in the 1920s on law and order. **(5 marks)**

(c) Use **Source G** and your own knowledge to explain why the Ku Klux Klan attracted substantial support in the 1920s. **(7 marks)**

EITHER

(d) The USA in the 1920s was seen as being very prosperous. Did all Americans share in the prosperity of the 1920s? Explain your answer. **(15 marks)**

OR

(e) The years 1929–32 are labelled as the Great Depression. Did all Americans suffer equally in the Depression in the years 1929–32? Explain your answer. **(15 marks)**

7 Britain, 1905–51

INTRODUCTION

In 1900, Britain was a nation divided into rich and poor. Booth and Rowntree had shown that something needed to be done to help the less well off people in society. People realised that poverty was not always the fault of the poor.

From 1906, the Liberal government tried to solve these problems by introducing new laws and ideas. By 1918, the beginnings of the welfare state had been set up, the system of government had been changed, women had got the vote and the Labour Party had become an important part of politics. The relationship between the government and the unions was troubled and eventually led to the General Strike of 1926.

During the Depression of the 1930s, many factories closed and many people lost their jobs despite the growth of new industries in the south. It was only after the Second World War, when the government **nationalised** (took over) some industries and set up the National Health Service, that economic and social conditions seemed to be getting better.

1906	Beginning of school meals
1908	Beginning of Old Age Pensions Act
1911	National Insurance Act Parliament Act
1918	Women over 30 get the right to vote
1926	General Strike
1929	Wall Street Crash leads to Depression
1936	Jarrow Crusade
1939	Second World War starts
1942	Beveridge Report
1944	Education Act
1945	Labour Party elected
1946	National Health Service Act
1947	Transport and coal nationalised
1951	Labour Party defeated in election

How far was the welfare state established by 1914?

Poverty in Britain

Life in Britain in 1900 was very different from life in Britain today. The rich and middle classes enjoyed a comfortable life, but the poor and unemployed had almost no help and often lived in very bad conditions. Workhouses had been set up in the nineteenth century to take in very poor people. Up to the end of the century it was not considered necessary for the government or society to do any more.

However, a **Royal Commission** in 1895 showed that people were simply not earning enough to live on. These findings were backed

Source A photograph of a London East End family at the beginning of the twentieth century.

up by reports published by **Charles Booth** and **Seebohm Rowntree**. Booth showed that many people were living in poverty in London; Seebohm Rowntree showed that many people were living in poverty in York.

To some extent people expected high levels of poverty in London, but were surprised to see such poverty in a small city like York.

In 1906, the Liberal government was elected and started to introduce reforms and new laws. It was the start of what is called the welfare state.

Children's health

From the late nineteenth century children had had to go to school. Teachers complained that children were too hungry to be able to learn properly. Charities were unable to help everyone, so the Liberal government brought in new laws.

1906 Education (Provision of Meals) Act
This meant that local education authorities could provide school meals for children. Meals were sometimes provided in school holidays. Providing some school meals was made compulsory in 1914.

1907 School Medical Inspection Service
Each child was inspected once a year by a doctor or nurse and doctors and nurses could visit schools regularly.

1912 School clinics opened
These clinics looked at children's eyes, ears and teeth.

This was how children's health was treated until after the Second World War.

THINGS TO DO

1 Look at **Source A**.
  (a) Do you think this family is rich or poor? Explain your answer.
  (b) What evidence suggests that this photograph was posed?

2 How did the Liberal government try to help young people?

Britain, 1905–51

Old age pensions

The Old Age Pensions Act was passed in 1908 to give **pensions** to everyone over 70 years of age.

- Pensions started on 6 January 1909.

- Pensioners got 5 shillings (25 pence) a week.

- You had to earn less than £21 a year to get one.

- Over 650,000 people applied for a pension in the first year.

- By 1914, there were almost one million pensioners.

Until 1908, if old people did not have any savings or receive help from relatives they frequently had to go the workhouse. Pensions meant that fewer people had to go to the workhouse. One pensioner who could now give his son some money for looking after him said: 'Now we want to go on living for ever because we can give them ten shillings a week.'

Friday was the beginning of a new life for the poor. In Norwich there were old people waiting for the doors to open at 8.00 am. When the post office opened at 9.00 am the first pensioners got out their books. They answered one or two questions, signed their books and then pocketed the money and walked out.

From the **Norwich Mercury,**
9 January 1909.

Source C Pensioners queuing inside a post office for their pensions.

THINGS TO DO

1 Twenty-five pence a week was not enough to live on but it did help. Write down one way this small sum of money would help a pensioner.

2 Study **Source D**. Do you think the journalist on the *Norwich Mercury* thought pensions were a good idea? Explain your answer.

3 Do you think the government would want a pensioner to 'go on living for ever'?

Labour exchanges

In 1909, the President of the Board of Trade, **Winston Churchill**, set up **labour exchanges** to stop people having to walk from factory to factory looking for work. By 1913, the unemployed could visit one of 430 labour exchanges to see what work was available in their town. We now call these places job centres.

Source E

A government poster advertising the National Insurance Act.

National Insurance

The **National Insurance Act** of 1911 was passed to help low-paid workers when they were sick or when they lost their jobs. As part of this scheme the worker paid 4d (2p) a week towards receiving help when ill (see Source E).

Not everyone got these benefits. Women workers could not join until 1920. Unemployment insurance was only available to labourers working in building, engineering and shipbuilding. Other workers were allowed to join in 1920.

THINGS TO DO

The welfare state should help everyone. Do you think it helped everyone by 1918? Explain your answer.

How far did the government change as a result of events between 1905 and 1919?

Helping the poor was very expensive so the Chancellor, **Lloyd George**, planned to increase taxes in 1909.

- For people earning over **£3000** per year, income tax went up from 5p to 7p for each pound earned.

- For people earning over **£5000** per year, income tax went up from 5p to 9p for each pound earned.

- Death duties (taxes on wealth of a dead person) were increased.

- Taxes on tobacco were raised.

- Taxes on alcohol were raised.

- Taxes were charged on the sale of land (if you had any).

The increases in taxes were very unpopular with many well-off people. When the **Finance Bill** to bring in the new taxes was being voted on in the House of Lords, peers (members of the House of Lords) came from all over the country to vote against it.

In November 1909, the House of Lords rejected the Bill. The Prime Minister, **Herbert Asquith**, then called for a general election to see if the government plans had the support of the country.

Source A Liberal Party leaflet in 1909.

Mr Lloyd-George: What are you using this acre field for?

Owner: Agricultural purposes, I turn my pony in here!

Mr Lloyd-George: It can't be worth more than £50 for that purpose – couldn't you do something better with it?

Owner: There's no need for me to do anything – the builders over there are doing it all for me. They'll be wanting to build here soon. Why, I could get £500 tomorrow for this acre!

Mr Lloyd-George: Then, surely, it won't hurt you to pay tax of a halfpenny in the £ on an increased value which you had nothing to do with making!

The general election, January 1910

The election was a draw between the Liberals and Conservatives but the Labour Party and the Irish Nationalists joined up with the Liberals, and formed a new government.

- Liberals (with Labour and Irish Nationalists) **397 seats**
- Conservatives **273 seats**

Now the new Liberal government made sure that the fuss over taxation of rich people could not happen again. It threatened to reduce the power of the House of Lords through a new **Parliament Bill**. The Lords gave in and the new taxes outlined in the '**People's Budget**' became law in April 1910.

The constitutional crisis

Now that the Finance Bill had been passed, the politicians started to look at proposals to reduce the power of the House of Lords. The new king, **George V**, had to find a way of ending the crisis about the future of the House of Lords.

Main events

- June: George V arranged talks to sort out the crisis.

- November: Talks failed. The Liberals asked the king to make 300 more Liberal Lords so they could outvote the Conservative Lords. This would make it possible to pass the Parliament Bill. The king agreed, provided that a general election was held to show the people approved.

- December: The Liberals won the general election and the Parliament Bill was passed in April 1911.

	1906	Jan 1910	Dec 1910	1918	1922
Liberal Party	377	275	272 *	146*	117
Labour Party	53	40	42 *	59	142
Conservative Party	157	273	272	338*	347
Irish Nationalists	83	82	84 *	–	–
Asquith Liberals	–	–	–	26	–

* Liberal Government
(needing support from Labour and Irish Nationalists)

* Lloyd George Coalition Government
(Liberals and Conservatives)

General election results, 1906–22.

THE PARLIAMENT BILL 1911

- Established that all money bills (budgets) passed by the Commons had to be passed by the Lords.
- Limited the power of the Lords over other bills.
- Said that MPs should be paid.
- Established that general elections take place every five years rather than every seven.

THINGS TO DO

1 List three ways the Liberals intended to pay for pensions.

2 Who would be annoyed at the new taxes?

3 Why might the poor be happy with taxes on wages? (Remember that a typical worker's wage for a year was £160–200.)

Women's right to vote

Before the First World War, women did not have the right to vote in general elections. They could not be MPs or members of the House of Lords. Many people, including Queen Victoria and the Prime Minister, Herbert Asquith, thought this was right.

However, a campaign by a group of women (called **suffragettes**) and events during the First World War changed all this.

G Women fire-fighters on a practice drill during the First World War.

Before the war
- slogan 'The Right to Vote'
- marches, petitions, own newspaper
- bombs and arson (setting fire to buildings)
- breaking shop windows
- hunger strikes
- disrupting public transport.

During the war
- slogan 'The Right to Serve'
- working on the land
- working in munitions factories
- working in shops and offices
- joining the armed forces
- working on buses and trains.

The Suffragettes

Suffragettes were women who fought for the right to vote in general elections. From 1903, this fight was led by the Women's Social and Political Union (WSPU). Emmeline Pankhurst and her daughters set this up. At first, they used peaceful methods – marches and petitions – and then in 1909 they turned to violence. This got them publicity but it also made some people think they were mad and should not get the vote. Some went on hunger strike and were force-fed to prevent them from dying. The Cat and Mouse Act was passed in 1913. It allowed prisons to free women on hunger strike and arrest them again when they were well enough. The women then went on hunger strike again, so it did not really work.

In 1913, a suffragette called Emily Wilding Davison tried to stop the Derby horse race by grabbing the reins of the King's horse. She was badly hurt and died a few days later. Her funeral was attended by thousands and gave the suffragettes a lot of publicity in the newspapers.

By 1918, many people in the country, including MPs, felt that women had earned the right to vote through their contribution to the war effort.

- 1918: women could vote from the age of 30 (men had to be 21 to vote).

- 1928: women could vote at the age of 21 (equal terms with men).

Keir Hardie and the rise of the Labour Party

Keir Hardie was the leader of the miners. The first time he stood for parliament (in 1888) he lost. He then formed the Scottish Labour Party. Four years later, he was elected as an Independent Labour MP for West Ham.

Important dates for the Labour Party:

- 1906: 53 Labour MPs were elected.

- 1911: MPs got paid for the first time – £400 a year. (This helped poor Labour MPs.)

- 1913: Trade unions were allowed to support Labour Party candidates under the Trade Union Act.

- 1918: 59 Labour MPs were elected.

- 1922: 142 Labour MPs were elected. (The Labour Party became the second biggest political party.)

- 1923: 191 Labour MPs were elected.

- 1924: in January, Ramsay MacDonald formed the first Labour government.

In fewer than 20 years the Labour Party had gone from being a small party with 29 MPs to being large enough and popular enough to form the government of the country.

SUMMARY

1909 Liberals introduce 'People's Budget'.
1910 Liberals win two general elections.
1911 Parliament Act passed.
1913 Trade Union Act.
1918 Women aged 30 and over given the vote.
1924 First Labour government.
1928 Voting age is reduced to 21 for women.

THINGS TO DO

1 How did women try to get the vote?

2 Why were women given the vote in 1918?

3 Draw a table to show the number of Labour MPs in 1906, 1918, 1922 and 1923. What does this table show us?

Source Keir Hardie.

Why was there a General Strike in 1926?

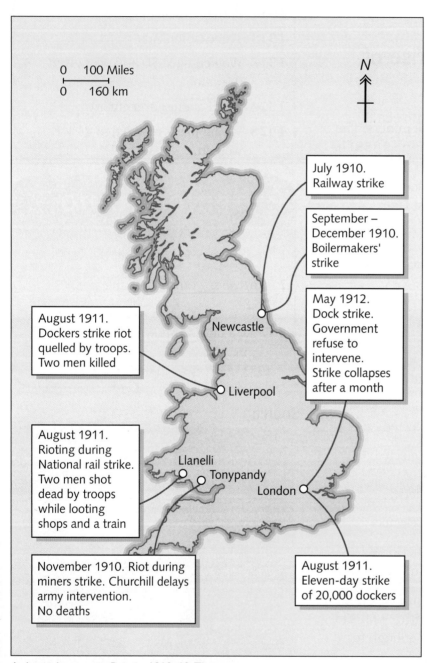

Industrial unrest in Britain, 1910–12. The map shows that strikes occurred all over Britain.

July 1910.
Railway strike

September – December 1910. Boilermakers' strike

May 1912. Dock strike. Government refuse to intervene. Strike collapses after a month

August 1911. Dockers strike riot quelled by troops. Two men killed

August 1911. Rioting during National rail strike. Two men shot dead by troops while looting shops and a train

November 1910. Riot during miners strike. Churchill delays army intervention. No deaths

August 1911. Eleven-day strike of 20,000 dockers

Newcastle

Liverpool

Llanelli

Tonypandy

London

Strikes, 1910–14

As we have seen, the Liberal government had passed laws to try to improve living and working conditions in Britain. Between 1910 and the First World War, there was a series of strikes which challenged the government.

- 1910: railways workers, boilermakers, miners and cotton workers
- 1911: dockers and railway workers
- 1912: miners
- 1913: miners, railway workers, transport workers all planned to strike together.

Why strike?
Some trade unionists thought that strike action was the only way of bringing about changes in society. They thought that if the workers controlled the industries things would improve. This was called **syndicalism**. When the miners, railway workers and transport workers joined together to increase their power in the **Triple Alliance** in 1913 the government was worried; but, with the outbreak of war, people's attention moved from this issue.

Strikes, 1914–21

Even the war against Germany did not stop men going on strike. Workers were still unhappy about their wages and working conditions. There were strikes in Clydeside, Glasgow, South Wales, Liverpool, Newcastle and London.

During the First World War Japanese and US goods began to be sold in countries which used to buy British goods. When the War ended Britain found it difficult to sell some things in these markets. Exports of British coal declined (fell), because Britain could not compete with the cheaper coal produced by countries such as America, Germany and Poland.

Giving back the mines

During the War the government took over the running of the mines. The miners preferred this but the mine owners wanted them back. The **Sankey Commission** agreed with the miners that the mines should be nationalised. But in 1921 the government decided to give the mines back to the owners anyway.

From bad to worse...

At this time the price of coal dropped; the mine owners were forced to cut wages and increase working hours. Angry miners called for a strike and asked the transport workers and railway workers, the other unions in the Triple Alliance, to join them. On Friday 15 April 1921 they refused to help. This became known as **Black Friday**.

Miners were forced to accept a cut in wages. Even railway workers, dockers and building workers faced wage cuts. Unemployment rose to over two million by June 1921. Workers left trade unions they thought had let them down; union membership fell from over eight million to about 5.5 million.

THINGS TO DO

1 Use the map on page 258 to explain how serious the strikes were between 1910 and 1912.

2 In 1914, coal provided heating and lighting and fuel for trains. Why would a miners' strike be worrying for the government?

3 Why is the writer of **Source A** in such a panic?

Events leading to the General Strike

In 1925, coal prices fell again and the owners cut wages and added another hour to the working day. The miners' leader, A. J. Cook, was furious and his reply, 'Not a penny off the pay! Not a minute on the day', became the miners' slogan.

This time it looked as if the transport workers and railway workers would join the miners on strike, so the government stepped in.

On Friday 31 July 1925, the government announced a **subsidy** (money to keep the miners' wages up) and set up an enquiry led by Sir Herbert Samuel to try to find an answer to the problems in the mines. As you can imagine the miners were delighted. This day became known as **Red Friday**. The trouble was that the subsidy was only for nine months.

The Samuel Commission 1926

- agreed with the mine owners' plan to cut wages

- thought that hours should stay the same.

Neither side was happy. Then the owners cut wages again. Miners refused to accept the pay cut and called on other unions to support them by coming out on strike. **The Trades Union Congress (TUC)**, the organisation which represents the unions, agreed with the miners. The stage was set for the biggest strike of the 1920s.

Source B

Yesterday was the worst day in the history of the Labour Movement. We cannot deny it. We have said that if the unions would fight together they would win. They have not fought together and they have lost.

*An article in the **Daily Herald, 16 April 1921, commenting on Black Friday. The newspaper was paid for by the trade unions.***

SUMMARY

1910 Series of strikes.

1913 Triple Alliance between miners, railwaymen and transport workers.

1919 Sankey Commission recommends mines stay under government control.

1921 Mines returned to mine owners. Black Friday.

1925 Red Friday. Government subsidy for nine months to keep up miner's wages.

1926 Samuel Commission fails to find solution.

Government withdraws subsidy.

Mine owners again reduce wages and increase working hours.

THINGS TO DO

1 **Source B** sees Black Friday as a disaster but this newspaper was paid for by the trade unions. Can we trust what the paper says? Explain your answer.

2 Why were miners unhappy with the results of the Samuel Commission? Explain your answer.

Why did the General Strike fail after only nine days?

The strike begins

- 30 April 1926: owners offered pay cut of 13 per cent and an increase in the working day of one hour.

- 1 May 1926: miners rejected the offer.

- 2 May 1926: the government called off talks with the miners and the TUC.

- 3 May 1926: General Strike planned to begin at midnight.

- 4 May 1926: no trains. No buses. Cities were silent About three million workers backed the miners and came out on strike. Even the TUC was surprised at the level of support.

Progress of the strike

At first the strike seemed to be working. This was because the strikers were well organised. They had no intention of asking hospital workers to strike or to stop essential supplies getting through as some people feared.

In some areas strikers and police got on well.

- In **Plymouth**, there was a football match between strikers and police.

- In **Lincoln**, all the special constables were also on strike.

- In **Yorkshire**, miners greased the railway lines and slowed down the trains.

But, in other areas, relations between strikers and police were more hostile.

- In **Glasgow**, strikers were arrested and imprisoned.

- In **Wales**, two strikers were arrested for having communist magazines.

- In **Hull**, the mayor called out the navy after attacks on trams.

- In **London**, armed convoys were used to protect food supplies.

Source C London's Waterloo station is deserted during the General Strike of 1926.

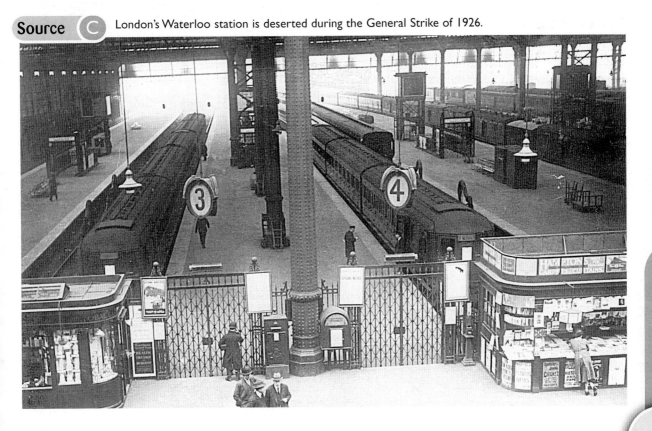

Volunteers play their part

Students, stockbrokers and office workers volunteered to help to keep essential services going during the strike. Some just wanted to have a go at being a train driver, fire-fighter or lorry driver. On one day alone, 6000 men and women volunteered to join the **Organisation for the Maintenance of Supplies** (OMS).

Special constables

Office workers queued outside local police stations to volunteer to be special constables.

If they were under 45 years old, healthy, strong and had stamina they were encouraged to join and defeat 'the enemy'.

The second week – it gets tough

As the strike went on violent clashes between the sides took place. Bus windows were smashed; trams were turned over; trains were held up when the tracks were blocked.

Rumours began to spread that the electricity workers would join in the strike.

The end of the strike

The TUC panicked. It had no intention of bringing the electricity workers out on strike.

It found it difficult to cope with the pressures that the strike had brought. On 12 May 1926, its leaders went to Downing Street and called off the strike. Why was this? No one is quite sure.

Why did the strike fail? – Part 1

1 Government prepared

Before the strike the government had:

- set up the OMS to make sure food supplies, gas and electricity were maintained
- set up a newspaper (*The British Gazette*) to tell its version of events

- organised lists of volunteers to carry out vital jobs
- planned to build up food supplies for an emergency.

The government's preparations meant that it was ready before the strike even started.

1926

Even greater British invention – television. John Logie Baird demonstrates his 'pictures by radio' in London. Meanwhile there is a 'General Strike' of miners, transport workers and many others. The government appoints 140,000 special policemen to sort the strikers out. The special police don't have enough truncheons to go round so they sent a lorry-load of chair legs. Ouch!

A humorous modern view of the conflict between police and strikers from a book designed to make history amusing for children.

2 Trade unions unprepared

- The trade unions made no preparations until five days before the strike.

- When the talks failed the government was already prepared.

- On 4 May 1926 the TUC could not get the government to reopen talks.

3 Reaction of middle classes

Middle-class people were gradually able to undermine the strikers.

- They volunteered to do essential work.

- They were protected by the army and navy.

- They wanted life to go on as normal. The secretary of the MCC (Marylebone Cricket Club) even said: 'As far as we can see we have no intention of allowing cricket to be interrupted.'

This made it difficult for the unions to win because so many people were against the strike.

Source E

We set out from Oxford early in the evening in an old Bentley, but from Doncaster onwards groups of strikers tried to interrupt our progress by throwing stones or trying to puncture our tyres.

On the next day those of us who were to work on the docks received our orders. Others went to drive trams or work the cranes. We were under the supervision of a Cambridge don, Mr Owen Morshead.

Some of the old hands who drifted back to work were surprised by the speed with which we unloaded the ships. We realised that it was a different story working for a few days as an adventure, compared to regular work over a period of years.

This is an account by an Oxford undergraduate of his experience as a volunteer working in the Liverpool docks during the General Strike.

Source F Women volunteer as postal workers during the General Strike.

Source G The front page of *The British Gazette*, a newspaper that supported the government, covering the strike.

Why did the strike fail? – Part 2

4 Propaganda

- *The British Gazette*, edited by Winston Churchill, told the government story.

- BBC radio broadcasts supported the government.

- The chairman of the BBC refused to allow the Labour leader, Ramsay MacDonald, to speak.

- The TUC responded by publishing its own newspaper, *The British Worker*.

With many newspapers and the radio against the strike it was difficult for the unions to get more support or to get across to the people why they were on strike.

5 Division among trade unionists

- Many members of TUC did not like the idea of a General Strike.

- Many feared that the government would be overthrown.

- The TUC refused to bring out on strike workers in essential services like health, sewerage or water.

When the miners refused to accept a cut in wages, recommended by the Samuel Commission, the TUC still went to the Prime Minister and called off the strike. The miners had to fight alone until November 1926. Some union leaders also lost their jobs because they had organised the strike.

THINGS TO DO

1 How did the government get ready for the strike?

2 Study **Source D**. How does it make fun of the strike?

3 Study **Source F**. Why do you think this photograph was taken?

4 (a) Write down five reasons why you think the strike lasted only nine days.
  (b) Which reason(s) do you think are the most important? Why?

The *British Worker* was the newspaper of the TUC. It gave the TUC's side of the story of the strike to the public.

THE BRITISH WORKER
OFFICIAL STRIKE NEWS BULLETIN
Published by The General Council of the Trades Union Congress

No. 1.   WEDNESDAY EVENING, MAY 5, 1926.   PRICE ONE PENNY

IN LONDON AND THE SOUTH

Splendid Loyalty of Transport Workers

EVERY DOCKER OUT

"London dock workers are absolutely splendid," said an official of the Transport and General Workers' Union.

"So far as they are concerned, it is a 100 per cent. strike. There is no trouble and everything is going smoothly."

POLICE HELP REFUSED

At Swindon the railwaymen are obeying Mr. Cramp's injunction to remain steady and to preserve order. The Great Western works are, of course, closed, and no trains are running.

It was stated at a mass meeting of the N.U.R. that Mr. Collett (the

The General Council suggests that in all districts where large numbers of workers are idle sports should be organised and entertainments arranged.

This will both keep a number

WONDERFUL RESPONSE TO THE CALL

General Council's Message : Stand Firm and Keep Order

The workers' response has exceeded all expectations. The first day of the great General Strike is over. They have manifested their determination and unity to the whole world. They have resolved that the attempt of the mineowners to starve three million men, women and children into submission shall not succeed.

All the essential industries and all the transport services have been brought to a standstill. The only exception is that the distribution of milk and food has been permitted to continue. The Trades Union General Council is not making war on the people. It is anxious that the ordinary members of the public shall not be penalised for the unpatriotic conduct of the mineowners and the Government.

Never have the workers responded with greater enthusiasm to the call of their leaders. The only difficulty that the General Council is experiencing, in fact, is in persuading those workers in the second line of defence to continue at work until the withdrawal of their labour may be needed.

WORKERS' QUIET DIGNITY

The conduct of the trade unionists, too, constitutes a credit to the whole movement. Despite the presence of armed police and the military, the workers have preserved a quiet orderliness and dignity, which the General Council urges them to maintain, even in the face of the temptation and provocation which the Government is placing in their path.

SOUTH WALES IS SOLID !

Not a Wheel Turning in Allied Industries

'MEN ARE SPLENDID !'

Throughout South Wales the stoppage is complete, and everywhere the men are loyally observing the orders of the T.U.C. to refrain from any conduct likely to lead to disturbance.

So unanimous has been the response to the call of the leaders, that not a wheel is turning in the industries affiliated to the T.U.C.

MONMOUTHSHIRE

Complete standstill of industries in the eastern valleys. Absolute unanimity prevails among the rank and file of the affiliated unions, and not a single wheel is turning in the allied industries.

Monmouth Education Authority—which has a majority of Labour representatives—has arranged to feed the school-children where required.

ABERDARE VALLEY

All railway and bus services are at a standstill. The miners' attitude indicates that they are absolutely loyal to the advice of their leaders to refrain from anything in the nature of riotous behaviour.

NEATH

Impact of the strike on trade unions

In 1927, the government passed a new law, the **Trades Disputes Act**. It made general strikes illegal. Workers could no longer come out on strike in sympathy with other workers. It also made it harder to give money to the Labour Party which supported the trade unions.

The General Strike was a disaster for the trade unions. Many workers left the unions and membership did not start to go up again for seven years. There were no more general strikes. The miners had to go back to work eventually and had to accept the terms offered to them by the mine owners.

SUMMARY

Reasons for the failure of the strike

- Government preparation.
- Middle-class opposition.
- Opposition from political parties and the churches.
- Division in the TUC.
- Government propaganda.

THINGS TO DO

1 Write down the headlines of *The British Gazette* (**Source G**). Explain how it says that the strike was not so good.

2 Write down some headlines from *The British Worker* (**Source H**). Explain how it says that the strike was a success.

3 How useful are newspapers like these to historians studying the past?

Britain 1929–39: A decade of depression and recovery?

How far did Britain experience a depression in the 1930s?

The Wall Street Crash

Wall Street is where the US stock market is based. The Wall Street Crash began on 24 October 1929 (see pages 231–3). Share prices dropped so much that when people tried to sell their shares they got less than they had paid for them.

Many Americans lost all the money they had. American banks had invested in the stock market and lost money too. They could no longer afford to lend money to Europe, and asked for their money back. Americans could no longer afford to buy European goods.

This did not help any British industry that made goods to be sold in America and so America's economic depression affected Britain too. At the same time, Britain had other problems of its own.

- British companies used old or out-of-date equipment.

- Britain depended on its empire for cheap raw materials.

- Britain depended on its empire to buy goods made in Britain.

- Other countries were getting better at making things for themselves so traditional industries like coal mining, shipbuilding, textiles, and iron and steel began to suffer.

The declining industries

- British mines could not compete with coal produced in other countries. The USA and other countries used better machinery than the British mining industry. In the mid-1920s, American coal cost 65p a

The American Depression hits Britain.

tonne compared with British coal at £1.56 a tonne. Who would want to buy British coal?

- About 1000 British textile mills closed in the 1930s. There was strong competition from Japan: Japanese workers were paid one-fifth of the wages of British workers and factories in Japan were more efficient.

New man-made fibres such as rayon began to replace cotton and shorter skirts meant less demand for fabric anyway.

- The shipbuilding industry suffered as less trade meant fewer ships. A decline in the numbers of ships being built meant a decline in the demand for the raw materials of iron and steel. Besides, American and German-built ships were cheaper, further reducing demand for British ships.

In all these industries Britain was finding it harder and harder to compete.

Poor north, rich south?

Most of the traditional British industries, like shipbuilding, coal mining and textiles, were in the north of England, Scotland, Northern Ireland and Wales. These areas suffered the highest unemployment. But at the same time towns in the Midlands and the South East of England did much better because they did not depend on the older industries for jobs.

Why set up in the south?
New industries and workers moved to the south. Why?

- More people still had jobs in the south and could afford to buy goods: factories wanted to be nearer to their customers.

- Electricity was used more: factories did not need to be near coal fields any more.

- Improved roads and railways could bring raw materials easily to the factories.

- After the General Strike of 1926, employers thought people in the south would be less likely to go on strike.

A good example of a company which moved to the south was the Ford Motor Company. It moved from Manchester to London taking over 2000 workers with it.

SUMMARY

Reasons for the Depression in Britain

Wall Street Crash.

Decline in old industries.

Lack of investment in modern machinery.

Competition from abroad.

THINGS TO DO

Explain how the following affected British industry after the First World War.

(a) Out-of-date machinery.

(b) Competition from abroad.

(c) New man-made fibres.

How did standards of living change?

- The employed had a good lifestyle; they could, for example, buy cheap, new electrical goods.

- For the unemployed life was difficult. There was hunger and despair.

The good life

- Four million new homes were built in the 1930s.

- An income of £200 a year was enough to buy your own home.

- New chain stores like Marks & Spencer and Woolworth's became popular.

- The quality of food improved as branded foods, breakfast cereals and canned food became available.

- Between 1924 and 1935 the price of cars went down at least 50 per cent.

- The entertainment industry grew – cinemas, radio and daily newspapers.

All these things made daily life more comfortable, for those who could afford them. While for those people who were unemployed life was hard.

Northern Ireland	26.2%
Wales	24.3%
North-East England	19.1%
Scotland	15.2%
Lancashire	12.9%
Yorkshire	9.2%
London	8.2%
South East	6.1%
Midlands	6.0%

Unemployment figures for 1937.

The increase/decrease in output and employment in Britain in the period 1920–38.

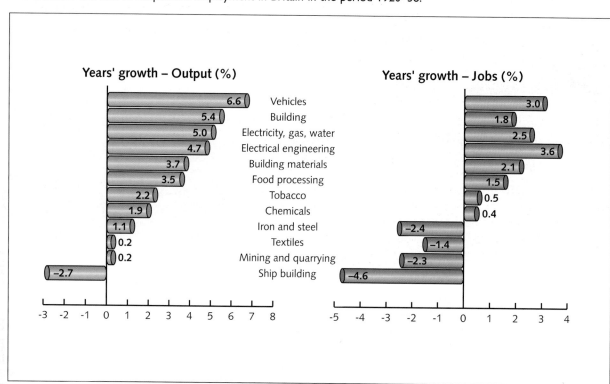

Modern World History for AQA

Despair for others

Miners, shipbuilders, steel workers and textile workers all faced unemployment. One in four men were unemployed in Britain in 1931.

Areas which depended on iron and steel, shipbuilding and coal mining were the worst off.

Not only did the workers suffer but so did their families who depended on wages to buy food and other goods. Even the local shopkeepers suffered.

In Merthyr Tydfil (South Wales) and Jarrow (Tyneside) there was more than 60 per cent unemployment. Further south, in Birmingham and Oxford, unemployment was less than six per cent.

How did unemployment affect an area?

- In some towns half the shops shut and shopkeepers joined the unemployed.

- Some people left the towns they had lived in all their lives and headed south for new job opportunities.

- Charities tried to help but struggled with too many people in need.

Source **B**

This traffic jam in Britain photographed in the 1930s shows how important motor transport had become. Of course, for many others owning a car was little more than a dream.

THINGS TO DO

1 What was good about living in the 1930s?

2 What was bad about living in the 1930s?

3 Explain why looking for a job in the south was a good idea in the 1930s.

Jarrow: a town 'murdered'

Jarrow was very badly hit by the Depression. Hebburn Colliery (a mine) was closed in 1930. The steel works (one of Jarrow's largest employers) closed in 1931. Palmer's shipyard was closed in 1934.

After the closure of the pit and the steel works, the town had depended entirely on shipbuilding. The government had been buying and then closing down shipyards, hoping this would help the remaining yards to stay in business. The people did not understand this policy. With so many people out of work and not much chance of finding work anywhere else, the town decided to fight back in 1936.

The Jarrow Crusade

A public meeting was held and the town council decided to march to London. One marcher thought they should take a bomb.

Most people wanted a peaceful, organised march. They began a **petition** to take with them.

The medical officer, a local doctor, helped to pick 200 men to go on the march. It was going to be tough. They planned to march between 15 and 25 miles each day. They set off from Jarrow with a cheering crowd.

The well-organised march made people across the country aware of the Jarrow workers' situation.

- The press gave the marchers mouth organs to play as they marched.
- They were given places to stay on the route.
- A rich lady gave them free cigarettes.
- The police praised the marchers for being well organised and obeying the law.

- Their Labour MP, **Ellen Wilkinson**, marched with them.
- They marched with the support of Jarrow town council.

Source C

I have seen nothing like it since the war. Misery is everywhere. One out of every two shops is shut. Everywhere men were hanging about: thousands of them.

A writer describing Jarrow in 1933.

Year	Unemployment
1927	2987
1928	3233
1929	3245
1930	3643
1931	6603
1932	6793
1933	7178
1934	6462
1935	6053
1936	4065

Unemployment in Jarrow, 1927–36. The total workforce in the town was 9700.

Reaction in London

The government refused, however, to let the marchers present their petition asking for work to Parliament. Their MP, Ellen Wilkinson, had to present the petition alone. Still, they did return to Jarrow (by train) as heroes. When they got home they discovered that their unemployment benefit had been stopped because they were not available for work when they were marching to London.

Was the march a success?

- The marchers returned home as heroes.

- Some men found work on new trading estates in Jarrow and Gateshead.

But:

- Many found no work.

- Many had to wait until the Second World War and the rearmament programme to get full-time employment.

Source D

Jarrow men on their march to London, October 1936.

Source E

1936 First BBC television broadcasts – if you can afford the £110 for a set. The unemployed can't. Two hundred unemployed men march from Jarrow in north-east England to London with a petition asking the government to create jobs. After weeks of marching they reach London... and Prime Minister Baldwin refuses to meet them. They go home to houses without the new television sets – or even a loo.

At the time the first television broadcasts were made, and a television set cost £110, the Jarrow men were marching to London to protest at having no jobs.

A modern view of the contrast between the life of an unemployed Jarrow worker and the improvements taking place in society. It was written in a humorous book on history for school children.

Source F

Amongst the marchers was Robert Winship. He was 42 and worked in Hebburn Colliery (coal mine) from the age of 13 until it closed in 1930. He did not have another job until the war started in 1939.

The year the colliery closed his wife was taken to a mental hospital and eventually died there in 1935. He had to bring up his two daughters on 95p a week. On one occasion when he was in hospital for fourteen days his dole was stopped as he was not available for work. He was brought home on a stretcher to fend for himself and his daughters as best he could.

An account of the life of one of the Jarrow marchers.

Source G

The use of marchers is wrong. They are just an organised mob. This is not a proper way of doing things.

A letter from the Bishop of Durham to The Times in October 1936.

THINGS TO DO

1 Why did the people of Jarrow decide to organise a march to London?

2 Read **Source C**. How did the unemployed men spend their day?

3 When was unemployment at its worst in Jarrow in the 1930s?

4 Study **Sources D** and **E**. Which picture do you think is the most accurate? Explain your choice.

5 Read the story of Robert Winship (**Source F**). Do you agree that the government was unfair towards him and his family? Explain your answer.

6 Do you agree with the Bishop of Durham (**Source G**) when he describes the marchers as an 'organised mob'?

How effective was the government in dealing with economic problems?

The **dole** (unemployment insurance money) had been set up for some workers in 1911. By 1920, if you were out of work and had been earning less than £250 a year, you could claim the dole for a total of 15 weeks. After that you were expected to find a job and could no longer claim the dole.

In November 1922, when it was clear that jobs were so hard to find, the government said benefit could be claimed until you found work.

But, in 1929 the government was paying out more money in benefits than it was receiving in taxes.

Unemployed Welsh miners marching to London in 1932 to protest about the lack of job opportunities.

Government spending cuts

The Labour government, elected in 1929, faced huge problems:

- Britain was selling a lot fewer goods abroad, so exports had fallen.

- Three million people were out of work and claiming the dole.

- The government was spending £2 million a day more than it could afford and had to look to other countries for loans.

- The USA and France did not want to lend Britain money.

The government could not agree on the cuts that had to be made, so a new, all-party National Government was formed to bring in the cuts.

- Judges' pay was cut by ten per cent.

- Teachers' pay was cut by fifteen per cent.

- Unemployment benefit was cut by ten per cent.

- A **means test** was brought in so that people did not get benefits if they had some money of their own left.

The Means Test

Local officials did the Means Test. If you were unemployed you had to tell them:

- who lived in your house, how much they earned.

- if they had any savings.

The Means Test officials even checked to see if you had anything worth selling to raise money.

In a family, if the father was out of work and children were working, the children were expected to look after the parents and even help look after their younger brothers and sisters. A father out of work would find all this very difficult. His pride as the bread winner would be destroyed.

Import Duties Act, 1932

The government tried to help British industry by making foreign goods much more expensive. It did this by bringing in a tax of 10 or 20 per cent on all foreign imports.

The government hoped that by making foreign goods more expensive it would encourage people to buy cheaper, British-made goods.

The idea behind this was:

- if more British goods were bought more goods would have to be produced

- this would mean that more people would be employed to produce them

- unemployment would then fall.

Special Areas Act, 1934

The higher import duties worked for new items like cars and electrical goods but failed to help people in the North of England, Scotland and Wales. The government introduced the **Special Areas Act**.

- This Act tried to get new factories opened in the old industrial areas.

- Two commissioners were given £2 million to build new factories, such as those on the Team Valley Trading Estate in Gateshead.

But, many companies still did not want to move to these areas. And small industrial estates alone could not replace the large coal and shipbuilding industries which had employed so many people.

THINGS TO DO

1 Read 'Government spending cuts'. Explain why the government had problems.

2 Why would parents and working brothers and sisters be unhappy with the means test introduced at this time?

Had the welfare state been fully established by 1951?

The Beveridge Report, 1942

The report was written during the war. It suggested ways in which life in Britain could be improved. It said that the state (government) should look after people from '**the cradle to the grave**', meaning from the moment they were born to the moment they died.

Beveridge thought there were **five giant problems** which had to be tackled to make Britain a better place to live in and he suggested solutions for each.

- **Want**: lack of basics including food. Introduce a system of national insurance.

- **Ignorance**: lack of proper education for all. Build new and better schools.

- **Disease**: lack of proper medical care for all. Provide a health service for the whole country.

- **Squalor**: lack of proper housing for all. Build more homes.

- **Idleness**: lack of jobs (unemployment). Help industry to create more jobs.

The general election, July 1945

Winston Churchill had been a great wartime leader and was still very popular, but many people wanted change. They thought that the Labour Party would be more likely to do something about Beveridge's five giants, so the majority of electors voted for the Labour Party in the general election of July 1945 (see the table). The first Labour government

Conservatives	213
Labour	393
Liberals	12
Other parties	22

Result of the 1945 general election.

began the task of tackling the problems of the country.

The attack on want

Family allowances were introduced in August 1946 to improve the standard of living.

- A family with one child received nothing.

- A family with more than one child received 5 shillings (25p) per week for each child after the first until the child was 16 or in full-time employment.

  The **National Insurance Act** of 1946 made everyone part of the scheme. It did not matter what job you did or how well paid you were.

- Employers, government and workers paid into the scheme.

- Everyone would receive money if out of work because of sickness, unemployment or pregnancy.

- There was no limit to sickness benefit.

- Unemployment benefit lasted for six months.

TACKLING THE FIRST GIANT

WANT · IGNORANCE · DISEASE · SQUALOR · IDLENESS

" WANT is only one of the five giants on the road of reconstruction " — The Beveridge Report.

Source **A** This 1942 cartoon shows Beveridge setting out to defeat the problems of British society.

The **National Insurance (Industrial Injuries)** Act of 1946 helped those who could not work because of injury at work:

- it gave benefits to those injured or disabled at work
- it set up tribunals to decide on the amount of compensation.

The **National Assistance Act** of 1948 gave help to those who were very poor:

- it helped people who were not covered by the National Insurance Act
- a National Assistance Board was set up. It dealt with a lot more cases than it was thought that there would be.

The attack on disease

The **National Health Service Act** of 1946 provided:

- free medical treatment and free medicine
- free dental treatment and free false teeth
- free hospital treatment
- free eye treatment and free spectacles.

Hospitals came under the control of the **National Health Service** (**NHS**). Local councils provided midwives, home nurses, health visitors and ambulances. Doctors were paid by the NHS and this encouraged general practitioners (GPs) to begin working in poorer areas without worrying if they were to get paid.

All this was paid for through taxes and National Insurance contributions.

Source **B**

The men and women of this country who have endured great hardships in war are asking what kind of life awaits them in peace. They need good homes, sufficient food and clothing, employment and leisure. They need help in case of accident, sickness and for old age. For their children they desire a system of education.

Part of a radio election speech by the Labour leader, Clement Attlee in 1945.

The NHS: the worries

Doctors and dentists worried that the changes would be bad for them. Some doctors thought they might be poorer if they worked for the government and some of them even organised a campaign against the new NHS. They should not have worried. The new scheme started on 5 July 1945. By the end of the first year 95 per cent of people had signed up for the NHS and 95 per cent of doctors had too.

The NHS: it worked

Very quickly people could see how the NHS made a difference.

- There was a fall in deaths from tuberculosis and diphtheria.

- Fewer babies died.

- Eight and a half million people had dental treatment in the first year.

- Just over five million pairs of spectacles were issued.

The NHS: it cost too much

In 1946, the NHS cost £400 million to run. This was much more than expected. The government could not afford this amount, so changes had to be made. In 1951, people had to start paying towards dental treatment, prescriptions and spectacles. The Minister for Health, **Aneurin Bevan**, was disappointed at the decision and resigned. He still thought it should be free for everyone.

THINGS TO DO

1 Study **Source A**. Why do you think Beveridge is small and want, ignorance, disease, squalor and idleness are big?

2 Study **Source A** and read **Source B**. Do you think Clement Attlee had read the Beveridge Report? Explain your answer.

3 How did the Labour government try to get rid of disease?

4 Read **Source C**. How does the story of the false teeth show that some money was wasted?

5 The doctor in **Source D** has a small pile of objections to the NHS. What do you think he is thinking?

Source C

When the National Health Service came in it was much easier to see a doctor, and it was free!. My teeth had been bad since I had a baby and I was now able to have false teeth at no cost.

Some of my friends got teeth because they were free but never used them. My mum got free spectacles and we all noticed how much better she could see.

An 83-year-old woman remembers the start of the National Health Service.

Source D

A *Daily Mirror* cartoon from May 1946.

THE PUBLIC'S VOTES IN FAVOUR OF THE NATIONAL HEALTH SERVICE BILL

Which other features of British society were changed in the period 1944–51?

The attack on ignorance

The **Education Act** of 1944 was introduced to provide free secondary education for all. Elementary schools which took children aged from five to fourteen were phased out. Children now stayed in school from five to fifteen. There were three types of secondary school:

- grammar (for academic education)
- technical (to train engineers and such like)
- secondary modern (for practical training).

These schools were supposed to be as good as each other but:

- grammar schools were seen as the best, and the way to a better-paid job
- competition was fierce for places at the grammar schools
- passing an examination at eleven (the eleven plus) became over-important.
- very few technical schools were built.

Other parts of the education system were improved.

- More full-time and part-time courses at colleges.
- More people going to university.
- New universities opened, such as Keele University in 1950.
- More grants provided for children whose parents could not afford to support them through university.

Source E

Mum and dad woke me up shouting: 'You've passed! You've passed!' I knew what they meant and I was very excited. I would be going to the grammar school.

My best friend was going to the local secondary modern school. She felt she had failed. I was sad because we would be going to different schools.

A 60-year-old woman remembers her feelings on the day she received her 'eleven plus' results.

Source F   Children in the playground of a school in a new town in 1954.

Modern World History for AQA

The attack on squalor

During the Second World War, bombs had destroyed many houses; no new homes were built during the war. There was therefore a housing shortage which had to be dealt with.

Families were put in temporary houses called **pre-fabs**. They were made out of concrete and, although they were only expected to last a few years, some are still being lived in today. New council estates were built so people could rent houses. Over one and a quarter million council houses were built between 1945 and 1951.

The New Towns Act, 1946

The government also decided to build 'new towns' to provide extra housing and stop the overcrowding of cities such as London. New towns had to:

- have a population of about 50,000 people
- be 30 miles apart
- have shops and schools within walking distance of homes
- be surrounded by countryside which could not be built on, called the 'green belt'.

The Act specified that twelve new towns were to be built. Eight new towns were built near London (including Stevenage and Hemel Hempstead), two were built in Scotland (East Kilbride was one), one in Wales and one in the North of England (Peterlee). Money was given to industry to set up new factories and offices in these new towns.

Some mistakes were made, such as too few garages and parking spaces. People did not know each other very well so at first there was a lack of community spirit. However, they were successful enough for more to be built in the 1970s and 1980s (for example, Washington).

Source G

An aerial photograph of Harlow, one of the new towns. Blocks of flats, streets of semi-detached houses, and playing fields can be seen.

Britain, 1905–51

279

Source (H)

An open-cast mine at Templenewsham, Leeds in 1944.

The attack on idleness

By 1950, the government seemed to have won the battle against unemployment. In 1947, there were over one million unemployed people. Within five years there were almost none! How did the government achieve this?

- **Winter of 1946–7**: Severe winter and fuel shortages meant one million workers were laid off work.

- **1947**: Marshall Aid (money from the USA) helped Britain's industries recover from the Second World War.

- **1948**: Trade unions accepted a wage freeze.

- **1949**: Reducing the value of the pound abroad encouraged foreigners to buy British goods.

- **1950**: There was almost full employment in Britain.

Nationalisation of key industries

Nationalisation is when the government owns and controls important factories or industries. The government had done this during the war to ensure that the needs of the country were met. The new Labour government thought it was a good idea to continue with this for a number of reasons.

- It had worked during the war.

- It would help the workers because workers' interests would come before the importance of making profits.

- Government money could be spent modernising the industries and improving working conditions.

Nationalised industries
- **1946**: Bank of England, cable and wireless and air transport.

- **1947**: electricity, gas, railways, road transport and coal.

- **1951**: iron and steel.

The National Coal Board

The National Coal Board took over the coal mines on 1 January 1947. The winter of 1947–8 was very bad. Coal shortages were blamed on the government.

The mines had been badly looked after before nationalisation, but the government did not want to have to put too much money into them. Coal production did increase but there were still shortages under the Labour government.

The iron and steel industry

The iron and steel industry was profitable, so the owners did not want to give it up to the government. However, the Labour government thought it was too important to the whole country to let it stay in private hands.

Although the Conservative Party and the House of Lords were against nationalising this industry, it was nationalised in 1951. In 1951, the Conservatives were elected to government and returned the iron and steel industry to the original owners.

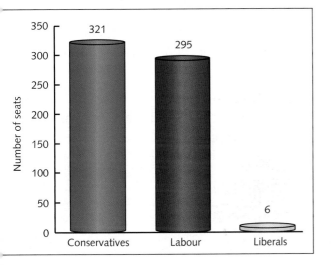

Result of the 1951 general election.

THINGS TO DO

1 What sort of school could a child go to before the Second World War?

2 What sorts of schools could a child go to in 1947?

3 What were the problems with the eleven plus exam? Use the text and **Source E** to help explain your answer.

4 List three good things and three bad things about the new towns.

5 Why was there full employment in 1951? Explain your answer.

6 Explain the term 'nationalisation'.

7 Was the government policy of nationalisation effective in all industries? Explain your answer.

SUMMARY

1942 Beveridge Report.
1944 Education Act.
1945 General Election.
1946 National Insurance Act.
   National Health Service.
   Industrial Injuries Act.
   New Towns Act.
   Beginning of nationalisation.
1947 Transport and coal nationalisation.
1948 National Assistance Act.
1951 Iron and steel nationalisation.

Britain, 1905–51

Exam-style assessment

These questions follow the pattern of questions to be set by AQA for Paper 2 of its new Modern World History specification.

SECTION A: Britain in the 1930s and 1940s

Study **Sources A** to **E** and then answer all parts of Question 4 which follow.

Source A: Number of unemployed (in millions) in Britain during the 1930s

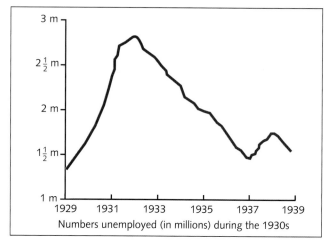

Numbers unemployed (in millions) during the 1930s

Source B: The difficulties of finding a job in the 1930s

He stared up at the huge building. 'Aw, God, just let me get a job. Ah don't care if it's only half pay.'

Some of the factories anticipated such callers as he. There were notices at the entrances: 'No hands wanted'.

He ignored them. You never knew but what somebody had just been sacked.

'Please sir, d'y' want any hands?'

A holding of the breath, an anxious stare.

'Do we hell as like. Can't you read? Blimey, we're sacking 'em ourselves. An' don't bang the door when y' go out, either.'

There were no more places to visit.

From *Love on the Dole*, a novel by WALTER GREENWOOD about life in the north of England and published in 1933

Source C: The Jarrow Crusade of 1936

Source D: Effects of the Means Test

An old-age pensioner, if a widower, would normally live with one of his children. His pension would go towards the household expenses, and probably he is not badly cared for.

Under the Means Test, however, he counts as a "lodger" and if he stays there his children's dole will be docked (reduced). So at seventy or seventy-five years of age, he has to turn out into lodgings, handing his pension over to the lodging-house keeper and existing on the verge of starvation.

From *The Road to Wigan Pier* (1937) by GEORGE ORWELL. The book is a description of the bad conditions in the 1930s in parts of northern England

Source E: The problems faced by British governments of the 1930s

It was not that there was unwillingness to help those who were suffering. What was lacking was any knowledge of what to do. The sheer magnitude of the problem was staggering. At the depth of the slump in September 1932 between six and seven million people were dependent on the 'dole' – men who could not find work, plus their wives and families. During the thirties one in three of all workers was out of work for some part of the time, many of them for long periods. The coal they mined, or the products they helped manufacture, could not be sold, so there was no work for them until 'times got better'.

From *From Workhouse to Welfare* (1971) by I. MARTIN. This book was published for use in schools

Question 4

(a) What can you learn about unemployment in Britain in the 1930s from **Source A**? **(5 marks)**

(b) Compare what **Sources B** and **C** are suggesting about attitudes to unemployment in the 1930s. **(6 marks)**

(c) How useful is **Source D** for studying the effects of government policies towards unemployment in the 1930s? Explain your answer by using **Source D** and your own knowledge. **(9 marks)**

(d) Is **Source E** an accurate interpretation of the extent of the economic and social problems faced by British governments in the 1930s? Explain your answer using **Source E** and your own knowledge. **(10 marks)**

(e) Using your own knowledge, how successful were the Labour governments of 1945–51 in getting rid of the economic problems of the 1930s? Explain your answer. **(15 marks)**

SECTION B: Britain 1905–26

Study **Sources F** and **G** and then answer parts **(a)**, **(b)**, **(c)**, and **either (d) or (e)** of Question 8 which follow.

Source F: Living standards in the early 1900s

The average family was better off at the end of Victoria's reign (1901) than it had been at the beginning (1837). Conditions of labour had improved and working hours were less, yet wages had risen. However, the root causes of poverty remained. Lower-paid workers could not afford to live decently.

From *Britain Since 1700* (1968) by R. J. COOTES. This was a textbook for use in British schools

Source G: The benefits of National Insurance

A government poster of 1911 advertising the National Insurance Act

Question 8

(a) What can you learn from **Source F** about living standards in Britain in the early 1900s?

(3 marks)

(b) Describe what Liberal governments in the years before the First World War did to help the welfare of children while they were at school. **(5 marks)**

(c) Using **Source G** and your own knowledge, how did Liberal governments help working and retired people? **(7 marks)**

EITHER

(d) Changes were made to Britain's system of government in the period 1906–18. To what extent did Britain become more democratic during this period? **(15 marks)**

OR

(e) Why was there a General Strike in Britain in 1926? **(15 marks)**

Index